THE ARK IN THE PARK

The Zoo in the Nineteenth Century

WILFRID BLUNT

THE ARK
IN THE PARK

The Zoo in the
Nineteenth Century

―――――――――――

Foreword by
Professor Lord Zuckerman
OM KCB DSc FRS
Secretary of
The Zoological Society of London

BOOK CLUB ASSOCIATES
LONDON

To the glorious memory of my grandmother
EMILY JANE BLUNT
née Simpson—of The Cedars, Upper Tooting
who one day
at the age of ninety-four and through my negligence
narrowly escaped death at the London Zoo

Contents

List of Colour Illustrations

In short, whatever folks might trace
    In Noah's famous ark
(If ever there was such a place,)
    Are in the Regent's Park

Zoological Keepsake, 1830

Foreword

THE widespread interest in science which was triggered by the Industrial Revolution led, in the latter half of the eighteenth and the first half of the nineteenth centuries, to the foundation of a number of learned societies concerned to promote studies in specialist fields. Among them were the Royal Astronomical Society, the Linnean Society, the Geological Society and the Zoological Society. Thomas Stamford Raffles, the founder of Singapore, who, in addition to being a great colonial administrator, was also an eminent naturalist, suggested in 1817 to Sir Joseph Banks, the somewhat authoritarian President of the Royal Society—he presided over its affairs from 1778 until his death in 1820—the possibility of establishing in London a collection of animals for purposes of study and because of their general interest. The project did not come to fruition until 1826, by which time Banks had been succeeded by Sir Humphry Davy, the distinguished scientist who is best remembered today as the inventor of the miner's lamp. He, with Sir Stamford Raffles, laid the foundations of the Zoological Society of London.

Two years later the Zoological Gardens were started in Regent's Park, and the Society now celebrates the 150th anniversary of its efforts to fulfil the purpose stated in its Royal Charter—'The advancement of zoology and animal physiology and the introduction of new and curious subjects of the animal kingdom.'

Throughout the nineteenth century, on which Mr Blunt concentrates in this book, many eminent men of science, including Sir Richard Owen, Thomas Henry Huxley, and Philip Lutley Sclater, participated in the Society's regular meetings, at which new findings in all fields of zoology were discussed. Much of our knowledge of the anatomy, taxonomic status and evolutionary relationships of animals is based on studies presented to the Society in the nineteenth century, or carried out on material provided to research workers by the Society. The various Superintendents, vets and keepers learned, often by trial and error, how to care for their exotic charges. The Fellows of the Society ranged from professional zoologists and amateurs with specialist knowledge, to persons to whom membership of the Society was little more than a means of granting patronage or, in some cases, gaining prestige or privilege. The Zoological Gardens soon became a popular feature of the fashionable Victorian scene and were well loved by Londoners, avid to see the animals they could otherwise know only from drawings, paintings and the stories told by travellers.

There is little wonder that in this tapestry of differing interests and activities there should be not only highlights of success, but also strains and stresses which were frequently seized upon and recounted in highly dramatic terms in the Press of the day.

Mr Blunt was left free to select his own topics in portraying a period picture of the nineteenth century, and has been clearly fascinated by the strengths and weaknesses of those who played their part in the development of the Society. As he says in his Preface, he wanted to 'get a period flavour' that would interest and amuse the reader. This he has undoubtedly achieved.

The history of the Zoological Society in the twentieth century has yet to be written. It will tell of the concern of zoologists to improve methods of animal management and to conserve the remaining fauna of the world, of the development of Whipsnade, the first zoological park in the world, of the reshaping of the Society's constitution to fit the present century, of the modernization of the London Zoo and the establishment of modern research institutes, of the development of its unique zoological library, scientific publications and, in recent years, international symposia. But that is another book.

Professor Lord Zuckerman, OM KCB DSc FRS
Secretary of The Zoological Society of London

Preface

When Lord Zuckerman, the Secretary of the Zoological Society of London, invited me to write a book about some aspect of the London Zoo, the publication of which would coincide with the sesquicentennial of the foundation of the Society, I must confess that the first thing I did, after recovering from my surprise, was to look up 'sesquicentennial' in the dictionary—to find that it meant 'one hundred and fiftieth anniversary'.

The Society's hundredth birthday in 1926 had been commemorated by a *Centenary History*, a useful work written by its learned Secretary and published by the Society in 1929. But it was not primarily directed at the general public; for one thing, its thirty or more illustrations consist entirely of portraits of officers of the Society, not of the non-human occupants of the Gardens which are of greater concern to the average reader. A book much nearer to my own heart is Henry Scherren's *The Zoological Society of London*, published in a limited, numbered edition by Cassell in 1905. The text is of far wider interest, and among its black-and-white illustrations are a number of delightful wood-engravings taken from nineteenth-century periodicals; the colour, however, was sadly squandered on insipid, amateurish Edwardian watercolours of the Gardens. At a later date there have appeared several 'popular' accounts of Regent's Park such as L. R. Brightwell's *The Zoo Story* (Museum Press, 1952), illustrated with pen-and-ink drawings by its versatile author, and Philip Street's *The London Zoo* (Odhams, 1956) with photographs principally of animals. Of all this material I have unashamedly made considerable use, as also of those countless books on animals in general and on zoos in particular which deal to a greater or lesser extent with the oldest Zoological Society and one of the earliest zoos (in the modern sense of the word) in the world.

Since the last War there has been a spate of zoological books illustrated with superb colour photographs of animals. I felt no desire to compete in this field, and in any case the steadily rising cost of colour-printing may soon make their production no longer commercially viable. It was not until I came across the press-cuttings volumes in the library of the Z.S.L., which Lord Zuckerman most kindly allowed me to carry off to Compton, that I discovered the kind of book that I wanted to write: a book based on the London Zoo in the nineteenth century, in which I could get a period flavour by supplementing my text with some scissors-and-paste use of contemporary newspaper accounts and their supporting wood-engravings. It was roughly around the turn of the century that photographs and half-tones began to replace wood-engravings, thus giving the illustrations a new—and in my opinion less attractive—look for many years to come.

After further consideration I decided that to attempt any kind of balanced account of the animals exhibited at Regent's Park in the nineteenth century would be impossible. I have therefore preferred to write at some length about a handful of those that, for the most part, had some particular association with the London Zoo—for example, the giraffe, the elephant, and the hippopotamus; but I have not hesitated to discuss them in a general way or to digress about their earlier or their more recent history. Even here I have followed no consistent pattern, mobilising my material in each case in the order that seemed to me most convenient. Interspersed among these portraits—or, if you prefer it, biographies—are chapters of a more miscellaneous kind, some of which, it must frankly be confessed, do not always show the Society and its officers in a very favourable light.

The reader, even if he consumes no more than a few pages of this discursive book, will hardly fail to discover that its author is not a professional zoologist. But I believe that this is not wholly a disadvantage, for the amateur is in a good position to know what might interest those other amateurs for whom his book is intended. In short, I have tried to write the kind of book that I, a mere lover of animals, would have enjoyed reading had someone else written it first. I have recorded what has interested or amused me in my zoological browsings, I have discarded what has bored me; and I have tried to write simply, avoiding the kind of 'zoologese' which I recently saw thus delightfully parodied:

> For my part, when tourists or other ranid cursorials seasonally disrupt the ecosystem, I retreat, following fossorial habit, with my felids and canids to our microhabitat, and aestivate.[1]

Should *The Ark in the Park* chance to fall into the hands of a professional zoologist, he cannot say that he has not been warned.

A further point. I am, as my readers will also soon discover, an unashamed addict of discreetly selected programmes on colour television, and those which deal seriously with animals in general, and with wild life in particular, seem to me to be for the most part beyond praise. Almost without exception the commentary is as lucid as the photography is brilliant.

I have, as always, many people to thank. First, I gratefully acknowledge the gracious permission of H.M. the Queen to quote passages from Queen Victoria's Diaries at Windsor Castle. The officials of the Z.S.L. gave me invaluable assistance and showed me great

---

1. Margaret Lane in *The Daily Telegraph*, 7 August 1975.

hospitality—and here I would particularly mention Lord Zuckerman, the administrator Miss E. M. Owen, the librarian Mr R. Fish, the director of zoos Mr C. G. C. Rawlins, and the curator of mammals Dr M. R. Brambell. Miss Sandra Raphael put her store of miscellaneous knowledge of the byways of zoology at my disposal, read my proofs and produced an excellent index. Mr John Holmstrom lent his sharp eye to spot inconsistencies and to tauten my script. I would also thank Mrs Richard Miles (for suggesting the title), Mr Daniel Freeman, the Hon. Aylmer Tryon, Mr W. Jordan (of the R.S.P.C.A.), Miss Susan Radcliffe, Mrs Arthur Harrison, Mrs Hubert Hartley, Mr Jeremy Marks (for some photography), Mr Raef Payne, Miss Caroline Tonson Rye (for invaluable help over the illustrations), and Mr J. R. Freeman for the large majority of the photographs.

I also acknowledge with gratitude the permission of Sir Rupert Hart-Davis and the Hogarth Press to quote two poems by William Plomer, Messrs Curtis Brown and the estate of Roy Campbell for eight verses of the poet's *Dreaming Spires*, Miss Sheila Scriven and the Editor of *Country Life* for a passage from an article on the French giraffe, the Museum Press for allowing me to reproduce a drawing from L. R. Brightwell's *The Zoo Story*, and Mr Jack Henderson for the famous painting of okapis by Sir Harry Johnston.

W.J.W.B.
August 1975

The Garden of Eden. Oil painting by Rubens and Jan Brueghel the Elder, *c.* 1620

1

Introduction

'GOD Almighty', wrote Bacon, 'first planted a garden'; indeed, He also created the first nature reserve—that earthly paradise so charmingly and whimsically re-created for us in the paintings of Jan Brueghel the Elder and other Flemish artists. No discord here; no snapping or snarling; not a 'sportsman' in sight. The lion lies down with the lamb, while the curator and his wife, naked both but unashamed, walk side by side in the cool of the evening devising the first and commendably simple system of zoological nomenclature. Then came that meddlesome serpent, the Fall, and the expulsion from the Garden. . . .

It was Noah who assembled the first menagerie, and conditions in the Ark must have been not unlike those obtaining in many a nineteenth-century zoo; there may or may not have been cages, but there must certainly have been overcrowding. The long, fascinating, but at times distressing story of the keeping of animals in captivity from the days of Noah onwards may be read in the three stout volumes of Gustave Loisel's *Histoire des Ménageries de l'Antiquité à nos Jours*, published in Paris in 1912. In them the author describes first the menageries of the ancient Egyptians, the Chinese, the Indians and the Romans. There follows a full account of the keeping of animals in Europe in the Middle Ages and the Renaissance, and of the gradual emergence in what he calls 'modern times' (i.e., the seventeenth and eighteenth centuries) of zoology as a precise science. In conclusion, he deals with the creation, all over the world in the nineteenth century, of zoos and zoological societies. Most of this cannot, of course, be told here; but we may reasonably make space in which to consider the part played by England since the time when William the Conqueror established or perhaps took over an already existing animal park at Woodstock, near Oxford.

Julius Caesar mentions in his *Commentaries* that even in those days rich English land-owners had parks in which they kept hares, geese and chickens, not for eating but almost as 'pets'. The Norman lords who came over with the Conqueror appropriated parks such as these and stocked them with deer for the chase and sometimes with less common animals also. There is a record of a nobleman receiving a bear from William Rufus, and William

The Tower of London Menagerie, *c.* 1820

of Malmesbury tells us that Henry I had at Woodstock lions, leopards, lynxes, camels and other animals, including a remarkable owl which had been sent him by William of Montpellier. Henry III, who in 1252 transferred the Woodstock collection to London, had a polar bear for whose maintenance at the Tower of London the City's sheriffs were made responsible; they were also obliged to furnish it with a muzzle and an iron chain, and a stout rope to hold it when, to save expense, it was taken down to the Thames to fish for its supper. In 1254 Henry was sent by his son-in-law, King Louis IX of France, a sensational present: the first elephant ever to be seen in England.[1] Again the unfortunate sheriffs had to bear the substantial cost of feeding it and of constructing a cage, forty feet by twenty, to house it.

Over the years the Tower menagerie had its ups and downs, flourishing only when a monarch (or his consort) was interested in animals, or upon the chance receipt of rarities as gifts from foreign potentates. In 1436 there was not a single lion left; but nine years later, after Henry VI's marriage to the zoophile Margaret of Anjou, there were enough to justify the appointment of a Keeper of the Royal Lions. Under Edward IV the lions were removed to a spot just beyond the present Lion Gate. Elizabeth I (an *aficionada* of bear-baiting) and James I, sharing the barbarous tastes of their subjects, enjoyed watching the combats between wild animals and dogs there. The animals at the Tower were miserably housed in Stuart times, and Evelyn, when in Florence in 1644, commented that the city's 'wolves, cats, bears, tigers and lions', kept in a deep walled court, were 'therefore to be seen with much more pleasure than those at the tower of London, in their grates'.

In the eighteenth century the public was admitted to the Tower menagerie on the pay-

1. The Macedonian historian of the second century A.D., Polyaenus (*Strategematum*, Bk VIII), is the only authority for the suggestion that Caesar used an elephant to effect a crossing of the Thames, near Chertsey. It seems improbable.

ment of three-halfpence or, alternatively, the provision of a cat or dog to be fed to the lions. George IV inherited only one elephant, one grizzly bear and a few birds, but by the end of his reign the menagerie was again well stocked. Then came William IV, who closed it down and presented the animals to the Zoological Society of London, suggesting at the same time that any unwanted duplicates might be passed on to the recently founded Zoological Society of Dublin. In the eighteenth century there were also small menageries at Kew, Richmond and Osterley.

At Windsor there had been, since the time of William the Conqueror or soon after, a large deer park—one of many such parks for which the British Isles are still famous. But it is not until the year 1764 that we hear of the existence of a menagerie in the Park, near Sandpit Gate, in which George II's odious son the Duke of Cumberland, the 'Butcher of Culloden', kept a variety of wild beasts. The Duke enjoyed animal combats, and on one occasion pitted a tiger against a fine stag. When the latter routed its adversary, he surprisingly ordered a silver collar to be made for it, engraved with an account of the fight, and granted the courageous animal its liberty.

Soon after his accession George III received from Lord Pigot, the Governor of Madras, a hunting cheetah whose prowess it was proposed to demonstrate by a hunt in Windsor Great Park; but, alarmed by the large crowd of spectators, the cheetah refused to play.

Polito's Royal Menagerie. Hand-coloured aquatint, 1812

The Surrey Zoological Gardens. Opened in 1831 and patronised by Queen Adelaide

The animal is, however, immortalised for us in one of the finest of all the paintings of George Stubbs, recorder also of our first, and also royal, zebra. As will be told in a later chapter, George IV kept England's first giraffe at Windsor until its death in 1829; but under his successor the collection suffered the same fate as that at the Tower.

Also famous in its day was Edward Cross's 'Exeter 'Change', a private menagerie off the Strand which had started life in the eighteenth century as 'Pidcock's Exhibition of Wild Beasts', then becoming 'Polito's Royal Menagerie' before passing under the management of Cross. C. R. Leslie, in his *Autobiographical Recollections*, mentions 'a curly-headed youngster' who in 1816 was 'dividing his time between Polito's wild beasts at Exeter Change and the Royal Academy Schools'; this was the fourteen-year-old Edwin Landseer, who was later to find at Regent's Park the models for his polar bear in 'Man proposes, God disposes', and his lions for Trafalgar Square.

In 1829 Cross transferred his animals from 'the disgusting receptacles of the Exeter 'Change' to the King's Mews, the site of the present National Gallery; so it is amusing to remember that where a St Jerome now sits beside his docile painted lion, real live lions once roared. But he was soon on the move again—this time to the grounds of the Manor House at Wandsworth, where he established and ran the Surrey Zoological and Botanical Society until the growing popularity of the London Zoo drove him out of business. Among Cross's most celebrated animals was Chunee the Indian elephant, one-time star of 'Blue Beard' at Covent Garden, who finally went berserk and, kneeling to make his execution the easier for his murderers, fell at last to the one-hundred-and-fifty-second bullet from a wildly incompetent firing squad.[1] There was also a mandrill named 'Happy Jerry' (of whom more later[2]), and a clouded tiger (clouded leopard) acquired from Sir Stamford Raffles, who first made it known to science.

Thomas Hood, a great animal lover, writes in 'The Monkey-Martyr' about

> . . . that intrusive pile,
> Where Cross keeps many a kind
> Of bird confin'd
> And free-born animal, in durance vile.

The hero of his poem is 'Pug', a monkey infected with a zeal for 'Animals' Lib' who decides to liberate Cross's lion—which immediately devours him. One verse describes the cramped conditions in which Cross's mammals were kept:

> Lord!–how it made him chafe,
> Full of his new emancipating zeal,
> To look around upon this brute-bastille,
> And see the king of creatures in—a safe!
> The desert's denizen in one small den,
> Swallowing slavery's most bitter pills—
> A bear in bars unbearable. And then
> The fretful porcupine, with all its quills
> Imprison'd in a pen!
> A tiger limited to four foot ten;
> And, still worse lot,
> A leopard to one spot!
> An elephant enlarg'd,
> But not discharg'd;
> (It was before the elephant was shot;)
> A doleful wanderoo, that wandered not;
> An ounce much disproportion'd to his pound.
> Pug's wrath wax'd hot
> To gaze upon these captive creatures round;
> Whose claws—all scratching—gave him full assurance
> They found their durance vile of vile endurance.

At the time of the opening of the London Zoo in 1828, the Tower, the Exeter 'Change, and Chiswick House (where the Duke of Devonshire had 'a particularly sagacious female

---

1. For a full and horrific account of this butchery see Hone's *Every-Day Book*. See also Thomas Hood, *Address to Mr Cross, of Exeter Change, on the death of the Elephant*, 1826, and F. Buckland, *Curiosities of Natural History*, third series, vol. ii, pp. 254–7.

2. See p. 95.

The Execution of Chunee, 1826. Contemporary wood-engraving

elephant'), were apparently the only places in London with wild animals on permanent exhibition. Travelling menageries, however, were enormously popular, and that of George Wombwell (1778–1850) by far the most celebrated. Wombwell had begun in a humble way by exhibiting a couple of boa constrictors, which within three weeks had reimbursed him for his initial outlay of £75. In 1825 he achieved notoriety by staging at Warwick a 'match' between his fiercest lion, Nero, and six mastiffs. When Nero declined to fight he was replaced by a smaller lion, Wallace; but this time it was the mastiffs which found discretion the better part of valour. At one time Wombwell had forty caravans and more than twenty lions, many of which he had bred; but his most famous exhibit was his 'Elephant of Siam'.

Hone dismisses Wombwell as 'undersized in mind as well as in form, a weazen, sharp-faced man, with a skin reddened by more than natural spirits'.[1] Though it is hard for us today to accept that anyone who staged such 'matches' could really have loved animals, it was widely asserted that he did; and according to his obituary in *The Times*, 'No one probably did more to forward practically the study of natural history among the masses.'

But these were caged animals; and though at the London Zoo the cage was for a long time to remain very much in evidence, here at last there was to be in England a zoological

1. William Hone, *Table Book*, 1827–8.

garden—and one which was soon to influence the keeping of animals all over the world. Such a project was not wholly new, for something of the kind, far more spectacular and at that time wholly unrealistic, had been advanced as early as the year 1800 by M. Verniquet, architect to the Jardin des Plantes in Paris. Of his ambition to display animals in a sort of super-Whipsnade, he wrote:

> It is desirable that the terrain should be uneven, with mountains, grottoes, valleys, plains, streams, ponds, lakes, springs and woods of different kinds of trees. It is also desirable for there to be land variously cultivated, heaths, sandy ground, marsh, vineyards and meadows—the whole enclosed by walls and by double fences for the containing of wild and dangerous beasts. . . .[1]

Though Verniquet's scheme was, needless to say, never carried out, the Jardin des Plantes did in fact make some advance in the direction of a garden-zoo; and as we shall see, Sir Stamford Raffles, co-founder and first President of the Zoological Society of London, was openly to admit that he had taken it as his model.

1. Loisel, *op. cit.*, ii, pp. 319–20.

Sir Stamford Raffles. Oil-painting by G. F. Joseph, 1817

❧ 2 ❧

The Zoological Society of London

Animals are such agreeable friends—they ask no questions, they pass no criticisms.

George Eliot, *Mr Gilfil's Love-Story*

How many, one may ask, of the two million or so of those who visit the London Zoo each year appreciate that what they see is no more than the shop-window, as it were, of a scientific institution—the Zoological Society of London? Or to put it another way: the Zoo is the flower which springs from invisible roots carefully planted and tended. Animals, like flowers, attract visitors; and the money contributed by visitors to the Zoo, and to the gardens and exhibitions of the Royal Horticultural Society, provides for the upkeep not only of what the public sees, but also for all the invaluable scientific research which is carried on behind the scenes.

The Zoological Society of London was founded on 29 April 1826, Sir Stamford Raffles being elected its first President.

This remarkable man—the creator of Singapore and, incidentally, the discoverer of the largest and one of the most malodorous flowers in the world, *Rafflesia arnoldi*[1]—was born in 1781, the son of a ship's captain. By his brilliant natural gifts and tireless industry he rose from the drudgery of an office desk in East India House to achieve, by the age of twenty-three, a position of responsibility as Assistant Secretary in the newly constituted Presidency of Penang (Malaya). During the five months' voyage he learnt Malay, and on his arrival set about making himself the leading authority on every aspect of Indonesia. After the capture by the British of Java (in which his knowledge and contacts played a decisive role), the Governor General of India, Lord Minto, appointed him Lieutenant Governor of the island.

Raffles was now thirty, and we may see him as he was at this time through the naïve eyes of Abdullah, one of his Malayan clerks, a hero-worshipper of this unusual type of

---

1. Elephant droppings found near a Rafflesia gave rise to the absurd myth that the flower was fertilised by these animals.

Englishman who took so deep an interest in local history, botany and zoology[1] and who, above all, treated the natives as human beings:

> Mr Raffles struck me as being of middle stature, neither too short nor too tall. His brow was broad, the sign of large-heartedness, his head betokened his good understanding, his hair being fair betokened courage, his ears being large quick hearing. His eyebrows were thick and his left eye squinted a little, his nose was high, his cheeks a little hollow, the sign of oratory and persuasiveness, his mouth wide, his neck was long, his breasts were well formed, his waist slender, his legs in proportion, and he walked with a slight stoop.

Abdullah added that he was 'most courteous in his intercourse with all men. He had a sweet expression on his face, was extremely affable and liberal, and listened with attention when people spoke to him. . . . If my experience be not at fault, there was not his equal in this world in skill or largeness of heart.'

We cannot follow Raffles through his distinguished though at times stormy career in India and Indonesia. In 1816 he returned to London (dropping in on Napoleon at St Helena *en route*), summarily recalled to answer charges which had been made against his administration. Overwork in a bad climate had by now undermined his health; but he made light of his illnesses and, after his personal honour had been vindicated, returned to Sumatra as Governor of Bencoolen.

In February 1824 Raffles took a final farewell of the Far East and sailed with his wife for England. Though he had already over the years sent a part of his collections home, he now had with him a vast accumulation of papers, books and maps, more than two thousand drawings, many botanical and zoological specimens, and a small zoo. A few hours out of Bencoolen the ship caught fire and he lost everything, counting himself fortunate to have been able to escape with his wife, both of them only half dressed, in an overcrowded rowing-boat. After the disaster, he wrote:

> There is scarcely an unknown animal in Sumatra, whether bird, mammal or fish, that we did not have on board. There were among them a live tapir,[2] a new clouded leopard and a set of splendid pheasants, which I had specially tamed for the voyage. In short, we had in this respect a perfect Noah's ark. Everything, absolutely everything perished! But, thank God, our lives were spared and so we must not complain.

Three months later they sailed again, reaching Plymouth in August with a substantial new collection which he had assembled while awaiting a passage.

*   *   *

1. Raffles had a Malayan Sun Bear of which he wrote: 'He was brought up in the nursery with the children; and when admitted to my table . . . gave a proof of his taste by refusing to eat any fruit but mangosteens, or to drink any wine but champaign. The only time I ever knew him out of humour was an occasion when no champaign was forthcoming.' *Transactions of the Linnean Society*, 1821.
2. For an interesting account of Raffles and the Malayan (or Banded) Tapir, see H. Wendt, *Out of Noah's Ark*, pp. 309 ff.

In 1817, during his visit to England, Raffles had taken the opportunity to make a short tour of France and Holland. In Paris he had, of course, visited the Jardin des Plantes (the Jardin du Roy), which had been founded by Louis XIV and transformed in the eighteenth century by Buffon from 'a mere jumble of plants and animals, got together for a king's plaything, into a scientific institution that for many decades led the world.'[1] It was then that the idea had come to him to create one day in London a similar institution but one that would far outshine it, and soon he was in touch with Sir Joseph Banks, the President of the Royal Society, about the formation of 'a zoological collection which should interest and amuse the public'. But Banks died in 1820, and six years later, when Raffles returned to England for good, he could no longer call upon the assistance of that generous and public-spirited doyen of English naturalists in the realisation of the last great dream of his life—the foundation of the Zoological Society of London (Z.S.L.).

The reader, unless he is a glutton for punishment, will hardly wish to become too in-volved in the tangled story of the origins of the Society, a full account of which may be read elsewhere.[2] There can be no doubt that Raffles was its principal promoter, and that the role played by Sir Humphry Davy, whom he generously calls joint 'projector', was less important than has sometimes been suggested; Davy, as President of the Royal Society, was too busy a man to take a very active part, but his backing was no doubt invaluable in giving respectability to a venture which many people considered rash, hardly practicable, or even absurd. Further, it is certain that though the Society was not a direct offshoot of the Zoological Club of the Linnean Society (formed in 1822), the two bodies were fairly closely associated.

By 20 May 1825 a brief prospectus had finally been agreed and was soon afterwards published. It consisted of a single sheet bearing on one side a list of the names of sixty-six subscribers, drawn mostly from the world of science but discreetly seasoned with a sprinkling of the more enlightened or influential aristocracy, and on the other the following:

It is proposed to establish a Society having the same relations to Zoology that Horti-culture bears to Botany, and upon a similar plan and similar principles.

The objects of this Society are,

1st.—To introduce, by means of a public Establishment, new varieties, breeds, or races of living Animals, such as Quadrupeds, Birds, Fishes, &c. which may be judged capable of application to purposes of utility, either in our Farm Yards, Woods, Wastes, Ponds, or Rivers.

2d.—To assist this Establishment and the general study of Zoology by a Museum of prepared specimens.

---

1. L. R. Brightwell, *op. cit.* Actually, live animals did not arrive there (from Versailles) until 1793, after Buffon's death.
2. See in particular the works of Chalmers Mitchell, Scherren, Street and Brightwell, and also John Bastin in *J. Soc. Biblphy Nat. Hist.* (1970) *5* (5): 369–88 and (1973) *6* (4): 236–41.

It is proposed to make the Annual Subscription from each Individual Two Pounds, and the Admission Fee Three Pounds.

Persons desirous of belonging to this Society, will signify their wishes, by letter, to Mr T. Griffiths, 21 Albemarle-street.

There is no mention here of 'amusing' the public, though in fact one at least of its members was amused by the reference to 'new . . . races of living animals'. 'What the dickons does this assertion mean?' he inquired of the *Literary Gazette*, a paper particularly concerned with the sciences and arts. 'Are we to have animals that never existed before?'

As will soon appear, the original aims of the Society were to be considerably amended and extended. But it is clear from a letter which Raffles had written in 1825 to a cousin, Dr Thomas Raffles, that from the very beginning he and Davy had envisaged something far more ambitious than simply the breeding of livestock useful to man and the formation of a museum of 'stuffed' animals. In it he spoke of 'a Grand Collection' of live animals which would far surpass that of the Jardin des Plantes; and such was his optimism that he anticipated a membership of twenty thousand—a number that has not been reached even today.

A site had already been found: the Commissioners of Woods and Forestry had offered the use of about five acres of Crown land at the northern end of Regent's Park. This little pocket-handkerchief of a plot—it is hardly as big as Grosvenor Square—was to become the nucleus of the present Gardens. It was, however, trebled in size in 1831 and a further ten acres were added in 1834, since when it has gradually expanded to its present size of about thirty-six acres.

The first General Meeting of the 'Friends of the proposed Zoological Society' was held on 29 April 1826 at the Horticultural Society's room in Regent Street. Forty-eight people attended, and among the resolutions adopted was one stating the amended aims: 'The formation of a Collection of Living Animals; a Museum of Preserved Animals; and a Library connected with the subject;' there is no mention of the 'utility' which, rather surprisingly, had figured so prominently in the prospectus of the previous year. The Society was to be directed by a President, Treasurer, Secretary and Council, Raffles's election as President being 'by acclamation'. Members (they were not yet called Fellows) were now to pay an admission fee of £5 together with an annual subscription of £2, or a composition fee of £25 for life-membership. It is interesting to note that in 1827 ladies were admitted as Members—something quite unusual in learned societies at that time[1]—and further (and perhaps because in those days girls were educated for little beyond matrimony) no 'intelligence test' was involved: you merely had to be recommended by three Members (after 1829, Fellows) and to pay your subscription; thus those authors who once proudly appended 'F.Z.S.' to their names did so out of vanity. This has now been forbidden.

1. It may, or may not, have been merely coincidental that Lady Raffles presented her late husband's Sumatran collection to the Society's Museum at this time and was elected a Member a few weeks later.

The Old Tunnel, Regent's Park. Lithograph by F. W. Hulme, 1848

A week after this first Meeting of the 'Friends' the Council held its first formal Meeting, at which it was announced that a house, no. 33 Bruton Street, was being taken for offices and a museum. *The Times* briefly reported this gathering and listed the more distinguished of those present (who, very gratifyingly, included a royal Duke); but only the *Literary Gazette* had anything of substance to say. The article was captioned 'ZOOLOGICAL, OR NOAH'S ARK SOCIETY', and its tone was mocking. If funds allowed, its readers were told, 'strange reptiles may be propagated all over the kingdom. But there is neither wisdom nor folly new under the sun'. After referring to Henry I's menagerie at Woodstock and the Romans' addiction to 'wild beast shows', the writer continued: 'Considering the advanced state of knowledge it is to be expected that the new Zoological Association will beat both the Romans and King Henry; though we do not know how the inhabitants of the Regent's Park will like the lions, leopards and linxes so near their neighbourhood.'

The first tasks of the President and Council were to appoint an architect and to get some

THE INDIAN WANDEROO MONKEY (SILENUS VETER).

Wanderoo Monkey. Wood-engraving, 1859

animals. For the former they turned to Decimus Burton (1800–81), a clever and ambitious young man who had already won fame by his Colosseum, a building with a dome larger than St Paul's which contained a panorama of London painted by a Mr Horner from drawings made as he clung to scaffolding at the summit of the Cathedral. There had followed the planning of Hyde Park, and the erection of the triumphal arch at Hyde Park Corner which Burton had been obliged to crown with an equestrian statue of Wellington in lieu of his projected quadriga. ('*Nous sommes vengés!*' a French officer had cried on seeing its ugliness.[1]) So Burton was looked upon in 1826 as 'up-and-coming', and the Zoological Society, considering itself fortunate to have acquired his services, appointed him in 1830 its official architect. But though his planning of the grounds was pleasant enough, his designs for the buildings were undistinguished, and in the event never to be more than partially carried out. Today all that remains of his work is the plainly functional Giraffe House (now considerably modified), the little Camel House with its clock tower,[2] an elegant Ravens' Aviary (originally the Macaw Cage), and the old tunnel which proved too low to allow the passage of an elephant and howdah. Piety alone has justified their survival.

As for the animals—since there were as yet no cages in Regent's Park, Cross of the

1. For many years Burton's will provided to the nation the sum of £2,000 if it would agree to the removal of the statue. This offer he eventually withdrew; but in 1885, after his death, Wellington was carted off to Aldershot.
2. Added in 1831, replaced by another of different design in 1845, and no doubt 'tinkered with' more than once subsequently for its present appearance is frankly grotesque. It was bombed in the Second World War, but 'rebuilt brick by brick—the Society's way of taking its hat off to tradition'. (James Fisher, *Zoos of the World*, p. 173, with two illustrations.)

Exeter 'Change agreed to take charge of any unruly acquisitions until the Zoo[1] was ready to receive them; but some that were relatively innocuous and reasonably house-trained were kept at Bruton Street. The first live animals received by the Society were a griffon vulture, a white-headed eagle, and a 'female Deer from Sangor [Sambar?]'. The eagle, known as 'Dr Brookes' after its donor, survived for more than forty years in horribly cramped captivity. Cross also twice offered to sell his entire collection to the Society—first (together with himself as manager) in 1826, which was far too soon from the Zoo's point of view, and again in 1829 (but now without his services) when he had to leave the Strand. On this occasion the price was more than the Society could afford, and an offer for a part of the collection was rejected.

Of the animals housed at Bruton Street we know details only of one—a wanderoo monkey whose pranks Broderip describes in his *Zoological Recreations* (1847):

There was one in the Zoological Society's collection, then in its infancy, in Bruton Street, and a right merry fellow was he. He would run up his pole and throw himself over the cross-bar, so as to swing backwards and forwards, as he hung suspended by the chain which held the leathern strap that girt his loins. The expression of his countenance was peculiarly innocent; but he was sly, very sly, and not to be approached with impunity. He would sit demurely on his cross-perch, pretending to look the other way, or to examine a nut-shell for some remnant of kernel, till a proper victim came within his reach; when, down the pole he rushed, and up again he was, in the twinkling of an eye, leaving the bare-headed surprised one minus his hat, at the least, which he had the satisfaction of seeing undergoing a series of metamorphoses under the hand of the grinning ravisher. . . .

It was whispered—*horrescimus referentes*—that he had once scalped a bishop, who ventured too near . . . and that it was some time before he could be made to give up, with much mowing and chattering, the well-powdered wig which he had profanely transferred from the sacred poll to his own. . . .

In July 1826 Raffles died suddenly of apoplexy; he was only forty-five. Davy, his natural successor as President, being already a sick man with only three more years to live, Lord Lansdowne was elected to fill the post, which he held until his retirement in 1831.

Though the Zoological Society was no more than a babe in arms, and the Zoo as yet unborn, Raffles died in the knowledge that these the last of his children would, like Singapore, long survive him. The Zoo now proudly boasts the Charles Clore and Michael Sobell

1. This vulgar but convenient abbreviation entered our language about 1847, when Macaulay used it of the Clifton Zoo; but it was not until some twenty years later that Vance, the famous music hall singer, made it popular by his 'Walking in the Zoo on Sunday':

> The Stilton, Sir, the Cheese, the O.K. thing to do
> On Sunday afternoon is to toddle in the Zoo. . . .

Pavilions, the Mappin Terraces and Mappin Wimpy Kiosk, the Cotton Terraces and the Snowdon Aviary, thus very properly commemorating four benefactors and an architect; but in the most recent *London Zoo Guide* (1973) you will search in vain for even a mention of the name of the Zoological Society's founder and first President, whose entire Sumatran collection also came, through the generosity of his widow, to the Society after his death. His statue by Chantrey is in Westminster Abbey, his portrait by George Joseph in the National Portrait Gallery; but another bust of him which formerly graced a niche in the Lion House has now been removed to the Society's offices.[1] *Si monumentum requiris, circumspice?* Maybe—but I would be prepared to bet that not one visitor in a thousand knows the name of Raffles in connection with the Zoo, whereas every visitor to Singapore knows it from the famous Raffles Hotel. That of the Regent is written large already over his Park; might not an *amende honorable* be made by re-christening the Regent Restaurant the Raffles Restaurant? It would be better than nothing, and even the alliteration would be preserved.

Burton got quickly down to work; in July 1827 his plan of the Gardens was lithographed for distribution to Members and reproduced in the *Literary Gazette*, which now abandoned its former bantering tone and predicted a great future for the new Zoo. Though this was not yet open to the public, Members and their friends were able, before the year was out, to inspect some two hundred animals already housed there 'in suitable dens, aviaries, and paddocks'. These included 'two beautiful llamas, a leopard, kangaroos, a Russian bear, ratel, ichneumons, &c., &c., besides a pair of emus, cranes, gulls, gannets, corvorants [*sic*], various gallinaceous birds, and many others', all in the charge of several keepers enticed from the Tower and Exeter 'Change.

The first of the so-called 'Occurrences'—report sheets sent daily to Bruton Street from the Zoo—appeared on 25 February 1828 and contained the following information:

> MENAGERIE.—Received eleven wild ducks from the Lake,[2] caught for the purpose of pinioning, and then to be returned.
> Received six silver-haired rabbits from Mr Blake.
> Otter died, in consequence of a diseased tail.
> Emu laid her fourth egg on the 24th.
> All animals and birds well.
> WORKS.—Pit for bear, house for llamas in progress.
> Boundary wall for supporting the bank next the Bear's pit begun.
> SERVANTS.—All on duty.
> NO. OF VISITORS.—Four
> PARTICULAR VISITOR.—Lord Auckland

1. There is also a portrait of Raffles, attributed to James Lonsdale, in the Council Room of the Society.
2. The Zoological Club of the Linnean Society had transferred to the Zoological Society 'a lake and its islands near Regent's Park' for waterfowl.

Meanwhile the scientific side of the Society's work was not being neglected. On 25 April 1827 its first Scientific Meeting was held, when the eminent anatomist Dr Joshua Brookes lectured on his dissection of the body of an ostrich which had lived for two years at Windsor and at death had been given to the Society by the King. The first books were presented to the Library, which was one day to become the finest of its kind in the world, and in due course there appeared the first volumes of the Society's *Proceedings* (1830) and *Transactions* (1835). The aid of the Foreign Office was invoked to inform British consuls abroad that a garden had recently been laid out 'for the reception of curious beasts and birds from all quarters of the world, in imitation of the Jardin des Plantes, at Paris', and begging them to seize every opportunity to send home 'any rare animals which may be worthy of a place in this rising establishment'.

All was now set for the opening to public scrutiny of what was soon to become, and what in spite of American riches and Swiss and German 'know-how' was to remain to this day, the most representative collection of wild animals in the world.

3

The Early Days of the Zoo

To offer hospitality or to accept it is an instinct which man has only acquired in the long course of his self development. Lions do not ask one another to their lairs, nor do birds keep open nests. When you give a dog a bone, he does not run out and share it with another, nor does your cat insist on having a circle of friends round her saucer of milk.

Max Beerbohm

ON 27 April 1828 the Zoo opened its gates for the first time to non-Members. Or rather, its gate: the only way in was between two little rustic sentry-boxes where the main entrance now is. 'Strangers' (as they were called) were admitted to the Garden[1] on the written order of a Member and payment of a shilling, the order allowing the holder to introduce, each for the same sum, as many of his friends as he liked; but there was no move to admit the general public, every care having been taken 'to prevent the contamination of the Zoological Garden by the admission of the poorer classes of Society'.[2] On Sundays the Garden was open to Members only.

Unfortunately the Press-cuttings volumes of the Society do not go back beyond 1849; but thanks to the delightful illustrations in *The Zoological Keepsake* (1830), G. Scharf's *Six Views of the Zoological Gardens, Regent's Park* (1835), and other such works, we can form a good idea of what the Zoo looked like in its infancy. At the actual time of its opening, though the condition of the Garden was described as being 'in considerable forwardness', no permanent buildings had as yet been erected, and even the pictures in the *Keepsake* were to anticipate certain features never to be realised; a year or two later, however, there was plenty to be seen.

At the end of the terrace, beneath which were housed an American tapir and an ostrich, came a bear-pit with three bears, and near to this a stall for the sale of 'cakes, fruits, nuts,

1. Only after the construction in 1829 of the tunnel to connect the original Garden with land on the other side of the Outer Circle was the plural form used.
2. Letter from 'Constant Reader' to Mr Tatler.

Bird's-eye View of the London Zoo, 1829. *Zoological Keepsake*, 1830

and other articles, which the visitor may be disposed to give to the different animals'.[1]
Among further prominent features were the camel house (used at first for llamas), the
elephant paddock and wapiti house, the monkey house, an open-air aviary, and a temporary
building containing a variety of animals which included three leopards[2] and other big cats.
The bird's-eye view (here reproduced) of the Garden in 1829 shows the layout.

As for the human fauna, the elegant ladies and gentlemen who stroll so nonchalantly
across the wide lithographs of Scharf, feeding the elephant or chatting up a pigtail macaque,
make it clear that here was a centre of fashion of a kind later to be associated with Ascot
and other smart venues of the London 'season'; not for nothing was it soon to be dubbed
'the most delightful lounge in the metropolis'. Many of the animals were, after all, royal
gifts; the King himself had been graciously pleased to become a Patron of the Society,

1. It may be mentioned here that the feeding of animals by the public—something so pleasurable to the donor,
so dangerous to the recipient—was very sensibly phased out from the middle of the present century and
finally forbidden altogether in January 1968.
2. 'A lady, Mrs Bowdich, now Mrs Lee, won the heart of one of these animals by lavender water, which it
was so extravagantly fond of, as to be trained into the habitual sheathing of its claws by the mere punishment
of the loss of this luxury when it did not.' (*London* by Charles Knight.)

and when you gazed at the scarlet ibis from the menagerie at Windsor, Queen Adelaide's three alpacas, or the Duke of Sussex's Persian lynx, you could almost feel that you were in the presence of royalty. Indeed, you might before long, if you were very lucky, even have run into young Princess Victoria in person, clutching the arm of 'dear Augustus' because 'the crowd was great'. It was already very much 'the O.K. thing to do' to visit the Zoo; today you can spend a whole long June afternoon there without catching sight of a single duchess or rubbing shoulders with a single 'television personality'.

In 1829 King George IV granted a Charter 'constituting and founding a society . . . for the advancement of zoology and animal physiology and the introduction of new and curious subjects of the animal kingdom by the name of "THE ZOOLOGICAL SOCIETY OF LONDON".' The first printed list of Fellows was issued, and fifty years later, in his Jubilee address, the President (Sir William Flower) drew attention to the number of persons 'eminent in science, art, literature, or social life' that it included; 'Indeed,' he added, 'there were not many people of distinction in the country at that time who are not to be found in it.'

This was no doubt true; but among the Fellows there were also one or two black, or at least silly, sheep. In that same year the Society had established 'at Kingston Hill beside Richmond Park' an experimental farm—something more ambitious and more scientific than the traditional deer-park, but falling far short of the Whipsnade of a century later. On this rural retreat there descended one summer Sunday evening a party of seventeen drunks, unwisely introduced by 'a Lady of Title', who 'dined on the lawn and amused themselves with hunting the zebras and kangaroos about—upsetting the coops and carrying the ducks about in their arms, and afterwards pouring Punch or something similar into their pans. The Men were kept till past 10 o'clock searching for the ducks after the Party had left, and seven ducks died the next day in consequence of the treatment they had received.'[1] One of the reasons for leasing the land had been to provide shy animals with peace and privacy for breeding, and it was possibly the difficulty of patrolling so large an area that led to the abandonment of the project after only four years.

In 1829 the Society also published its first Guide to the Zoo. This was the joint work of its scholarly Secretary, Nicholas Vigors, and the more discursive William Broderip, and Scherren is no doubt right in seeing the hand of the latter in the description of another potential alcoholic—the Crab-eating Raccoon:

> Strange stories are told of its fishing for crabs, with its tail, and opening oysters with its feet; and Pennant says 'that it loves strong liquors and will get excessively drunk.' It seems to be attached to good cheer in general, from ''Possum up a gum tree' to sugar cane, and appears to have a penchant for turtle; for our friend here, who is extremely amiable, playful and caressing, was admitted one day into a room with a land tortoise, which he no sooner saw than he flew at it with the zeal of an alderman.

1. Letter from Mr Papps, the Superintendent, to the Assistant Secretary.

A century later (1933 *Guide*) we are informed merely that the Common Raccoon *(Procyon lotor)* and the Crab-eating Raccoon *(P. cancrivorus)* are 'small tree-loving omnivorous mammals, allies of the Coatis', which 'should be looked for high up on the branches of the tree as well as on the ground', while in the 1973 *Guide* raccoons (so far as I can see, for it has no index) seem to have become too vulgar to be accorded a mention. This is not really a reflection on the latest *Guide*, which is a gay and handsomely illustrated booklet, but rather on a public brought up on television and scared of the printed word.

Vigors and Broderip were also among the contributors to the two volumes of *The Gardens and Menagerie of the Zoological Society Delineated* (1830, 1831), edited by Edward T. Bennett and illustrated with charming wood-engravings, some of them after drawings by Edward Lear.[1] The following notice of the first volume (mammals) appeared in the *Athenaeum* on 23 October 1830:

> This book will be invaluable to the sick, to the infirm—and, indeed, to all those persons who from weakness of constitution or the severity of our English summers, are unable to go upon their travels so far as to the Zoological Gardens, in the back settlements of the Regent's Park—where the wild beasts of the desert, and the wild birds of the wood and rock abound. The Zoological Gardens may be visited in this singularly faithful and beautiful work to the perfect satisfaction of the eye; and perhaps the holiday which the ear and nose enjoy in this pictured visit is not without its pleasures and relief. . . . The publication of a work so spiritedly, yet so carefully got up as this, is a real treasure to science. Anyone may now have his own menagerie in his own room—every gentleman be his own Wombwell.

In 1832, in an *Ode to N. A. Vigors, Esq. on the Publication of 'The Gardens and Menagerie of the Zoological Society'*, Thomas Hood suggests that the book might have been provided with practical zoological advice of the kind offered to horticulturists. For example:

> About the middle of the month, if fair,
> Give your Chameleons air;
>   Choose shady walls for Owls,
>   Water your Fowls,
> And plant your Leopards in the sunniest spots;
> Earth up your Beavers; train your Bears to climb;
> Thin out your Elephants about this time;
> And set some early Kangaroos in pots. . . .

In 1831 the attendance at the Zoo for the first time passed a quarter of a million, and for the next five years the figure never dropped below 210,000; then a more or less steady decline set in, which continued until the late forties. The novelty of the venture, and in

1. See chapter 5.

Escaped Kangaroo at Regent's Park. Hand-coloured etching by R. Cruikshanks, *c.* 1840

particular the royal gifts of 1831, had got the Zoo off to a good start, and the acquisition of a number of animals of special interest had sustained the momentum until 1836, when the arrival of four giraffes[1] attracted a record 263,392 visitors. But after the death in that year of Edward T. Bennett, since 1833 the Society's distinguished and energetic secretary, came a succession of men—William Yarrell (1836–8), the Rev. John Barlow (1838–40) and William Ogilby (1840–7)—who were either too ill or too busy to give much attention to the affairs of the Society. It must not be forgotten that the post was unpaid.

It would also appear that an unhappy atmosphere prevailed in the zoological world at that time, for Darwin, in a letter to John Henslow in 1836 explaining his reasons for *not* giving to the Society the vast collection of specimens he had brought back in the *Beagle*, wrote:

> The Zoological Museum is nearly full, and upwards of a thousand specimens remain unmounted. I dare say the British Museum would receive them, but I cannot feel, from all I hear, any great respect even for the present state of that establishment. . . . I am out of patience with the zoologists, not because they are overworked, but for their mean,

1. See chapter 7.

quarrelsome spirit. I went the other evening to the Zoological Society, where the speakers were snarling at each other in a manner anything but like that of gentlemen.[1]

Certainly the Zoological Department of the British Museum had long been in a very unhealthy state. Dr William Leach (1790–1836) had, it is true, begun to clear up the mess; but before long his health deteriorated and 'his habits became irregular'. His working hours were devoted to his collections of skulls and bats (kept in what he called his Scullery and his Battery), his leisure to 'leaping over the back of a stuffed zebra . . . over which we have seen him vault with the lightness of a harlequin'.[2] As for Regent's Park—rivalries, jealousies and petty bickerings are not uncommon in learned societies, and, as we shall see, the Zoological Society has had, over the years and as recently as during the Second World War,[3] at least its fair share of them. Nothing was too trivial to provoke dispute: for example, when in 1829 the regulation of the affairs of the Society was under discussion, there was heated argument even over whether or not 'Bye-laws' should be spelt with an 'e'. Very distinguished men can, on occasions, be very silly.

The Museum had all along been something of a headache to the Society: a considerable expense with very small financial return. The Council reported in 1836 that it had 'rather the confused air of a store than the appearance of an arranged museum', and even after the move that year of the Society's headquarters to a larger house in Leicester Square,[4] chaos and overcrowding remained. The obvious solution might have seemed to be the transference of the entire collection to the British Museum; but as Darwin had said, this was at that time in an almost worse state. About 1840 the Society's preserved specimens were put in store, then briefly housed at the Zoo, and in 1843 taken to the Society's new premises in Hanover Square.

In the meantime the British Museum had been putting its house in order, and in April 1850 the Council was able to record that both it and the provincial museums now presented 'so striking a contrast with their condition at the time when the Zoological Society was founded' as to render 'the maintenance of our own museum as a separate collection no longer an object of the importance which it formerly possessed.' Five years later the Council recommended that the specimens be offered to the Government 'for a fair equivalent'. In the event the 'type' specimens were presented to the British Museum, which also purchased other desiderata at an agreed price, while the bulk of the collection passed by purchase to provincial museums. Thus what the *Literary Gazette* called 'the mere wild-beast-show part of the Society' finally triumphed over the dead.

$$* \qquad * \qquad *$$

1. *Life and Letters*, vol. 1, pp. 273–4. There was little demand for unnamed specimens; but Darwin did in fact present to the Society's museum in 1836 an extensive collection of named specimens of mammals and birds collected chiefly in South America.
2. W. Swainson, *Taxidermy*, see bibliography.
3. See bibliography under Clark and Huxley.
4. Where the Alhambra now stands. The house had once belonged to the famous surgeon, John Hunter.

Among the animals that created particular interest in the early days of the Society was England's first orang-utan, a young male sent in 1830 from Calcutta by a Mr Swinton, who had previously given the Museum a female specimen preserved in spirits:

> The vessel which conveyed the poor little orang to a climate always fatal to its race, stopped some time at the Isle of France [Mauritius] to take in fresh provisions. The orang accompanied the sailors in their daily visits to the shore, and their calls upon the keepers of taverns. . . . To one of these, kept by an old woman who sold coffee, &c., for breakfast, the orang was accustomed to go, unattended every morning; and by signs easily interpreted, demand his usual breakfast, which was duly delivered. The charge was scored up to the captain's account, which he paid before his departure.[1]

The orang was on friendly terms with all on board except the butcher, whose knife he had seen in action and of whom he was mortally afraid. In his opinion the property of his friends was as much his as theirs; he therefore helped himself to the sailors' bedding and whatever else took his fancy, and fought fiercely to prevent their recovery. He was quick to learn:

> His conduct at table, to which he was familiarly admitted, was decorous and polite. He soon comprehended the use of knives and forks, but preferred a spoon, which he handled with as much ease as any child of seven or eight years old.[1]

On his arrival in London he lived for a time 'in the house of a gentleman residing in Regent's Park'. But the animal sickened and was moved to the Society's offices in Bruton Street, 'where one of his favourites, I believe the cook, attended as his nurse. He would raise his head from his pillow, turn his eyes on his attendant, with an expression as if entreating him to do something for his relief. He would at the same time utter a plaintive cry, but he evinced nothing like impatience or ill temper, and was compassionated by all who saw him.' But within a few days, without ever having been exposed to public scrutiny, he died.

His successor, Jenny or 'the first Lady Jane'—'apparently amiable, though grave and of a sage deportment'—came in 1837, and when exhibited attracted a good deal of attention until her death eighteen months later. She was followed in 1839 by a second and more famous Jenny, who survived for nearly four years—at that time a record—in captivity. Queen Victoria, who visited her on 27 May 1842, noted: 'The Orang Outang is too wonderful preparing and drinking his tea, doing everything by word of command. He is frightful & painfully and disagreeably human.'[2]

Actually the first anthropoid ape to be seen by visitors to the Zoo was Tommy the

---

1. Edward Jesse, *Gleanings in Natural History*, 2nd series, 1834.
2. It will be remembered that the murderer in Poe's *The Murders in the Rue Morgue* (1841) proved to be an orang-utan. Hollywood made it a gorilla.

Tommy, the Zoo's first Chimpanzee. Lithograph by G. Scharf, 1835

chimpanzee, who reached Regent's Park from the Gambia in 1835 and survived there for six months. One of the keepers was sent to collect him at Bristol, where some difficulty was experienced in persuading a coach proprietor to provide two inside places in the night coach. This newcomer also created a stir at the Zoo, and Theodore Hook, that 'prince of lampooners' whom Coleridge called 'as true a genius as Dante', wrote in lines hardly Dantesque:

> The folks in town are nearly wild
> To go and see the monkey-child,
> In Gardens of Zoology,
> Whose proper name is Chimpanzee.
> To keep this baby free from hurt,
> He's dressed in a cap and a Guernsey shirt;
> They've got him a nurse, and he sits on her knee,
> And she calls him her Tommy Chimpanzee.

Tommy lived as a guest in the keeper's house until his death, and in January 1838 this rather belated obituary by Broderip appeared in the *New Monthly*:

Poor dear Tommy, we knew him well, and who is there who was not at least his visiting acquaintance? . . . Peace be with him! Everybody loved him; and everybody was kind to him. In his last illness he was suffered to come forth for a closer enjoyment of the kitchen-fire; and there we saw him sit, 'leaning his cheek upon his hand', watching the gyrations of a depending shoulder of mutton, as it revolved and hissed between him and the glowing grate—no, not with prying mischievous eyes of ordinary monkeys; but with a pensive philosophic air that seemed to admit his own inferiority, and to say, 'Ah! man is, indeed, *the* cooking animal.'

In 1839 came the first gibbons, allowing Londoners the chance to see the third of the four anthropoid apes; of man's closest relatives there now remained only the gorilla. But the gibbons soon fell victims to an outbreak of tuberculosis which decimated the inhabitants of the new monkey house. The old building, erected in 1833, had been a failure from the start, and soon after its opening the Council had received the following letter:

> The front of the monkey house is constructed with taste and judgment; it is everything that could be wished for the exercise of the animals and the amusement of the company, but the house or back part of the building is low and defective, it is unhealthy and inconvenient; there is not room enough for the company; they are suffocated from the confined air and the stench of the animals, and the animals suffer in return. Ladies have frequently their veils and dresses torn by being pressed too near the dens.

As an article (probably by Richard Owen[1]) in the *Zoological Magazine* of 1833 pointed out, Cross's monkeys were much more sensibly housed, and it may well have been Owen's campaigning that led to the building in 1839–40 of the better, though still far from satisfactory, new monkey house.

Another important acquisition, purchased in 1831, was a quagga. This member of the horse tribe, zebra-like before and donkey-like behind, was once visible in vast numbers on the wide plains of the Cape Colony and no less audible by the harsh cry of 'oug-gaaa..., oug-gaaa...' which gave it its name. A pair brought to England in the twenties had been sufficiently domesticated for a Victorian exhibitionist, a Mr Sheriff Perkins, to drive them spectacularly in Hyde Park. In 1858 Sir George Grey, Governor of Cape Colony, presented another specimen, a male, to the Zoo. By this time the quagga, thanks to its persecution by Boers and big game hunters, had become such a rarity that his gift of this and other South African animals won him the Society's Silver Medal.[2] By about 1870 the quagga was declared extinct in the wild, though one at Regent's Park[3] lived until 1872 and another at Amsterdam—the last in the world—until 1882. Today we can do no more than regretfully gaze at the stuffed specimen in the museum at Tring.

The Zoo's first elephants will be discussed in a later chapter.[4] A more unusual giant was

1. For Owen see p. 80.
2. Designed by Thomas Landseer, Sir Edwin's elder brother, in 1837, but not first awarded until ten years later.
3. Acquired in 1851, and the only quagga ever photographed alive.
4. See p. 163.

a four-year-old Indian rhinoceros, purchased in 1834 for a thousand guineas.[1] This was the second attempt to import one: twenty years earlier another had been shipped from Calcutta, but it had worked such havoc during the voyage that 'a storm coming on, the captain thought it only prudent to throw him overboard'. The great one-horned Indian rhino had been known in Western Europe since the year 1513, when King Manoel of Portugal received one by sea from India; and it was from a rough sketch of this that Dürer had made his famous but fanciful woodcut which shows the animal apparently armour-plated and riveted.[2]

Today there may be no more than a few hundred of these splendid beasts remaining in the swamps of Assam, Bengal and Eastern Nepal; thus it is particularly satisfactory that since 1956 several births have occurred in captivity at Basel and Whipsnade. But, except for the giant panda, it remains the most expensive purchase a zoo can make. The Indian rhino takes kindly to prison life, one which came to Regent's Park in 1864 surviving there for more than forty years.

Such were some of the more important acquisitions of the London Zoo in the first decade or so of its existence. The success of Regent's Park soon led to the foundation of three other zoos in Great Britain and Ireland: in Dublin (1831), Bristol (1835) and Manchester (1836); all these, though they too have passed through difficult days, are now flourishing. On the Continent came Amsterdam (1837), Antwerp (1843), Hamburg (1860), Budapest (1865) and Basel (1873); but no further British zoos were established in the nineteenth century. Indeed, by the forties the popularity of Regent's Park itself had begun to wane. In 1843 the attendance dropped for the first time since 1828 to below a hundred thousand, and the account of the Zoo given by Charles Knight in his *London* (1843) is misleadingly rosy. Brightwell was only too justified in entitling the third chapter of his history, 'Downhill, 1841–50'.

1. For his death, see p. 163.
2. This animal was drowned in February 1516 off Porto Venere on its way to the Pope, and so reached the Vatican stuffed. Leo X, who had hoped to match it against his recently acquired elephant, Hanno (see p. 160), was bitterly disappointed. London's first rhino, which arrived in 1684, was described by Evelyn as looking like 'a greate coach overthrowne'.

Sir Edwin Landseer working on one of the lions for Trafalgar Square.
Oil-painting by John Ballantyne, 1866

4

Butlers, Astons, and Poor Charlie

The guides hitherto published have been of too scientific a description to assist the youthful mind. . . . It is to remedy this inconvenience this little work is put forth.

J. Bishop, *Henry and Emma's Visit to the Zoological Gardens* . . .

'A day at the Zoo'! Those five words conjure up many happy childhood memories.

To the young, the national collection of animals was so much more exciting than, for example, the national collection of pictures. Landseer's lions did not roar as one was steered reluctantly across Trafalgar Square to the National Gallery—they just sat there like enormous dead black pussycats; and within its doors it was much too like being in church. You could not give peanuts to Crivelli's peacock; there was no thrilling 'feeding-time' for Titian's leopards.[1] And there were no surprises: you did not find that a Goya had died in the night (though today you might well find that it had been stolen in the night); and though there might be an occasional acquisition there was no chance that a Tintoretto had given birth to several little Tintoretti since one's last visit. In short, to the very young the National Gallery was very dull indeed; one saw the point of it later on.

The Edwardian child went to Regent's Park to enjoy itself; and I, at all events, was never subjected to parental zoological lecturing—for which, in any case, my parents were not qualified. But in 1828, when London first got its Zoo, it was considered immoral for youth to taste the jam of pleasure unless it served to cloak a bolus of 'uplift'. Victorian 'earnestness' was already in the air long before the Queen ascended the throne, and one of its dreary but relatively harmless manifestations was the forced-feeding of the young with knowledge served up in catechismal tabloid form. There was, for example, Mrs Jane Marcet's *Conversations on Botany* (1817), which brought the sexual system of Linnaeus almost to the infant's cradle. Far better known are the *History of England* (1823) and other didactic works by Mrs Markham, of whom it was written that even in girlhood she 'devours folios of history with much more appetite than her meals, except when we have bantam eggs; then, indeed, she is like a conjuror swallowing his balls'.

1. 'Bacchus and Ariadne'. The animals appear to be leopards, but are spotted like cheetahs.

Emma, Henry, and Mr Butler.
Pen-and-ink drawing
by L. R. Brightwell,
The Zoo Story, 1952

I have seen it stated that the new Zoo stimulated Mrs Markham to an opusculum, *A Visit to the Zoological Gardens* (1829); but the British Library denies its existence, and I think there must be confusion with a little book of that same year by Mr J. Bishop, entitled:

HENRY AND EMMA'S
VISIT
to the
ZOOLOGICAL GARDENS
in the Regent's Park
with an
ACCOUNT OF WHAT THEY SAW THERE:
interspersed with
A Description of the peculiar Manners and Habits
of the various Animals contained therein.

The following year came the already mentioned anonymous *Zoological Keepsake*—a stouter duodecimo enlivened (if that is the right word) with 'original poetry'. Both these works are charmingly illustrated with 'elegant and appropriate engravings'.

Mr Bishop's book deals with a single visit to the Zoo, made by Mr Butler, his wife and their two wretched children, Henry and Emma, as Henry's promised reward for a good half-term report.

So lovely were the flowers that, even before the first animal hove in sight, Henry 'thought himself in Fairyland', while Emma declared that with so much floral beauty on every side, animals seemed almost superfluous. But Mr Butler, who had no prepared lecture on delphiniums, urged his loitering party onwards towards the bear-pit, where he immediately proceeded to deliver the first of a succession of windy and inaccurate homilies. Indeed, there is surprisingly little catechism in this particular book; for it would seem that Mrs

Butler and Emma were cowed into silence, while even Henry could rarely do more than 'thank his papa for kindly telling him the history of the bears' before dear Papa propelled his captives to the tumbler pigeons and embarked upon his next monologue.

Mr Butler was a past master of the obvious. 'The greater part of the birds you see there,' he informed his family when they reached the pond, 'are called water-fowl, from their subsisting principally in the water'. And of the polar bear: 'This bear was brought from that part of the world, called the Polar Regions, and on that account is called the Polar Bear. . . . There, on large fields of ice, Bears similar to this are to be seen, wandering about in search of food, which consists of fish and snow, and now and then the dead body of a whale, or a sea-horse, or some such dainty.' The occasional unavoidable interruption of the discourse—for the author has to keep his puppets moving—creates a suspense that is almost unbearable. For example: 'Our party having reached the tunnel which unites the two Gardens, and feeling themselves fatigued, sat down on chairs placed for that purpose; and, after resting a time, again proceeded forward'—for a portentous lecture on the ostriches. 'They have the singular power,' Mr Butler observed, 'of being able to eat almost any thing, however hard, and from which no other animal could possibly derive nourishment.' And no doubt he put his theory to the test, 'thus [comments Brightwell] providing the Zoo's anatomist with another subject for dissection'.[1]

The chance to point a moral is never missed; but on occasions Mr Butler's zoological ignorance leads him into surprising errors. Having slandered those blameless vegetarians the macaws and cockatoos by assigning them to 'the hawk tribe—that cruel race, living on other birds which they tear to pieces with their hooked bill', he begs his charges to observe that 'the loveliest birds, like the prettiest children, have not always the best disposition'.

In short, Mr Butler is a pompous old bore, and one cannot help wishing that in those days the elephant, whose intelligence he so highly praises, had been uncaged and so at liberty to commit the Zoo's first and most commendable murder.

*   *   *

The Butlers had to *go* to Regent's Park, and one hardly likes to hazard where they set out from; but the Astons, the family who grace the pages of the *Zoological Keepsake*, *lived* there— no doubt in one of those fine Nash terraces—and visited the Zoo regularly, often in the company of Mr Dartmouth (Mrs Aston's brother) or their old friend a certain 'well-informed and hearty Admiral'. One hates to say it, but there seems the distinct possibility that the Butlers may have been 'trade'.

Mr Aston never appears—presumably he has some high office which demands his constant attention; but Mrs Aston is accompanied by her two daughters, Charlotte (almost eighteen) and Jane (eight), and her eleven-year-old son George. Living so near, they make

1. In 1953 at the Chester Zoo a mine detector, operated by engineers from the local garrison, confirmed the presence in an ostrich's stomach of a missing padlock.

a point of going to the Zoo early, when it is less crowded and when the animals are 're-freshed by sleep'; indeed, one morning they started out to find that 'the blushing tints of the clouds at sun-rise had not yet wholly vanished'. But even at that hour they could usually count on finding Mr Dartmouth already there, waiting to pounce and suffocate them with information of every kind.

Mr Dartmouth is a bore of such calibre that Mr Butler seems by comparison almost entertaining. On the occasion of the Astons' first recorded visit he is in an etymological mood, and no less than eighteen pages of the *Keepsake* are devoted to his explanation of the derivations of 'zoology', 'garden', 'horticulture', 'husbandman', 'farmer', and so on. Sometimes Miss Jane, who is 'a piece of a chatter-box, but a very clever little girl,' pertly interrupts:

> 'Our maid, Susan, says she is sure *Zulogical* (as she calls it) is some kind of tree that grows here, as mangel-wurzel grows in the Park; and that a *Zulogical* Garden must be full of *Zulogicals*, as flower-gardens are full of flowers! Only think, Uncle, how silly Susan is!'
>
> 'Not silly, my dear, but uninformed. Susan has not been so lucky as you, in being told the meaning of such a fine word as this ZO-O-LOGICAL, of which, as I suspect, three-fourths, at the least, of all the good people in town and country, knew neither the meaning nor the pronunciation, some three or four years ago!'
>
> 'What, Uncle,' cried Jane, 'was the word Zoological made only three or four years ago? Why, la! I am twice as old as *Zoological*.[1] Who would have thought it!'
>
> 'Not twice as old as *Zoological*, little Jane; but, at least, twice as old as the familiarity of any part of the English public, and especially of the London, with the use and meaning of the term. . . .'

Mr Dartmouth proceeds to explain that 'zoology' is a 'term compounded from the Greek,' whereupon George recalls that ζῶον is the Greek word for an animal. But instead of being praised he is immediately snubbed: 'ζῶον', replies Mr Dartmouth, 'does not particularly signify an animal, nor even a living being, but a being of any kind whatever . . .' They wasted so much time in this way that they got no further that day than the pelicans—of which Mr Dartmouth remarked, 'those unwieldy birds are particularly brisk this morning'.

Mr Dartmouth had promised to tell the children next day about the foundation of the Zoological Society, and this thrilling prospect brought them to the Zoo almost at crack of dawn. But for some unaccountable reason Mr Dartmouth was very late that morning, and 'George and Jane had run many times round the Garden, and Mrs and Miss Aston had paid long visits to the Paca and Guanaco, and to the Beaver House, and to the Emoos', before he appeared. The lecture finally at an end, one of the children boldly ventured to suggest that 'the necessity that Strangers must either be introduced by Members, or else

1. I might mention, in passing, that I am just half as old as the Zoological Society of London.

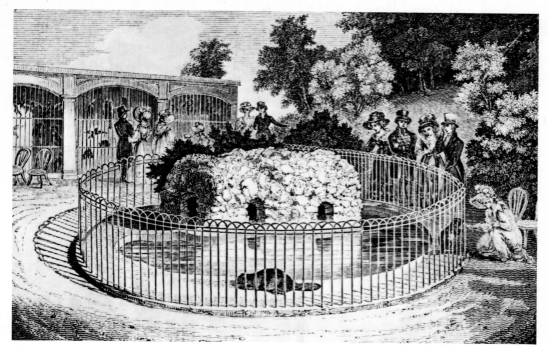

North American Beavers. *Zoological Keepsake*, 1830

provided with their orders', must be 'productive of some inconveniences'. But Mr Dartmouth, while admitting this, feels such restrictions to be more than justified:

> The vulgar are too fond of irritating the fiercer animals, and of teasing and hurting those which are gentle; and both vulgar and others are often exceedingly rash, in introducing their hands into the dens and enclosures, or careless in placing themselves so near the bars, as to defeat the effect of every precaution for their safety. Upon the first subject, as you all know, we have had to caution George; and I believe both George and Jane are indebted to some risks which they have run for the respectful distance which they now keep. Only the other day, too, as we saw, one of the Wolves, though so well guarded in the kennel, bit the arm of a little boy that had taken much pains to introduce it through the bars. You see, therefore, that caution is needful. . . .

On the third day the party was joined by the Admiral—'a very Gallant officer' whose duties had often taken him to South America. This conveniently qualified our 'veteran voyager and sailor' to discourse at enormous length on the llama, quoting extensively from Molina, Shaw, Shelvocke, Zarate and other authors whose works he evidently had by heart. Finally he felt obliged to touch upon the llama's regrettable habit of 'discharging saliva of a very bad odour' at any who offended him. 'In this manner finishing his remarks, the Admiral, after making a courteous bow to the ladies, and taking a cordial leave of the children, proceeded toward the gate of the Garden, and drove home to dinner.'

Charlie.
Beata Francis, *The Child's Zoological Garden*, 1880

And so, day after day, the visits continue. Perhaps the Admiral had an inkling that he was something of a bore, or perhaps his zoological knowledge began and ended with llamas; at all events, he soon fades out of the story into which he has in any case been dragged principally to let the reader know what fine friends the Astons have. But Mr Dartmouth is irrepressible, and on page 262 (where we must take leave of him) he is still in his pulpit, preaching now—and for once amusingly—about the diet of the beaver. 'Beavers,' he tells us, 'are remarkably fond of rice and plum-pudding . . .'

*   *   *

The Child's Zoological Garden by Beata Francis, authoress of *Slyboots, and other Farmyard Chronicles*, deals with the visit—or rather the non-visit—to Regent's Park in the seventies of Charlie, 'a little boy in a sailor's suit, with a very curly head'.

Aunt Alice had promised to take Charlie and his sister Nelly to the Zoo as soon as 'the east wind changed and the weather was warmer'. On 17 May Charlie pointed out to his aunt that it had, and it was; but Aunt Alice ordained that they should wait until the first of June: 'I don't trust the wind yet,' she said. The waiting was almost unbearable to the eager child. But at last the great day came, and 'Charlie's delight manifested itself in the performance of a feat in which he indulged on grand occasions, namely, hopping down-stairs backwards;' and so grand was this occasion that he attempted two steps at a time. This was a mistake: he fell, and 'terrible minutes followed, for all at first feared that he was killed'. The doctor, hastily summoned, decided that he was not; but he had injured his back and would have to spend many months in bed.

In the circumstances it must at first seem rather callous of Aunt Alice to have gone ahead with the expedition; however, the Brown children and some young cousins were also to be of the party, and Charlie's mother insisted. The other youngsters soon forgot

The Camel House.
Hand-coloured lithograph by G. Scharf, 1835

The Bear Pit.
Hand-coloured lithograph by G. Scharf, 1835

The First Monkey House.
Hand-coloured lithograph by G. Scharf, 1835

The Elephant Paddock and Wapiti House.
Hand-coloured lithograph by G. Scharf, 1835

all about Charlie and were 'in the highest spirits'; but poor Nelly could not raise a smile, and 'as she fed the Polar bear a big tear fell on the bun she dropped him. There was no pleasure in seeing the wild beasts dine without Charlie to share the excitement. . . . Kind Aunt Alice saw how sad poor Nelly felt, and thought of a plan to cheer her':

> 'I'll tell you what we will do, Nelly,' she said, 'you and I. We will look at all the animals very carefully, and when we go home I will begin to draw them, and you shall help me to remember what we saw, and then I'll make them all into a scrap-book for Charlie, and write little descriptions of the creatures and their habits to amuse him with when he is better . . .' And this was how the *Child's Zoological Garden* came to be made.

Many months, two hundred and fifty pages and a whole zoological encyclopaedia later came 'a bright summer day' when Charlie was pronounced strong enough to go out in a bath-chair. And where did he want to go? 'The first place he begged to be taken to was the Regent's Park Gardens. Aunt Alice and Nelly walked by the chair, and Nelly was wild with delight at having her brother out with her once more. She danced about by his side, and pointed out all the creatures she liked best, but she found that he knew very nearly as much about them as she did!'

❧ 5 ❧

Two Birds of a Feather

I shall not ask Jean Jacques Rousseau,
If birds confabulate or no. . . .

William Cowper, *Pairing time anticipated*

WHEN, on the fifth and sixth days of Creation, the Almighty dipped his paintbrush in the celestial colour-box to tint the animals, he reserved his most brilliant hues for the birds, the butterflies, the lizards, and the little fishes; for the big mammals he turned chiefly to earth colours, and indeed it is hard to conceive of an elephant from trunk to tail an iridescent kingfisher blue.

There is in the aquarium at the London Zoo a tiny fishlet—of its name I remember merely that it was longer than its owner—of so unbelievable and piercing an electric blue that it takes the breath away. There are flamingoes of a vermilion that Messrs Winsor and Newton do not, and could not, supply. There are macaws which almost demand dark glasses for the eyes (and certainly cotton-wool for the ears). And there are humming-birds that pass in a flash of amethyst, sapphire, emerald or ruby. The colour film of the Bourton-on-the-Water bird sanctuary, shown more than once on television, is of such beauty that a single viewing of it would justify the payment of a whole year's colour TV licence; and the same might be said of some of those films of the coral world of the tropics.

Two distinguished young artists with a particular interest in ornithology were associated with the London Zoo in its earliest days: Edward Lear (1812–88) and John Gould (1804–81). The former made most of the drawings there or at the Society's offices in Bruton Street for his superb *Illustrations of the Family of the Psittacidae, or Parrots* (1832); but later, though he worked occasionally for Gould and also for Lord Derby at Knowsley, he gradually drifted away from serious zoological illustration to eventual fame in the fields of landscape and nonsense. Gould, on the other hand, who came to work for the Society in 1827 as 'Curator and Preserver' of the Museum, remained officially or unofficially associated with it until his death. The first of his magnificent folios, *A Century of Birds from the Himalaya Mountains*, also appeared in 1832, to be followed over the years by a whole succession of works—forty-one volumes in all, with nearly three thousand plates—no less sumptuous and no less gigantic.

In this chapter, after brief biographies of the two men, we shall look at Lear's *Parrots*, and at a single example of Gould's vast output—the five volumes (and posthumously published sixth volume) of his *Monograph of the Trochilidae, or Family of Humming-Birds* (1849–87); they may also provide us with the excuse to gossip a little about two of the most dazzling of all the families of birds.

Edward Lear—that strange, brilliant, unhappy owl[1] of a man, homosexual and epileptic, youngest of the twenty-one children of a bankrupt London stockbroker—found his way to the Zoo at the age of eighteen. There he was soon producing the finest drawings of birds— and we are not forgetting Barraband, Audubon or Bewick—that had yet been made. The plates of the *Parrots* were lithographed by Lear himself, hand-coloured, and issued in parts, the total number completed being forty-two; the volume was dedicated to Queen Adelaide and, for want of a backer, published at the artist's own expense.

While at work on his *Parrots*, Lear had been introduced by Dr Gray of the British Museum to Lord Stanley, President of the Linnean Society and (from 1831–51) of the Z.S.L., soon to become the thirteenth Earl of Derby. Much impressed by what he saw, Stanley, an ardent zoologist, invited the young man to Knowsley, where he made the drawings used to illustrate a volume entitled *Gleanings from the Menagerie and Aviary at Knowsley Hall* and began an association with the Stanley family that was to endure through five generations. Lear also contributed to several other zoological publications including those of the Z.S.L.; but, as we have already said, he eventually abandoned this kind of work altogether. Was this a tragedy? When one imagines such might-have-beens as Lear's *Tropical Fish*, his *Humming-Birds* (at all events better than Gould's), or his *Big Cats* (he would of course have called it *Illustrations of the Larger Members of the Family of the Felidae*) one is tempted to say yes. But, looking at what he did achieve, we are forced to admit that the world would have been the poorer without his elegant landscapes, and the duller without his endearing whimsicalities.[2] Perhaps he was right after all.

Though driven by ill health to spend much of his life abroad, Lear never forgot in exile the happy days spent at the Zoo, which he revisited whenever he had the chance. 'Those Gardens,' he wrote in 1863, 'are such a Milestone & Landmark in my life that I like to go there when in England.'

It is pleasant to learn that what is believed to be the oldest extant specimen in the world of a stuffed bird is a parrot, and as pleasant as it is surprising to find that it rests today within the precincts of Westminster Abbey. This was the pet Grey Parrot once belonging to La Belle Stuart, favourite mistress of King Charles II and the original of the figure of

1. '*Que vos grandes lunettes vous donnent l'air d'un grand hibou*', a little girl once said to him in Corsica.
2. The Knowsley book has a plate captioned 'The Whiskered Yark', which sounds—and indeed looks—like nonsense Lear.

Britannia on our coins. The devoted bird did not long survive her death in 1702, and in obedience to her instructions it was stuffed and in due course placed beside her 'Effigie, as well done in Wax as can bee', which is now in the Norman Undercroft Museum at the Abbey.

Stepping back into the remoter past, we find that the ancient Egyptians did not know the parrot, nor is the bird mentioned by name in the Bible; but Aristotle wrote of 'the Indian bird, the parrot'—a great mimic which 'after drinking wine becomes more saucy than ever'. The Romans kept parrots in silver-wired cages of tortoiseshell and ivory; Ovid wrote an elegy on Corinna's dead pet; and Pliny, who should have known better, advocated (or at all events condoned) beating them over the head with an iron rod to teach them to talk.

At the time of the Crusades, French ladies who in the absence of their husbands were disinclined to take a lover, or precluded by a *ceinture de chasteté* from deriving full satisfaction from so doing, solaced themselves with the company of their parrots. The companions of Christopher Columbus brought back from the New World gaudy macaws— formidable birds whose beaks can crack a Brazil nut—which were soon the rage with the rich merchants of Augsburg and Vienna, while the Portuguese introduced into Europe the little Senegal Parrot from West Africa. Marie Antoinette received one of these charming, talkative pets which was bilingual in French and Senegalese, and which had been coached in advance to say, '*Ou est la reine? Je veux la voir. La voilà! Ah! qu'elle est belle!*' and suchlike *politesses*.

Parrots probably first reached England towards the end of the reign of Henry VII, where they were 'shown as a great curiosity'. There were macaws at Regent's Park from the very first, a Red-and-Blue being a gift to the Society from the young Queen of Portugal. But it was the introduction, in 1840, by John Gould of the Australian budgerigar that was to lead to a member of the parrot family ultimately becoming, along with the dog and the cat, the most popular of British pets.

Mention of budgerigars—which, incidentally, Gould was the first naturalist to see in the wild 'as they flew to water-holes in flocks up to a hundred strong'—may serve as the excuse to introduce the most celebrated animal-dealer in London in Victorian days, a German named Johann Christian Carl Jamrach (1815–91). Charles Jamrach—as he was always called after taking British nationality—came to London in 1840 and set up shop in premises in the notorious Ratcliff Highway (now 180 St George Street), facing the entrance to the London Docks, where he soon acquired a virtual monopoly of the wild animal trade in this country, and where his remarkable resemblance to Prince Albert was at times an advantage, at times an embarrassment. His stock was enormous, for his runners bought from sailors as their ships came in, and he also had agents in many ports in England and on the Continent. A man of remarkable strength and bravery, he once recaptured, virtually single-handed, a tigress which had escaped from his store and seized

Budgerigars. John Gould, *Birds of Australia*, 1848 (detail)

a nine-year-old boy in its jaws.[1]

Both Bartlett, the Superintendent at the Zoo, and his friend Buckland[2] knew Jamrach well, for he usually let the Society have first refusal of anything special that came his way. One day in March 1861 Buckland received a note from Jamrach summoning him urgently to Ratcliff Highway:

'Well, Jamrach, what now?'

'You shall see, sir.'

He took me upstairs, and opened the door of a room, and there I saw such a sight as really made me start. The moment the door-handle was touched I heard a noise which I can compare to nothing but the beating of a very heavy storm of rain upon the glass of a greenhouse: I cautiously entered the room, and then I saw it was *one mass*, windows and walls, of living Australian grass parakeets. When they saw me the birds began to chatter, and such a din I never heard before. I could hardly hear Jamrach's voice amidst the terrible din.

Advancing a step into the room, all the birds flew up in a dense cloud, flying about the room just like a crowd of gnats on a hot summer's evening, their wings causing a considerable rush of air, like the wind from a winnowing machine. Such a lot of birds I never saw before in all my life.

'Why, Jamrach, *how many*, for goodness' sake are there?'

1. The boy soon recovered, but the ensuing lawsuit cost Jamrach £300.
2. For Bartlett and Buckland see chapter 9.

'Well, sir, you see, two ships, the Orient and the Golden Star, came in from Port Adelaide, Australia; both ships had birds on them; I bought the lot, and now have *three thousand* pair of them. There are plenty of people about who would buy twenty – thirty, or a hundred pair, but I took the lot at a venture, and I am pleased to say we are doing very well with them. . . . You see, sir, I have put them in *two* empty rooms'; saying which, he opened the door of another room, and there I saw another edition of the first room, viz, a living mass of these beautiful little birds.

Jamrach had fitted up a series of common laths from the floor of the room to near the ceiling, the laths being one above the other; and when the birds got a little quiet, there they sat all of a row—eight to the foot I counted—just like a number of our noble selves on the benches at a public assembly, making a *continuous* clatter and noise.[1]

These 'grass parakeets' were, of course, the now ubiquitous 'budgies' which bring happiness into the lives of innumerable impoverished and lonely widows and spinsters, probably few of whom are aware that the male budgie is among the most shamelessly immoral of all birds. A Jamrach today could purchase a million budgies and still find little difficulty in disposing of his stock.

Budgerigar (*betcherrygah*) is a native name, said by some authorities to mean 'good cockatoo' and by others 'good food'. Even when abbreviated it is far from euphonious; yet I find that an owner never invites one to admire his or her *Melopsittacus undulatus*. However, though the scientific names of many birds are as tongue-twisting as any in the whole animal kingdom, their popular names are in general well-chosen; and among the most felicitous of the latter are those attached to the parrots. For example: the Turquoise-rumped Parrotlet, the Double-fronted Amazon, the Bloodstained Cockatoo, the Blossom-headed Parakeet, the Blue-crowned Hanging Parrot, the Yellow-thighed Caique, the Moustached Parakeet, the Funereal Cockatoo, the Hyacinthine Macaw, the Orange-bellied Grass Parakeet, the Peach-faced Lovebird, the Purple-chapped Lory and the Queen of Bavaria's Conure.

Another native name is kea, the so-called 'sheep-eating parrot' from the snow mountains of the South Island of New Zealand. In the spring of 1881 the Zoo acquired one of these rum creatures, the hardiest of all the parrots—a bird about the size of a raven, drab olive-brown but showing when in flight a rosy rump and a flash of tangerine orange under the wings. It has a schoolboy's love of destruction, insatiable curiosity, innate cunning and crude sense of fun; with its ferocious beak it can rip open a corrugated iron roof—which few schoolboys can do. In 1856, when it was first made known to science, it was, like all parrots, a vegetarian. So, too, had been the earliest specimen to reach the Zoo—the gift in 1872 of the Prince of Wales. But it was alleged that with the development of sheep farming in New Zealand the kea took to mutton as a savage might take to whisky when

1. Frank Buckland, *Curiosities of Natural History*, third series, vol. ii.

Kea. John Gould, *Birds of Australia*, 1848

a happy chance put it in his way; and certainly the new arrival showed from the first a marked preference for raw mutton chops.[1]

It must be said, at the start, that though zoologists of course accept that some keas are now omnivorous, opinion is still divided as to whether they are actually sheep-*killers*; in the guarded words of the latest London Zoo Guide (1973), their reputation as such 'has not really been proved satisfactorily'. It is possible that among keas, as among humans, there may be 'bad hats' which take to murder, choosing for victims the ailing or the cornered. But the evidence adduced by George Marriner in his fascinating little book, *The Kea: a New Zealand Problem*, published in New Zealand as long ago as 1908, makes very persuasive reading. Marriner thus describes the tactics of the kea when out for blood:

> The usual mode of attack seems to be as follows. The bird settles on the ground near its quarry, and, after hopping about here and there for some time, leaps on to its prey, usually on the rump. . . . Then the murderer begins cruelly to pull out the wool with its powerful beak, until it gets down to the flesh. The sheep, which for some time has been moving uneasily about, gives a jump as the beak enters the flesh, and then commences to run wildly about here and there in vain efforts to rid itself of its tormentor. When, however, the poor beast discovers that it cannot dislodge its enemy, it seems to lose its head, and rushes blindly about, usually at a high speed.

1. Another strict herbivore, a Bactrian camel at the Glasgow Zoo, suddenly developed a curious passion for fish.

Sometimes the birds run the sheep to death, and then gorge themselves on the dead body. At other times they never really reach a vital part of the animal's anatomy, but, after severely wounding it, they leave it, and the poor brute wanders about with a large gash, some four or five inches across, on its rump. . . . The sheep struggles along until blood-poisoning, caused by filth and exposure, sets in, and the unfortunate beast lies down and gives up the struggle.

The most recent account of the kea and its habits seems to be that of J. R. Jackson, writing in *Notornis*, the New Zealand bird journal, in 1962. His considered opinion is that keas do feed on carrion and attack live prey such as mice and opossums. 'It is credible that [they] do attack sheep trapped in the snow, sick sheep, sheep injured by falls or sheep they mistake as dead. . . . If such occurs, the evidence suggests it must be very rarely; so rarely, that the destruction of Keas is not justified.' One would think that the matter might easily be settled once and for all by—*pace* the R.S.P.C.A.—a simple if disagreeable experiment: put a very succulent sheep and a very hungry kea together in a cage, and await results. Has this ever been done?

But it is not the kea, remarkable though it is, which will catch the attention of the casual visitor to the Parrot House at the Zoo. For here he will first be irresistibly drawn by the dazzling plumage of the Red-and-Yellow, Blue-and-Yellow, and Red-and-Blue Macaws, and the less gaudy but no less beautiful Hyacinthine Macaw—all denizens of tropical Central and Southern America. (And how odd that they all hatch from pure white eggs!) Surprising, too, that these exotics gracefully accept our hostile English climate. Lear's Macaw, unlike the artist whose name it bears, is exceptionally hardy; but like Lear it can be a good talker, one at the Belle Vue Zoo in Manchester earning its keep for many years by crying 'Guides and catalogue, a penny' at the entrance. Another famous talker, 'Aunt Emmie', taken to a public shelter in Vienna during air-raids in the Second World War, learned so perfectly to imitate the whine of a falling bomb that she was ultimately refused admission.

Aunt Emmie may not have appreciated the despondency she was causing, but parrots can also be intentionally mischievous:

An incident of the day [Good Friday] was the adventure of Miss Vashti Earle and Miss Harriet Lena Bradford, two New York chorus beauties now at the Apollo, in the parrot house. Miss Earle was feeding nuts to one of the raucous-voiced birds, when he espied a glittering diamond cluster in her corsage and snapped at it. He caught it in his powerful beak, tore it loose, and tried to swallow it.

Miss Earle nearly fainted at the thought of losing her ornament, but Miss Bradford retained her presence of mind and cuffed the gaudy thief so hard that he dropped the sunburst and fell backwards off his perch. The attendant chided Miss Bradford for using such harsh measures, as in any case the jewel was too large to swallow. 'I don't care,' replied the fair American, 'I reckon that cluster is worth 500 dol., while that measly bird is dear at 30c. I'm not taking any chances, thank you.'

The parrot still lives.[1]

And not surprisingly, no less remarkable than their brilliance is the great age to which some parrots survive, though stories of their longevity are often much exaggerated. Jennison[2] trustingly writes:

Cocky Bennett, a cockatoo famous throughout Australia, was a mere featherless scarecrow, but he still flapped his stumps and croaked, 'Welcome, gentlemen,' at 117 years of age. This proved [*sic*] longevity may help the reader to believe our concluding tale. [Alexander von] Humboldt, the great explorer, discovered on his travels an Amazon parrot, grey with age, teaching the astonished natives the language of the Atures, a race long vanished from the face of the earth.

Cocky Bennett, who spent his old age as the guest of Mrs Sarah Bennett, licensee of the Sea Breeze Hotel at Tom Ugly's Point near Sydney, moved with the times, enlarging and enriching his vocabulary through daily contact with the bar's fluctuating and uninhibited clientele. He regretted nothing now but the loss of most of his fine plumage, which grounded him and shamed him to his dying day. 'One more fucking feather, and I'll fly', he screamed somewhat enigmatically—and forthwith expired.

*   *   *

John Gould was the son of a gardener who in 1818 became a foreman gardener at Windsor Castle. Here the boy worked for a time under his father, picking 'many a bunch of dandelions for Queen Charlotte's dandelion tea' and in his spare time stuffing birds for young Etonians. His skill at this led in 1827 to his appointment as taxidermist to the Zoological Society, where one of his tasks was the mounting of King George IV's giraffe on its death in 1829.[3] In this same year he found the perfect wife in a Miss Coxon—a capable artist and his devoted collaborator until her death twelve years later. Of her part in her husband's books, Professor Newton has written:

The earlier of these works were illustrated by Mrs Gould,[4] and the figures in them are fairly good; but those in the later, except when (as he occasionally did) he [Gould] secured the services of Mr Wolf,[5] are not much to be commended. There is, it is true, a smoothness and finish about them not often seen elsewhere; but as though to avoid the exaggerations of Audubon, Gould usually adopted the tamest attitudes in which to

1. *Daily Express*, 6 April 1901. 4. Edward Lear also helped.
2. George Jennison, *Noah's Cargo*.
3. See p. 76. 5. For Joseph Wolf see chapter 19.

represent his subjects, whereby expression as well as vivacity is wanting. Moreover, both in drawing and in colouring, there is frequently much that is untrue to nature, so that it has not uncommonly happened for them to fail in the chief object of all zoological plates, that of affording some means of recognising specimens on comparison.

One cannot but agree with Newton's judgment.

John Gould had all the less pleasant qualities of an ambitious parvenu. Wolf described him as 'a shrewd old fellow, but the most uncouth man I ever knew'; and after Gould's death Lear wrote: 'He was one I never liked really, for in spite of a certain jollity & Bonhommie he was a harsh and violent man . . . hard working toiler in his own (ornithological) line, but ever as unfeeling for those about him. In his earliest phase of this bird drawing, he owed everything to his excellent wife,—& to myself, without whose help in drawing he had done nothing.' All this was probably true; but we must also allow for a measure of jealousy. As Brian Reade[1] has pointed out, 'Lear was predisposed to be hostile to business men'—especially if, unlike himself, they were financially successful. When one subtracts from Gould's enormous output what he owed to others, including those who made the lithographs for his innumerable folios, his stature is greatly diminished. How much pleasanter would it have been had he devoted to the acknowledgement of the help he had received, some of the space allotted in one of his prospectuses to a snob list of his distinguished subscribers, whom he classifies as follows:

> Monarchs, 12; Imperial, Serene, and Royal Highnesses, 11; English Dukes and Duchesses, 16; Marquises and Marchionesses, 6; Earls, 30; Counts, Countesses, and Barons, 5; Viscounts, 10; Bishop [Worcester] 1; Lords, 36. . . .

and so on, to a total, including 'Miscellaneous', of 1008.

In 1830 Gould received a collection of bird-skins from the Himalaya which led to the production of his first great work, for which his friend Nicholas Vigors, the Society's secretary, provided the descriptions. It was while examining zoological specimens brought back by Darwin in the *Beagle* in 1836, that Gould decided to go with his wife to Australia on a two-years' voyage which resulted later in the publication of his *Birds of Australia* (1840–69), *Mammals of Australia* (1845–63), and a monograph on the kangaroos. On his return to England he bought a house in Charlotte Street, from where he continued to issue his great folios until his death more than forty years later. The stock of his works—more than thirty tons of it—was then purchased by Messrs Sotheran, the booksellers, in whose basement much of it lay unopened for half a century.

In 1849 there appeared the first volume of the *Humming-Birds*, and two years later Gould's remarkable collection of fifteen hundred mounted specimens of these birds was displayed at the Zoo in a temporary 'saloon' near the Lion House, where it became one of the major

---

1. *Edward Lear's Parrots*, Duckworth, 1949.

The Humming-bird House at Regent's Park. *Illustrated London News*, 12 June 1852

The Humming-bird House (exterior). *Illustrated London News*, 12 June 1852

attractions during the year of the Great Exhibition. Queen Victoria noted in her Diary for 10 June 1851 that she and Prince Albert drove 'with our 3 girls, Alexandrina, & the 2 Ernests' to the Zoo to inspect 'a collection (in a room specially arranged for this purpose) of Gould's stuffed Humming Birds. It is the most beautiful & complete collection ever seen, & it is impossible to imagine anything so lovely as these little Humming Birds, their variety, & the extraordinary brilliancy of their colours.'

Admission to the collection, which it had cost Gould between two and three thousand pounds to acquire and prepare, was sixpence, and this money very properly went to Gould. The birds attracted seventy-five thousand visitors in 1851; and since they remained on display the following year also, Gould must have been recouped for most if not all of his expenses. After his death in 1881, the Society succeeded in getting a Treasury grant of £3,000 to purchase them, together with 3,800 unmounted skins and 7,000 of those of other birds. They are now divided between the British Museum's natural history collections at South Kensington[1] and Tring.

To the Americans, with their taste for magnitude, there should surely have been allotted the elephant and the giraffe rather than the Queen's-dolls'-house-sized humming-bird. (But at least they have their whales.) According to the Rev. Thomas Heyrick (1649–94), Nature turned to making the humming-bird as a relaxation from heavier work:

> I'me made in sport by Nature, when
> Shee's tir'd with the Stupendous weight
> Of forming Elephants and Beasts of State . . .[2]

The humming-bird has been known to the Western world since the sixteenth century, and as such in English since 1637. Some of its names in other languages are more poetical. The Spaniards and Portuguese call it *picaflor* (flower-picker), *beijaflor* (flower-kisser), or *tominejo*—a *tomin* being a weight equal to a third of a gram. The Germans have opted for *kolibri*, a Caribbean word; the French say *colibri* or *oiseau-mouche*, fly-like bird. There are evocative names too, though their meanings elude me: *chuparosa*, *guainumbi*, *ourissia* . . . but surely the most beautiful of all is *beijaflor*. The humming-bird houses in Berlin, Frankfurt and New York are rather pretentiously known as 'Jewel Rooms' and their occupants as 'flying jewels'.

The first humming-bird to be publicly shown in Europe[3] was a Sparkling Violet-ear, which came to Regent's Park in November 1905; it survived there for only a fortnight because no one then understood how to feed it. Nectar alone was not enough; it also needed

---

1. One of Gould's enormous show-cases, formerly black but now painted white, may be seen (very poorly lit) in the Bird Room.
2. 'On an Indian Tomineios, the least of Birds'.
3. Gould had had one in 1857, which lived two days and died in his house.

insects or some substitute for them.[1] But in those brief fourteen days this pioneer created a sensation. Now most important zoos, and some bird-gardens, have at least one or two species. At Regent's Park the Humming-bird House is discreetly—and no doubt intentionally—tucked away where the casual visitor will not stumble upon it; but no one ought to miss it. One's first humming-bird in the wild is something never to be forgotten; the house in Regent's Park, where the birds are free-flying, is the next best thing.

There are two fairly common misapprehensions about humming-birds. First, that they are also to be found in the Old World: this is the result of confusion with the not dissimilar sun-birds of Africa and Asia. And second, that they are confined to the Tropics: in fact, though they increase in numbers and variety of species as they approach the equator—half of the three hundred and twenty or so known species are to be found in Ecuador and northern equatorial Brazil—they range from Alaska to the southernmost tip of South America. Even New York can boast of one: the Ruby-throated Humming-bird. For all their apparent frailty, some of them are remarkably tough. The tiny Alaskan Rufous Humming-bird may sensibly winter in Central America; but *Eustephanus galeritus* was seen by Captain Philip King 'flitting about the fuchsias of Tierra del Fuego in a snowstorm', while the Chimborazian Hillstar (more delightful names!) apparently enjoys life at fifteen thousand feet, in almost constant sleet and rain, on the slopes of the famous Andean volcano.

I have never known the *Encyclopaedia Britannica*[2] wax more lyrical than in the article by Professor Alfred Newton on Humming-birds. 'Ornithologists,' writes the Professor with almost Sitwellian abandon,

> have been compelled to adopt the vocabulary of the jeweller in order to give an idea of the indescribable radiance that so often breaks forth from some part or other of the investments of these feathered gems. In all, save a few other birds, the most imaginative writer sees gleams which he may adequately designate metallic, from their resemblance to burnished gold, bronze, copper, or steel, but such similitudes wholly fail when he has to do with the *Trochilidae*, and there is hardly a precious stone—ruby, amethyst, sapphire, emerald, or topaz—the name of which may not fitly, and without any exaggeration, be employed in regard to humming-birds.
>
> In some cases this radiance beams from the brow, in some it glows from the throat, in others it shines in the tail-coverts, in others it sparkles from the tip only of elongated feathers that crest the head or surround the neck as with a frill, while again in others it may appear as a luminous streak across the cheek or auriculars. The feathers that cover the upper parts of the body very frequently have a metallic lustre of golden-green, which in other birds would be thought sufficiently beautiful, but in the *Trochilidae* its

---

1. The London Zoo is said to mix the following 'cocktail': 1000 g. water, 130 g. honey, 2 g. Hepovite (liver extract), 40 g. Complan (proprietary food) and 2 drops vitamins. Every Zoo has its favoured elixir.
2. Eleventh edition.

sheen is overpowered by the almost dazzling splendour that radiates from the spots where Nature's lapidary has set her jewels. . . .

But the Professor had not yet finished, observing of the tail-feathers that they 'often exhibit a rich translucency, as of stained glass, but iridescent in a manner that no stained glass ever is—cinnamon merging to crimson, crimson changing to purple, purple to violet, and so to indigo and bottle-green. . . .'

Newton saw live humming-birds when he visited the West Indies in 1857; but in the above-quoted passages his raptures stem principally from the study of mounted specimens and his picture is a still-life. Richard Burton paints the living bird when describing his Brazilian explorations made in the sixties:

> Humming Birds, little larger than dragon-flies, red-beaked, and with plumage of chatoyant green, now stared at the stranger as they perched fearlessly upon the thinnest twig, then poised themselves with expanded tail feathers and twinkling wings, whilst plunging their needle-bills into the flower-cup, or tapping its side;[1] then darted, as if thrown by the hand, to some bunch of richer and virgin bloom. . . . The little bodies contain mighty powers of love and hate—they fight as furiously as they woo; and no unplumed biped ever died of 'heimweh' so readily and so certainly as the humming bird imprisoned in a cage . . .[2]

After such rhapsodies, dry facts may suggest an anticlimax; moreover, the figures given by various authorities do not always agree. None the less, these humming-birds are so extraordinary that their achievements and 'vital statistics' are worth recording. Size: the smallest of them—the smallest, of course, of all birds—is the Cuban Bee Humming-bird, known also as 'Helena's Humming-bird' and 'The Fairy Hummer'; its body is just over half an inch long, its overall length about two and a quarter inches, and its weight—seven-hundredths of an ounce—less than that of a Sphinx Moth. It also has the smallest eggs, which are laid in a nest soft as thistle-down and little larger than a thimble.

Wing-beat: up to one hundred (some say, two hundred and fifty) wing-beats per second have been recorded for several of the smallest species. Heart-beat: variously estimated at from five hundred to twelve hundred a minute. Speed: some humming-birds can fly at fifty-five miles an hour, and plunge at much greater speeds. Moreover, not only can they hover, stop dead in mid-flight, spin, and U-turn—they can also (Nature's only helicopters) fly backwards; and in aerobatics they surpass the most audacious performances of the Red Devils. Here is perfection in flying. Frau Scheithauer even maintains that they can wink, but her husband refuses to subscribe to this.[3]

And how varied are their forms! For sheer fantasy they may be surpassed, by, for instance,

---

1. I have found the hill fuchsia pierced in the lower part of the cup. (R.F.B.)
2. Richard Burton, *Explorations of the Highlands of Brazil*, Tinsley, 1869.
3. *Hummingbirds: Flying Jewels*, by Walter Scheithauer, transl. by Gwynne Vevers.

some of the Birds of Paradise and Lyre-birds, and in total splendour by the peacocks and the parrots. But how extraordinary is the Racket-tailed Humming-bird with its tail like tiny garden secateurs, or the Sword-billed Humming-bird whose beak is far longer than its body! The Black-throated Train-bearer has long tail-feathers, the White-lipped Sickle-bill a curved beak, the Purple-crowned Fairy a snow-white breast that contrasts strangely with the richness of colour elsewhere. Their variety is infinite.

Such a galaxy of iridescent beauty was a challenge to any artist, and even Lear, for all his success with his *Parrots*, would here have met his Waterloo. For no one could paint the humming-bird, just as no one—not even Van Gogh—could paint the sun high in the sky. Sacheverell Sitwell has justly described Gould's *Trochilidae* as 'an incomparable catalogue and compendium of beauties'; but he adds a warning:

> The humming-birds are so beautiful in themselves that the ecstasy of delight into which they throw one should not let it appear that the *Trochilidae*, in aesthetics, is other than among the most beautiful of Victorian illustrated books. . . . To argue more than that would be equivalent, in other context, to saying that Audubon was a greater artist than Albrecht Dürer.[1]

In short, if we see in Lear's *Parrots* a not too difficult success, then Gould's *Humming-Birds* must be counted a magnificent failure.

1. *Fine Bird Books, 1700–1900* by Sacheverell Sitwell, Handasyde Buchanan and James Fisher, Collins and Van Nostrand, London and New York, 1953.

6

Kangaroos

'Do you know, Mr Hopper, dear Agatha and I are so much interested in Australia. It must be so pretty with all the dear little kangaroos flying about.'

The Duchess of Berwick in *Lady Windermere's Fan* by Oscar Wilde

THERE were kangaroos at Regent's Park from the very first.

In Mr Bishop's opusculum we read that 'the young party were delighted at seeing the young Kanguroos sport about with their mother, and at the least alarm jump into a kind of pouch nature had furnished her with, for the purpose of protecting them from danger', and there is also a woodcut showing 'The Kanguroo Shed'. The *Keepsake* of 1830 reproduces an engraving of a kangaroo, copied without acknowledgement from Stubbs's famous painting now at Parham, and a long poem of almost unbearable facetiousness, 'The Migration of the Beasts', mentions

A curious Kangaroo,
Who stands upon the *strangest tail*,
The *tale*, though *strange*, is true.

In the same year thirteen more kangaroos were included among the animals presented by William IV; presumably all these were Great Grey Kangaroos—the species known in Australia as the 'boomer', 'old man' or 'forester'.

Everyone knows what a kangaroo is like: an almost woman-sized grey or rufous animal that moves in gigantic hops on gigantic back-legs, but which when stationary dangles its wizened 'arms' over its extensive chest like a nervous contralto. This image fits the Red or Grey Kangaroo or the Mountain Kangaroo (Wallaroo) well enough; but to imagine that all kangaroos are big, is as if to imagine that all dogs are the size of wolfhounds. For the Kangaroo family is very extensive and includes the Wallabies, some of which are about the size of a corgi, and the Musk Kangaroo which is far smaller than the tiniest chihuahua—no bigger, indeed, than a large rat.

It is also commonly believed that the kangaroo was discovered by some of Captain Cook's sailors on the eastern coast of Australia. In fact, one of the wallabies had been

Cheetah and stag, with two Indians.
Oil painting by George Stubbs, *c.* 1765

'The Kongouro from New Holland'.
Oil painting by George Stubbs, 1771 or 1772

Blue and Yellow Macaw.
Hand-coloured lithograph from Edward Lear's
Illustrations of the Family of Psittacidae, 1830-32

sighted and briefly reported upon in 1629 by a Dutch sea-captain, Francisco Pelsaert, on an island off the coast of Western Australia; but possibly his story was given little credence, for it aroused no interest and was soon forgotten. Dampier, too, relates that he had eaten 'a sort of racoon with very short fore-legs' in the same area in 1697, and this can only have been some species of kangaroo.

But with Cook in the *Endeavour* was (Sir) Joseph Banks, and no one was prepared to dismiss Banks as a Münchhausen. The astonishment of several of the crew on first seeing one of these extraordinary animals is hard to imagine. They had landed on 22 June 1770 near what is now Cooktown 'to shoot pigeons for the sick' when they caught sight of 'an animal something less than a grey hound, it was of a Mouse Colour very slender made and swift of foot'. Two days later Cook saw one for himself, and early in July Banks made an extended excursion on shore during which he came upon several more. Eventually two were shot and eaten, their meat proving excellent. After the shooting of the first of these, Banks wrote in his Journal:

> To compare it to any European animal would be impossible as it has not the least resemblance of any one I have seen. Its fore legs are extremely short and of no use to it in walking, its hind again as disproportionately long; with these it hops 7 or 8 feet at each hop in the same manner as the Gerbua [jerboa], to which animal indeed it bears much resemblance, except in Size, this being in weight 38 lb and the Gerbua no larger than a common rat.

The second animal was much larger, weighing 84 pounds; kangaroos are, however, often far bigger still, Gould at a later date shooting one that weighed 200 pounds. Cook's two skins were sent to England, and from them in 1771 or 1772 Stubbs painted the picture previously mentioned, 'The Kongouro from New Holland', which was exhibited at the Society of Artists in 1773. Though the existence of the pouch had long been recognised in the Old World opossum and certain other marsupials, Banks seems to have overlooked it in the kangaroo; no doubt the animals shot by Cook's sailors were males.[1]

Cook asked a native the name of these animals and understood him to reply, 'kangaroo'. It was long maintained that, like the word 'tulip', this name which has passed into almost all European languages was the result of what today is called 'a failure to communicate': that the native had in fact replied, 'I don't understand'. However, it has recently been alleged that a word sounding like *gangaroo* is still used by certain aboriginals for the Great Grey Kangaroo; so perhaps Cook was not so wrong after all.

In 1802 on Kangaroo Island, about a hundred miles south of Adelaide, the kangaroos came out to greet Captain Matthew Flinders and his merry men as if they had been long-lost brothers and, though capable of more than fifty miles an hour over short distances, allowed themselves to be massacred with sticks. It was believed that they were dim-witted

1. See Wendt, *op. cit.*, pp. 248 ff.

animals: in fact, they are something far more dangerous for their survival—they are *trusting* animals. They are also full of curiosity, unable when running away to resist the temptation to stop in mid flight and look round, with eyes disarmingly human, to see how things are going. This could, I suppose, be called stupidity; it certainly gives the marksman a sitting target. Today, with swift cars and more lethal weapons, some half a million kangaroos are killed annually in Australia for sale as cat and dog food, shoe leather, or material for ski-ing clothes.

In spite of all this slaughter, most of the kangaroos are very far from extinct. But not, alas! another delightful marsupial, the Tasmanian wolf. These elegant creatures, so prettily striped on the rump, were a menace to the colonists' livestock, and a price was once put on their heads; but they were innocent of all malice towards men, the only charge ever having been made against one in this respect being the biting of a certain Miss Murray in 1900. Even here there was probably some misapprehension; for the wolf in question was blind in one eye, and very likely mistook Miss Murray's arm for something tastier that it was already familiar with in the farmyard. The last of a dozen or so of these wolves

Tasmanian Wolf or Thylacine. Joseph Wolf, *Zoological Sketches*, first series, 1861

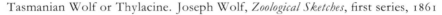

kept at one time or another at Regent's Park died in 1931, and since 1933 there has been no undisputed sighting of one in the wild. Statutory protection came in 1938, with a heavy fine replacing the former reward; but it came too late. As Michael Sharland, Tasmania's leading zoologist, has said of this unique animal, 'It has reached the point of no return, and the best intentions will not save it now'. Well—we rid ourselves in 1876 of the last pure-blooded Tasmanian aboriginal; have we any right in 1976 to shed tears over the extinction, or approaching extinction, of the Tasmanian wolf? Plautus wrote more than two thousand years ago: '*Homo homini lupus*'—'Man is a wolf to man'. And also, it would seem, to wolf.

The first live kangaroo to reach England was the gift in 1792 of Arthur Phillip, the Governor of New South Wales, to King George III; and not long afterwards there could be seen in the Haymarket, on payment of a shilling, another, billed as 'The wonderful Kangaroo from Botany Bay! This amazing, beautiful and tame animal is about 5 feet in Height, unparalleled from the Southern Hemisphere, that almost surpasses belief.' Soon there were 'several almost wild in the Park at Kew' (probably Richmond Park), where a birth occurred in December 1793; indeed, they bred so well in this country that the Exeter 'Change usually had a few on show. At a later date kangaroos were treated in some parts of Europe almost like deer, and are in fact approximately their Australian equivalent. Bernhard Grzimek[1] mentions a herd kept by Baron Philipp von Böselager near Bonn at the close of the last century, and Lord Rothschild also had both Grey Kangaroos and Bennett's Wallabies in complete freedom at Tring. Prince Gerhard Blücher von Wahlstatt's fine herd on the island of Herm, near Guernsey, was eaten by British troops during the First World War.

I first became 'hooked' on marsupials by seeing a film, shown on television a few years back, of the birth of a kangaroo.[2] Of all the many splendid zoological programmes sponsored by the BBC, this was for me by far the most brilliant, revealing, extraordinary. Had I been asked, before seeing it, how large I imagined a kangaroo to be at birth, I confess with shame that I would probably have hazarded, 'about the size of a baby rabbit'; in fact the infant kangaroo is only an inch or so long, its weight a mere fraction of an ounce. For the kangaroo, like all marsupials, is born an unformed embryo[3] and completes its development and kindergarten education in its mother's pouch.

1. See his splendid book, *Four-legged Australians*.
2. This film, supported by a paper by G. B. Sharman and Phyllis E. Pilton entitled 'Reproduction in the Red Kangaroo', was first shown at one of the Society's Scientific Meetings in April 1963.
3. An embottled embryo and a tiny kangaroo in its mother's pouch may be seen in the Hunterian Museum at the Royal College of Surgeons, Lincoln's Inn Fields, London. There is much else there of interest and of beauty: the wax-impregnated tracheobronchial tree of a horse is more lovely and more intricate than the finest coral, and among improbable exhibits is the heart of a human foetus preserved in turpentine and presented by Queen Victoria.

But how on earth does it get there? It is blind and it is deaf; it finds itself suddenly ejected from its mother's body without, one would have imagined, a clue as to what to do next. The question was long and hotly debated by zoologists and to this day puzzles the very young: 'How does a kangaroo get into its mummy's pocket?' inquired Elise, aged four, of BBC Wildlife. 'Is it very fluffy inside?' For though births had been witnessed at zoos, it had never been possible to get close enough to see exactly what happened. It was thought probable that the mother transferred what Maurice Burton has called the 'animated haricot bean' to her pouch with her lips, teeth or forepaws;[1] but this remarkable film, taken at Canberra by two Australian zoologists, G. B. Sharman and H. J. Frith, showed that the tiny mite *finds its own way* from the birth-canal to the pouch, prompted presumably by an inborn 'excelsior' urge[2] and steered by the only senses serviceable for the purpose that it then possesses—those of smell and of touch. Now it was remembered that as far back as 1832 a naval surgeon had maintained that he had personally witnessed exactly this—but only to be ridiculed for his pains.

An hour or two before giving birth, the mother spring-cleans her pouch and licks the approach to it; then, propping herself up against a rock or a tree, she awaits the moment of what must be an agreeably painless parturition. Now there is about to begin the most amazing journey in the world: a crawling journey of exploration, lasting four or five minutes, through a dense jungle of fur to the entrance of the pouch. Yet it is also an alpine ascent, the climber roped, as it were, by an umbilical cord. Watching the infant's purposeful, calculated endeavour I felt almost tempted to cry out, 'Bravo! You've made it!' when finally, like a good putt, it 'dropped into the hole'.

Once within—and here the photographer presumably had to use a female which had been killed or anaesthetised—the tiny creature noses its way to one of the four teats, to which it attaches its mouth like a press-button. In this warm darkness it remains for many months, growing and developing until the brave day comes when 'Joey' ventures its little head above the lip of the pouch—this 'womb with a view', as someone agreeably though inaccurately dubbed it—to take its first amazed look at the strange outside world in which it will soon be fighting for survival.

For many other marsupials the procedure is much the same; but for some, including most of the burrowers, there is a particular problem. As Grzimek says, 'the kangaroo's pouch reposes against its belly like a housewife's clothes-peg bag'—an arrangement sensible enough in an animal that normally stands upright. But for a burrower, a pouch opening thus would obviously soon get filled with sand. So the wombat, for example, has a pouch which faces *backwards*, and great was the amazement when in 1914 the first wombat to be

1. On 14 November 1844 Richard Owen received a letter from Lord Derby saying that a kangaroo at Knowsley 'was seen taking the new-born tiny kangaroo in her fore-paws and putting it in the pouch'. Either the observation was defective or the mother was a freak.
2. When an opossum was held upside down immediately after giving birth, the infant still climbed upwards—and so away from the pouch.

Dante Gabriel Rossetti
mourning his dead Wombat.
Pen-and-wash drawing by
Rossetti, 6 November 1869

*I never reared a young Wombat
To glad me with his pin-hole eye,
But when he most was sweet & fat
And tail-less, he was sure to die!*

bred in captivity (at Halle) was in due course seen peering out between its mother's *back* legs. The shorter crawl from vagina to pouch is an advantage to the infant wombat, but a back-facing pouch is difficult for the mother to clean.

Robert Brown, the famous Scots botanist who accompanied Matthew Flinders on his voyage to Australia, brought a wombat back to England with him in 1805.[1] It lived for two years with Sir Everard Home, behaved admirably with visitors, bit nobody in earnest (in spite of its formidable rodent-like teeth), and allowed Home to write a treatise on it. Dante Gabriel Rossetti, a regular visitor to Regent's Park where he would arrange to meet his friends at the 'Wombat-Lair', kept what was little less than a small zoo in Cheyne Walk in the sixties. Among his animals, which he bought from Jamrach, were kangaroos and what he called 'a Joy, a Delight, a Madness': a wombat. He preferred (said his brother) 'quaint, odd, or semi-grotesque animals', and found the wombat 'engagingly lumpish'. It slept in the bowl of a large hanging lamp, and once disgraced itself by eating the hat of a

1. Bewick's wood-engraving, in his *General History of Quadrupeds* (1790), of what he calls 'a bearlike marsupial rat', was made from the skin of a wombat which had been found dead on board a wrecked ship a year before.

Mrs Virtue Tebbs, a solicitor's wife, who was sitting to Rossetti for her portrait. It died after only two months and was stuffed, thus continuing posthumously to greet visitors as they entered the hall.

There is usually a wombat on display at Regent's Park, where one lived in captivity for nearly twenty years. Wombats soon learn to fend for themselves if need arises; two in the Florence Zoo escaped and set up house contentedly in the nearby Borghese Gardens until their recapture four months later. The second recorded birth of a wombat in captivity took place in 1931 at Whipsnade, where today many marsupials, including more than two hundred Bennett's wallabies from Tasmania, can be seen. These breed well, and the offspring are sent to zoos all over the world. 'The first little head is usually peering from its mother's pouch at Christmas and there is great competition amongst the Zoo staff to be the first to see a baby wallaby.'[1]

1. *Whipsnade Zoo Guide* 1972.

❧ 7 ❧

Dreaming Spires[1]

..... Giraffes!—a People
Who live between the earth and skies,
Each in his own religious steeple,
Keeping a lighthouse with his eyes. . . .

Roy Campbell, *Dreaming Spires*

MY cousin, Judith Wentworth, once took Edith Sitwell on a very thorough tour of inspection of her famous Arab stud. Stall after stall, but not a word from her guest. At last Lady Wentworth said, 'Perhaps you do not care for horses, Miss Sitwell?' The answer came with a sigh, 'No. But I simply *adore* giraffes.'

It is not difficult to sympathise with that formidable lady's enthusiasm for the giraffe—in general one of the sweetest-tempered and most charming animals in the world.[2] The loftiest, too, it is also the most unmistakable, though Dr Johnson's definition (under 'camelopard'), 'An Abyssinian animal, taller than the elephant, but not so thick,' is terse rather than definitive. Those who cannot tell a leopard from a jaguar or a chimpanzee from an orang-utan can never confound a giraffe with any other of God's creatures—and certainly not with its only surviving close relative, the okapi.[3]

There is something effeminate about the giraffe. Its dark brown, huge and lustrous, soft and melting eyes are shaded by lashes so long that they dwarf even those artifacts sometimes worn by women in the belief that they enhance their sex appeal. Like man and almost all other mammals the giraffe makes do with no more than seven neck vertebrae, whereas the tiny wren indulges extravagantly in fourteen (and, incidentally, a name to match: *Troglodytes troglodytes troglodytes*); unlike the whole human race it possesses a handy arrangement of sphincter muscles which enable it to close its nostrils as readily as it can

---

1. I have made considerable use in this chapter of two articles which appeared in *Country Life*: 'A Giraffe for George IV' by L. S. Lambourne (2 December 1965) and 'The Year of the Giraffe' by Sheila Cunningham Scriven (12 July 1973).
2. How can so-called 'sportsmen' shoot them 'for fun', or native poachers to provide fly-whisks for tourists? For some revolting accounts see C. A. Spinage's admirable and well-illustrated *The Book of the Giraffe* (Collins, 1968), pp. 90–3.
3. For the okapi see chapter 22.

close its eyes. It has four stomachs, and follows Mr Gladstone's advice to chew each mouthful forty times. Thanks to television we are all now familiar with its sedate 'pacing' (as it is called), and its brisk, lolloping gallop when the legs on each side move forward together; how odd that it has never learnt to trot!

Giraffes tend by nature to be timid and stupid—though Diana (of the Manchester Zoo) did learn how to shut her front door when she wanted privacy, and another to undo a bolt with her lips and tongue. No doubt it was fright or stupidity, rather than malice, that caused a giraffe to kick Carl Hagenbeck's brother unconscious on the water-front at Alexandria, and another to miss by inches the head of its keeper at the London Zoo, leaving a dent in one of the gateposts that was carefully preserved for many years.[1] They themselves also suffer from their stupidity, which makes them accident-prone and liable to break their necks when danger, real or imaginary, causes them to panic; and from their timidity: one is known to have dropped dead from fright when given an injection. Hagenbeck also tells us that they are liable to 'housemaids' knee'.

Spinage discusses a problem which had long perplexed zoologists. When a giraffe drinks —and to do this it inelegantly straddles its legs—it lowers its brain some seven feet below the level of its heart; when it jerks its head up again it brings its brain suddenly to a height of ten or eleven feet above its heart: then why does not this sudden rush of blood induce giddiness and blackouts? Certain experiments were carried out at Regent's Park—disagreeable ones involving yards of catheter and miniature radio transmitters implanted in the animal's arteries—in the hope that they might prove of value in the study of fainting and blackouts of crews of aircraft travelling at high speeds. Only a trained physiologist can grasp the details of what was learned; the layman must be satisfied with the explanation that the equivalent of valves keeps this blood-rush under control.[2]

*   *   *

The ancient Egyptians were, of course, familiar with the Nubian (or 'reticulated') giraffe,[3] a native now of Somalia and northern Kenya but once, as ancient rock-drawings show, much more widely distributed. It occasionally figures on temple walls, and at Deir el-Bahri, near Luxor, there is a fine though mutilated relief of one that was brought back by the expedition sent by Queen Hatshepsut in the eighteenth dynasty to the land of Punt (Somalia). But Europe was not to see this 'loftiest and most harmless of creatures' until the year 46 B.C., when one created a sensation in Julius Caesar's triumphal procession. Thereafter these

1. 'The three most powerful things in the animal kingdom are said to be—firstly, the stroke of a whale's tail, secondly, the kick of a giraffe, and thirdly, the "pat" of a lion's paw.' (F. Buckland, *Curiosities of Natural History*, third series.)

2. At an earlier date A. H. Garrod, prosector at Regent's Park from 1872 to 1880, had tried out his improved sphygmograph (blood-pressure recorder) on a giraffe (Brightwell, *op. cit.*).

3. The Nubian giraffe can be distinguished from other races or sub-species by the markings, which take the form of a network of whitish lines on a fawn ground, and by the presence in the male of a distinct third horn.

gentle giants appeared for several centuries from time to time on festive occasions in Rome, but rarely in the arena since they provided poor 'sport'; then for a millenium they vanish from sight in the West.

In the thirteenth century, however, Frederick II ('Stupor Mundi') managed to acquire one from the Sultan of Egypt, in exchange for a white bear, for his zoo at Palermo; and two centuries later several giraffes reached Italy as gifts from Oriental potentates. Lorenzo de' Medici,[1] for example, received one from the Mamluk Sultan of Egypt, which was praised by court poets and aroused the cupidity of Anne de Beaujeu, daughter of Louis XI of France. It seems that Lorenzo succumbed in the end to her importunity and promised to give it to her; but then he changed his mind, and her passionate appeal for the instant despatch of the '*girafle*—of all the beasts in the world the one I most long to see', was unavailing.

In the fifteenth century we also hear of giraffes reaching Central Asia and China. In 1404 the Sultan of Egypt sent an ambassador to present one (together with nine ostriches) to Tamerlane at Samarkand—an overland journey of several thousand miles. Those that went to China were luckier: they travelled by sea. Laufer[2] reproduces a splendid Chinese painting of the period, showing the animal patterned, not as in nature like 'crazy paving', but in the neat hexagons of a honeycomb.

Around 1600 a good place to see giraffes—or 'camelopards', as they were often called[3]—was Istanbul, and Fynes Moryson thus describes one he was shown there in 1597:

> His haire is red coloured, with many black and white spots; I could scarce reach with the points of my finger to the hinder part of his backe, which grew higher and higher towards his foreshoulder, and his necke was thinne and some three els long, so as hee easily turned his head in a moment to any part or corner of the roome wherein he stood, putting it over the beames thereof, being built like a Barne, and high. . . . by reason whereof he many times put his nose in my necke, when I thought my selfe furthest distant from him, which familiarity of his I liked not; and howsoever the Keepers assured me he would not hurt me, yet I avoided these his familiar kisses as much as I could. . . . The Janizare my guide did in my name and for me give twenty Aspers to the Keeper of this Beast.

Topsell's woodcut of a giraffe in his *History of Foure-footed Beastes* (1607), which is based on a drawing made in Istanbul in 1559 by Melchior Luorigus, gives an impressive, indeed a somewhat exaggerated idea of the animal's size.

*   *   *

1. This prince, in many respects so civilised, had wild animals herded in enclosures in the Piazza della Signoria so that he could spear them to death. *Autres temps, autres moeurs!*
2. 'The Giraffe in History and Art' (*Field Mus. Anthrop. Leaflet 22*), Chicago, 1927.
3. Hence the animal's scientific name, *Giraffa camelopardalis*.

In 1827 King George IV received from Mehemet Ali, Viceroy of Egypt, for his menagerie in Windsor Park, the first live giraffe ever seen in England.[1]

This ambitious and unpleasant Egyptian was little loved in Europe, and the English, in particular, can hardly have forgotten that less than thirty years had passed since he had decorated the streets of Cairo with the impaled heads of British soldiers. So it was diplomacy, rather than any enthusiasm for the promotion of zoology, that had prompted him to present a Nubian giraffe to the heads of each of the three most powerful countries in western Europe: England, France and Austria.

The English giraffe was one of a pair of youngsters which had been captured near Senaar, in the Sudan, and given by the local Governor to the Viceroy. It had made a part of the long journey to Cairo lashed to the back of a camel, 'and when they huddled it together for this purpose they were not nice in the choice of cords or the mode of applying them.' After spending some six months in Malta, it was put on board the trading ship *Penelope*, which had been fitted out with a 'suitable awning of tarpaulins'; with it travelled two Arab keepers, an interpreter, and two milch cows to provide sustenance during the voyage.

On 11 August 1827 the *Penelope* berthed at the wharf by Waterloo Bridge, and two days later, at dawn, the giraffe set out for Windsor in a vehicle drawn by four horses. On arrival, said the *Literary Gazette*, 'The King himself hastened to inspect his extraordinary acquisition, and was greatly pleased with the care that had been taken to bring it to his presence in fine order. . . . On the following morning His Majesty and his suite paid two other visits to examine the giraffe more attentively.' On these and subsequent occasions the vast, futile and dropsical old monarch was always accompanied by the last great love of his pointless life, the equally steatopygous Lady Conyngham.

Among poets who hailed the advent, yet lamented the confinement, of the newcomer was Thomas Hood, whose *Ode to the Cameleopard* begins:

> Welcome to Freedom's birth-place—and a den!
>   Great Anti-climax, hail!
> So very lofty in thy front—but then,
>   So dwindling at the tail!
> In truth, thou hast the most unequal legs![2]
> Has one pair gallop'd, whilst the other trotted,
> Along with other brethren, leopard-spotted,
> O'er Afric sand, where ostriches lay eggs? . . .

1. The 'camelopard' displayed by a London showman in 1810 was merely 'a white camel artificially spotted' (*Literary Gazette*, 25 August 1827).
2. In fact, back and front legs are almost exactly the same length. The illusion is the result of the high shoulders and sloping back.

'State of the Giraffe' (George IV and Lady Conyngham). 'I suppose we shall have to pay for stuffing him next'. Hand-coloured etching by William Heath

By the time it reached England the animal seemed to have completely recovered from the effects of its desert journey. At first it was 'exceedingly playful', delighting the King 'by its harmless disposition and uniform gentleness'; but as its height increased (by eighteen inches in less than two years) it grew each day more languid and more feeble:

> Its legs almost lost their power of supporting the body; the joints seemed to *shoot over*; and at length the weakness increased to such a degree, that it became necessary to have a pulley constructed, which, being suspended from the ceiling of the animal's hovel, was fastened round its body, for the purpose of raising it on its legs without any exertion on its own part.[1]

In the autumn of 1829, in spite of expert care and royal solicitude, it died in that utter silence that is the lot of almost all giraffes from their first breath to their last.[2]

Had the royal animal lived a little longer it would undoubtedly have passed to the London Zoo in 1830, when King William IV presented his entire collection to the Zoological

1. Professor Richard Owen in the *Zoological Magazine*, 1833.
2. Giraffes have been known on rare occasions 'to bleat, grunt, bellow, moo, and snore'; but they have little need to give voice since they are always visible to one another. Then why do they have such a big voice-box? Could it be that they use ultrasonics?

Society of London. The giraffe did, in fact, come to the Society—but only after Gould had stitched it and stuffed it, thus restoring to it the power to stand unaided and affording it at long last the opportunity of showing itself to the public. It had been further immortalised in a fine oil painting by the Swiss animal artist Jacques Laurent Agasse, in which it stands beside its native keepers and Cross, the animal dealer. In this picture, which belongs to H.M. the Queen, the frontal horn of the giraffe is shown as not yet fully developed.[1]

The Viennese giraffe, a young male, died within a year—of emaciation following upon caries in the joint of one of its hind-legs; but for a few glorious months it held the Austrian capital in its thrall. A great 'giraffe festival' was held in the suburb of Penzing, at which every lady present received a bouquet crowned with a giraffe's head made of sugar. 'Excellent music conducted by Mr Friedl soon invited the guests to dance—a polonaise followed by waltz, cotillion, gallopade *à la giraffe*, and others. . . . Beautiful transparencies, executed by Mr Eduard Gurk, depicting the giraffe attended by an Arab, were to be found in a copse at the bottom of the garden. The Arab, Cahi Alli Sciobary, who accompanied the giraffe to Vienna, himself appeared at the ball. Deeply moved with amazement and delight at the transparencies of himself and the giraffe, he indicated by gestures of his hands and feet that the dances were so much to his liking that he would fain tread a measure himself.'[2] A specially composed operetta, 'The Giraffe in Vienna', was staged at the Leopoldstadt theatre; but if the giraffe took part in it[3] he must presumably have been as silent as the heroine of *La Muette de Portici*—the opera which Auber was beginning to compose at that very moment.

The adventures of the French giraffe were even more fantastic. It appears that the English and French consuls in Cairo had drawn lots for the two siblings from Senaar, and that the French consul had got by far the better bargain. His animal, a very healthy female, was shipped from Alexandria in October 1826 in an Italian brigantine whose forward deck had been substantially modified to provide her with every comfort. A dormer window, padded with straw and shaded with an awning, enabled her to survey the ocean, whose waves were supposed to be subdued by the influence of a *saphie*[4] strung round her interminable neck. Her 'cabin steward' was the chief groom of the French consulate, who was assisted by three Sudanese keepers in native dress and always at her beck and call; and three milch cows had been taken on board to provide her with the twenty-five litres of

1. There is another giraffe painting, also in the Royal Collection, by R. B. Davis, dated 'September 1827'. It is entitled 'Two giraffes belonging to George IV', and on the back is inscribed, 'Portrait of a Giraffe belonging to his Majesty'. In fact it shows what seems to be the now extinct 'Cape' form, and was probably made from a stuffed specimen in the British Museum.
2. Contemporary account quoted by Dr Rosl Kirchshofer, *The World of Zoos*.
3. Giraffes are musical only in so far as that the natives use their leg-tendons as strings for musical instruments.
4. 'The Muslim equivalent of a St Christopher's medal' (Spinage).

The French Giraffe *en route* for Paris. Oil-painting by J. R. Brascassat, 1827

milk that she needed daily. On this VIP treatment she throve exceedingly.

The brigantine reached Marseilles in mid-November, where it had been wisely decided that the fashionable young lady should winter and acclimatise herself. Here she became the object both of scientific study and of universal adoration. Experiments made with her diet showed her to be '*ou très-délicate ou capricieuse*'. She would never touch a drop of water, and after a brief and disdainful sniff rejected almost all the fruit and vegetables offered her. Vast quantities of milk and of a kind of porridge made from maize and barley seemed to be all she required. The Prefect of the city, who called her '*ma pupille*' and '*cette belle enfant des Tropiques*', threw innumerable parties for her, and with the coming of spring she was paraded daily through the streets, preceded by a platoon of mounted gendarmes with bared sabres to clear the way, and reassured by the presence of her three cows.

At last the time came for her to leave for the capital—a journey that was to be made on foot. Her wardrobe was put in hand: a tailor-made poncho, buttoning at the front, to protect her body, and a hood emblazoned with the arms of the Pasha and King Charles X to cover her neck. Presumably these were for use only in wet weather, for Brascassat's painting of the triumphal progress shows her naked. Then Etienne Geoffroy Saint-Hilaire, director of the Paris Natural History Museum, arrived in Marseilles to collect her, and one sopping morning in May a rather bedraggled cortège set out on its five-hundred-mile journey.

The progress was truly royal: everywhere crowds lined the roads, and overnight stops were made at inns swiftly renamed '*La Girafe*'. The prima donna took the strain of the journey and the publicity in her ample stride, staring disdainfully down on the ridiculous goggling humanity of whom by this time she had lost all fear; it was poor Geoffroy Saint-Hilaire, perpetually fussed, who wilted and who was finally to end up in hospital. Nearly two months passed before the cavalcade reached the gates of Paris, to continue through cheering crowds to the Jardin des Plantes.

Charles had wanted to come to the city gates to welcome in person his distinguished guest, but his daughter-in-law, the duchesse de Berry, had dissuaded him. So the giraffe and her weary escort were obliged to march on to Saint-Cloud, where she was fed on rose petals from the King's own hand and garlanded with flowers by the duchesse. The two Sudanese keepers (the third had long since returned, homesick, to his native land) were handsomely tipped, while Geoffroy Saint-Hilaire was subjected to an exhausting interro-

French faience plate, *c*. 1827

gation—the *coup-de-grâce* that finally landed him in a hospital bed.

Now followed six months of what Sheila Cunningham Scriven has aptly described as 'giraffomania'. Six hundred thousand Parisians flocked to the Jardin, and Miss Scriven informs us that one day the animal was taken to the top of a mound so that the distinguished French naturalist Jean Bory de Saint Vincent, lodged at that moment in a nearby debtors' prison and refused leave on parole, was enabled to see her from the roof through a telescope.

> The giraffomania industry flourished [writes Miss Scriven]. Plates in Faience and Limoges, soap stamped with giraffes, cake moulds, paper weights, toothpick holders, wall-paper, all proclaimed the year of the giraffe. There were toy giraffes with articulated necks and Images d'Epinal for children. A medicinal ointment used the giraffe as a trademark. The fashionable colours were *ventre du girafe* and *girafe en exil* [presumably shades of beige]. Fashion gazettes presented their clothes on giraffe models. Hair was arranged in the giraffe style, higher in front than at the back. There were giraffe sleeves and giraffe parasols. Ladies wore a choker collar with an amulet like the giraffe herself. There were gold trinkets and brooches, and for men collar buttons, foulards and waistcoats, petit-point slippers and tobacco boxes decorated with the symbol of novelty.
>
> A woman who had large soft black eyes was said to have the eyes of a giraffe, a strain of flu was named *la girafe* and people died of '*une girafe vraiment sévère*'. Songs were written: a waltz for the piano, an 'Afro-French' piece for the guitar. . . . A medal was struck with a giraffe on it and an inscription that parodied what Charles had said of the Restoration: '*Rien n'est changé en France, il n'y a qu'une bête de plus*'. . . . There was even an abortive project for a gas lamp in the Place de la Bourse in the shape of a giraffe with a lantern in her throat.

But Parisians are notoriously fickle. With the arrival of a family of Red Indians the 'year of the giraffe' came to an end, and thereafter her luxury apartment in the Grande Rotonde was visited only by what Balzac called the '*provinciale arrière, la bonne d'enfant désoeuvrée, et le jean-jean simple et naïf*'. She had better have died at the peak of her popularity; but, like the *passé* singer or the faded actress, she lingered on, unloved and unremembered, until 1845—a virgin still at what was, for a giraffe, the considerable age of twenty-one.

According to *Larousse*, the word *girafe* is popularly used in France not only for a lanky woman and a high diving-board (as is fairly reasonable) but also as '*une injure grossière à une femme*'. One would like to know more. Was this the animal that brought the species into disrepute? And if so, what did she do to earn such a reputation?

So Paris had a giraffe, and London did not; an end had to be made to this disgrace, and the Zoological Society let it be known that it was ready to pay handsomely for a specimen in good condition. But at first all attempts failed. 'The giraffe on board the *Lady McNaughten*[1] is dead', came the news in the spring of 1831 of one potential acquisition; and in September

1. Macnaghten?

of the same year another died at sea off the Cape, though 'its appetite was good within half an hour of its death, and until then it appeared quite healthy'. In 1834 yet another was offered by a dealer for collection in Genoa, the price asked being ten thousand Spanish dollars (nearly £2,000); but the Council was 'unwilling to treat for the purchase at a high price of an animal at a distance from London'.

Meanwhile a certain M. Thibaut, a French trader in the Sudan, had been commissioned by the Society to go in search of giraffes. His two expeditions to Kordofan resulted in the capture of eight animals, half of which died of the cold even before reaching Dongola. But the remaining four—three males and one female—were shipped down the Nile, and after acclimatisation in Malta were finally landed at the Brunswick Wharf, Blackwall, before dawn on the morning of 25 May 1836.[1] Next day the *Morning Herald* reported:

> These interesting animals were conveyed yesterday morning from Blackwall to the Zoological Gardens. They left the former place at three o'clock, attended by Mr Bennett, the Secretary of the Society; M. Thibaut, who was attired in an Arab dress; the Nubian and Maltese attendants; and a detachment of the Metropolitan police to keep the road clear of obstructions, and they arrived at the Gardens about six o'clock. The cavalcade had altogether a very novel appearance; but it appeared that the precautions were absolutely necessary, as the animals started at the slightest noise, and the different cabs and other conveyances on the line were solicited to remove into the adjacent streets, which was in every case attended to without objection. Some alarm was occasioned to the animals in passing a field in the Commercial Road, where a cow was grazing; and it required some inducement to cause them to go forward, but they were conducted to the Gardens without much difficulty.

Caroline Owen—wife of Professor (later Sir Richard) Owen, the famous zoologist and comparative anatomist—also described in her diary their arrival at Regent's Park:

> 25th.—A lovely bright morning; up before 3 a.m. R[ichard] and I started at 4, and after waiting about near the Gardens till about 5 saw the most lovely procession imaginable. The four graceful, bounding, playful giraffes, attended by M. Thiebaut and four Africans in native costume. Two policemen were there to clear the road, but in the neighbourhood of the Gardens there was nothing to clear except an early market cart or two. . . . When the giraffes got on to that part of the road in which the trees are on both sides, they could scarcely be held in by the attendants. One animal got so excited that M. Thiebaut called out, 'Laissez aller', &c., and they allowed the pretty creature to bite some of the young shoots off the tree. They were delighted apparently to get into the Gardens, and were soon safe and unhaltered in the elephants' new house. One of the attendants had his cheeks gashed for ornament—three cuts on each side.

1. According to the *Transactions* (vol. II, p. 244) three further giraffes reached the Surrey Zoological Gardens in that same year.

Sir Richard Owen and the skeleton of a Giant Moa. This huge extinct New Zealand bird is said to owe its name to the misunderstood, exultant cries of Maori collectors: '*More* bones!'

Thibaut's Giraffes (Zaida, Mabrouk, Selim and Guib Allah) with their three native attendants and (extreme right) M. Thibaut. Hand-coloured lithograph by G. Scharf, 1836

June 6th.—R. told me today the names of the new giraffes. The one with a talisman round his neck is called Selim (fortunate). The others are called Mabrouk (favourite), Guib-allah (God's gift) and Zaida (happy).

The giraffes, for which Thibaut received the stipulated sum of £700, took kindly to their new surroundings, enthusiastically welcoming the enormous crowds and showing their pleasure by snatching and eating the flowers from the hats of any women who came too close. The Owens were regular visitors, and on 16 June Caroline witnessed one of those little tiffs which are not infrequent among the animals and not unknown even among the Fellows of the Society:

June 16th.—To-day one of the giraffes lifted to his own height a peacock in full spread, and, after giving the bird a shake, which left a mouthful of long tail-feathers in his mouth, let him drop, and the peacock ran off with his train shut up in a great fright. The giraffe lifted him by seizing some of the middle feathers (where the Argus eyes are) as the peacock was proudly displaying them, and then began chewing them with much satisfaction. The keeper gave him a whipping for his trouble. The peacocks were in the same enclosure as the giraffe.

Rather rash, one would have thought! And in 1837 the giraffes were transferred to the house built for them in that year by Decimus Burton.

The first recorded instance of the birth of a giraffe in captivity took place in the Gardens in June 1839, after a pregnancy of 444 days. Caroline Owen wrote:

June 18th.—Accouchement of Madame Giraffe [Zaida] at her residence in the Zoological Gardens, of a son. The mother standing licking some salt. The nurses had given the young gentleman some warm cow's milk out of a sucking bottle. It is wonderfully well formed for so recent an animal. It is like a big one reduced in size. Its mother will not allow it to go near her. . . . The keepers said we need not hurry away, as the mother rather liked company than not.

The infant lived for only ten days; but before the Thibaut stock finally died out in 1881, no less than seventeen births had taken place. The Queen records in her Journal seeing one of these infants when it was only a few hours old: 'March 31 [1852]. We took the two eldest girls to the Zoological Gardens today, looking at several animals we had not seen [on a visit four days before] *& vice versa*.[1] A little giraffe was born at 5 this morning & was lying in the straw.' Of these seventeen young giraffes, one was presented to Dublin (in 1844), five were sold, and two—unable to cry for help or, like elephants in a similar situation, to stamp out the flames—perished in a fire in the giraffe house in 1866.

Seven other Nubian giraffes of different strain had also been acquired over the years; but on the death of the last of these in 1892 there was for the first time since 1836 no giraffe

1. My italics. Brave animals indeed!

in the Zoo, and the troubles in the Sudan made it impossible to get another from there. However, a female 'southern' giraffe, 'Daisy', was purchased in 1895, and two years later the Queen presented a male she had received as a Diamond Jubilee gift from Chief Bathoen of Bechuanaland. Unhappily this potential mate for Daisy died immediately upon arrival at the Gardens.

In the present century the Zoo has never been without its giraffes. At the time of writing it has four, while there are others at Whipsnade, and many more to be seen in innumerable safari parks up and down the country. Indeed, there have never been so many in England. But even in safari parks, giraffes too often just stand and stare and rarely show their paces; for those, therefore, who cannot visit Africa, television still provides the best means of observing these glorious creatures in action.

*   *   *

Giraffe and her young.
Illustrated London News,
24 February 1849

It is impossible to resist quoting, as an *envoi*, a few more stanzas of Roy Campbell's splendid poem on the giraffe:

> Each his own stairway, tower, and stylite,
> Ascending on his saintly way
> Up rungs of gold into the twilight
> And leafy ladders to the day:
>
> Chimneys of silence! at whose summit,
> Like storks, the daydreams love to nest;
> The earth, descending like a plummet
> Into the oceans of unrest,
>
> They can ignore—whose nearer neighbour
> The sun is, with the stars and moon
> That on their hides, with learned labour,
> Tattooed the hieroglyphic rune.
>
> Muezzins that from airy pylons
> Peer out above the golden trees
> Where the mimosas fleece the silence
> Or slumber on the drone of bees;
>
> Nought of this earth they see but flowers
> Quilting a carpet to the sky
> To where some pensive crony towers
> Or Kilimanjaro takes the eye.
>
> Their baser passions fast on greens
> Where, never to intrude or push,
> Their bodies live like submarines,
> Far down beneath them, in the bush.
>
> Around their heads the solar glories,
> With their terrestrial sisters fly—
> Rollers, and orioles, and lories,
> And trogons of the evening sky.

8

A New Broom

I t may be recalled that in the middle forties the Zoo had been going steadily downhill.[1] The three honorary secretaries who had followed in fairly quick succession after the death of Bennett in 1836 had looked upon their office chiefly as a position of scientific dignity, preferring to leave the day-to-day work to a paid assistant who, however keen and diligent, carried little weight. On Ogilby's resignation in 1847 it was therefore very sensibly decided to replace him by a full-time paid[2] secretary, and it seemed at first that the choice of David William Mitchell to fill the post could not have been bettered, for Mitchell was capable and active, and it was largely due to him that the decline was arrested.

Then something went wrong. Chalmers Mitchell, in his *Centenary History*, states that in April 1859 his namesake resigned to become Director of the new Jardin d'Acclimatation in Paris, where a few months later he died 'in very painful and melancholy circumstances'. Sir Peter leaves it at that; but the facts, which have not previously been published, appear to have been as follows:

> The Society heard of Mitchell's death when they received a letter from a group of British residents in Paris, saying that they had not been able to get into touch with his relations. They reported that when Mitchell was dying he had been taken from his own house to a 'madhouse' and on his wife's instructions buried as a French pauper. It was suspected that he had committed suicide. After his death, the officers of the Society found that certain sums of money collected by him on behalf of the Society (for instance, Fellows' subscriptions) had not been entered in the books and had apparently been appropriated for his own use. More than £600 was never recovered. . . .[3]

But all this still lay in the future; meanwhile, as a leading article in the *Athenaeum* of 16 June 1849 shows, the Press was not slow to observe that the Zoo was being given a 'new look':

> Three or four years ago the faded appearance of these gardens, the diminishing number

1. See p. 35.
2. With a salary of £250 *per annum*. This was doubled in 1852.
3. Mr R. A. Fish, Librarian of the Z.S.L., in a letter to the author.

of animals, and above all the decrease of visitors, led us to fear that as 'every dog had his day' so had the animals in Regent's Park. But the great improvement that has taken place in the aspect of the grounds, the building of several new houses for their tenants, the enlarging of others, the addition of new plots of land, the increase in the number of visitors, and the variety of new species of animals lately added to the collection, have induced us to make inquiries into their present condition. By these means we have learnt some of the details of the improvements that are so obvious, and so creditable to the parties having the management of the Gardens—more especially to the secretary, Mr. D. W. Mitchell.

About this time a printed 'Letter to the President' was circulated among the Fellows, every copy of which seems to have disappeared; but its substance is known to us from a review of it in the *Literary Gazette* which the conscientious Scherren managed to track down. The writer of the review states that the letter

> went to expose the vicious system of forming Councils of men of wealth and station, unaccustomed to habits of business, possessed of every desirable qualification, except an acquaintance with the matter in hand, and contented to place themselves in the hands of an honorary secretary while incurring the mismanagement that insensibly arises out of a compact, in which one party takes all the power, the other all the homage.

The reviewer, comments Scherren, 'approved of the matter contained in the "Letter", but condemned the style'.

It would be possible, but it would be tedious, to list every novelty that reached Regent's Park in the late forties and the fifties, every first breeding record, every addition to or reconstruction of the houses; and we will not attempt it. Among the zoological sensations of the period were the arrivals of the hippopotamus,[1] a great ant-eater,[2] and of a young elephant named Betsey;[3] but one or two other newcomers deserve to be mentioned, one or two events to be recorded. The innovation whose ripples were to extend the furthest, was undoubtedly the establishment in 1853 of the world's first public 'Marine and Fresh Water Vivarium'[4]—or, as we call it today, Aquarium.

What had set the ball rolling had been the discovery that by keeping fish and aquatic plants together in a tank a kind of 'mutual aid society' (symbiosis) was formed: the fish absorbed the oxygen in the water and replaced it by carbonic acid; this the plants absorbed, returning the oxygen to the water. A surgeon named Ellis, in his *The Chemistry of Creation* (published by the S.P.C.K. in 1850), had apparently been the first to observe this; but it was the chemist Robert Warington and the naturalist and writer Philip Henry Gosse who explored its potentialities, and Gosse who put it to practical use.

1. See p. 106.   2. See p. 124.   3. See p. 164.
4. Latin for 'fish pond' or any kind of animal enclosure or park. Now normally applied to dry tanks for small reptiles, etc.

Sea-horses at Regent's Park.
Illustrated London News,
23 July 1859

Gosse, that dreadfully dour and intolerant Plymouth Brother immortalised for us in the pages of his son's *Father and Son*, had been driven in January 1852 by 'nervous dyspepsia induced by excessive brain work' to exchange the turmoil of London for the restorative calm of the seaside. Here, incapable as always of idleness, he had at once begun to study the local marine life. The fruits of this *villeggiatura* at St Marychurch and Ilfracombe were *A Naturalist's Rambles on the Devonshire Coast* (1853) and the construction of fish tanks in which he contrived to do what had hitherto been thought impossible: to keep marine animals alive in confined captivity for many months. On his return to London at the end of the year he immediately set out with his fish-tanks for Regent's Park. The Society was impressed. A kind of glorified greenhouse was immediately run up and put at his disposal, and in May the first Vivarium opened its doors to the public.

To those familiar with fine modern aquaria, especially that at Regent's Park, Gosse's Vivarium must seem humble indeed. The tanks, the majority of which contained marine animals (swimming in North Sea water delivered in small casks by the Great Eastern Railway), were divided into compartments:

In these, to speak in plain language, a variety of seaweeds and plants, of the most various and beautiful descriptions, rise from a soil of marine pebbles, shells, and rocky and mossy fragments. Within the recesses of these appear all manner of strange fishes—marine sticklebacks, crabs of every kind, and some with periwinkle shells upon them, scorpion-looking prawns by scores, strange molluscae, with their lungs on their outsides, baglike creatures which attach themselves to the said periwinkles, and live upon sucking their shells; strange animals, too, like bunches of living maccaroni; ugly little fishes all out of shape; other ugly little fishes with no shape at all—all swimming creatures, adhering creatures, crawling creatures, creatures with horns, creatures with great eyes, creatures sparkling in brilliant suits of scales, creatures of a clammy white—all these moved or hung in their different fashions to suck such substances as suited them—water-weeds, stones, and sometimes like suckers clung to the smooth plate glass of the tank.[1]

The writer found the fresh-water tanks less exciting, though he admitted to being impressed by 'some villainous looking pike, floating side by side with cannibal eyed and aldermanic perch, hardly able to carry about their fat proportions', and by a 'variety of minnows [that] looked more golden than goldfishes'. But the public was thrilled by everything. 'The secrets hitherto known only to fishes and mermaids', said the *Daily News*, 'are laid open to all who choose to know them . . . and those who formerly ran after the hippopotamus[2] may now perhaps find equal amusement in the more remote but not less curious novelties of this new glass house.'

The repercussions of the Vivarium were enormous. Not only did it prepare the way for the foundation of biological stations, fresh-water and marine, where systematic work could be carried on by trained observers; it also set in motion a craze for the domestic aquarium. From seaside holidays hundreds of families now returned home with jars brimming with fishlets and water-weed, and clutching one or more of the innumerable practical handbooks that had been rushed from the presses to satisfy this new demand.

But in fact the fish had never had it so bad, for the fish-cum-plant alliance was not as simple a matter as had at first appeared. If there was insufficient light, the plant died and polluted the water; if the water was changed too frequently, the fish resented it and sickened; and if there was too much light, then the fish died. At the Zoo there were men constantly pulling blinds up and down, and hand-syringing the water to regulate the supply of oxygen; but in the home, after the novelty had worn off, the wretched fish were left to fend for themselves. And there, among their ghastly 'china castles, sunken galleons, china mermaids and tropical shells', they died like flies. Even *Punch* shed a whimsical tear.

The time eventually came when the Zoo also found the difficulties of keeping a satisfactorily balanced aquarium too great to justify the labour and the expense involved. 'The ultimate failure of this quite heroic attempt', wrote Brightwell, 'was entirely due to the lack of those convenient gadgets, electric aerators, thermostats, etc., which every home aquarist may now purchase from a hundred dealers.' By the early seventies the fickle public had in any case already lost interest, and the Vivarium—henceforth curtly dismissed as 'the old Fish House'—was closed. Fifty years were to pass before a new Aquarium came into being; but the lessons learnt in the fifties and sixties were of the utmost importance, for the Regent's Park Vivarium was at all events the indirect begetter of Döhrn's now world-famous Stazione

---

1. *Morning Chronicle*, 21 May 1853. I hope the reader is familiar with Leigh Hunt's curious sonnet 'To a Fish', which opens:

> You strange, astonished-looking, angle-faced,
> Dreary-mouthed, gaping wretches of the sea . . .

2. See p. 106.

Domestic Aquarium. Shirley Hibberd,
Rustic Adornments for Homes of Taste,
1895

Zoologica at Naples and of the aquaria at Brighton and Hamburg.

Lastly, it was at Regent's Park that in 1853 a fish, the first ever thus to be immortalised, sat for its portrait to a photographer—Count Montizon.[1]

Regent's Park did not succeed until 1913 in getting a wine and spirits licence—a matter which caused the Society some irritation. But many visitors brought their drink with them, while one or two found it simpler to arrive already drunk; as a Zoo custodian once said, 'What they keeps in the cages is tame enough; the wild ones walks in through the turn-stiles'. The orgy in Richmond Park has already been described, and one can only hope that the following occurrence, reported by *The Times*, was exceptional. On 28 September 1852 'two well-dressed young men', John Gosney and George Tayton, were charged at Marylebone Police Court with 'drunkenness and disorderly conduct . . . and with wantonly injuring a badger by administering to it some gin':

William Nixey, 19, Windsor-street, City-road, deposed that on the previous afternoon, about 4 o'clock, he was in the gardens, and there saw the prisoners, one of whom (Gosney) gave some gin from a bottle to a wolf, after which he gave the animal a biscuit, and then threw some gin into its mouth. He then gave some of the like spirit to an Esquimaux dog, by throwing it from a glass; and in addition to these freaks he offered a piece of biscuit to a badger. Upon the animal opening its mouth to seize the morsel he introduced therein the neck of the bottle, from which no doubt a quantity of gin had passed down the animal's throat; it rolled and floundered about in its cage, and he (Gosney) then struck a blow at it between the wires. . . . The prisoners were both drunk. . . .

The magistrate, concluding that 'no real mischief was intended towards the animals',

1. I have failed to find a print of this.

Silver Medal of the Z.S.L. Designed by Thomas Landseer, *c.* 1837, but first awarded in 1847

fined Gosney thirty shillings, or a month's imprisonment, for assaulting the officer, and Tayton five shillings for being drunk.

In 1847 the Society awarded its first two silver medals. They went to Sir Roderick Murchison and to a Russian, M. Dolmatoff, Master of the Imperial Forests in the Government of Grodno, for their part in securing a pair of European bison (wisents[1]) for Regent's Park. Murchison, who had been helping in the making of a geological survey of Russia, persuaded Tsar Nicholas I to present two of these rare animals, while it was Dolmatoff who had organised the team of fifty foresters and three hundred beaters who captured them.

The European bison, once distributed over much of western Europe and recorded on cave walls at Altamira and Lascaux, was by this time restricted to two populations (possibly different races) in the forests of Lithuania and the Caucasus. Both became extinct in the wild soon after—and as a result of—the First World War; but some forty or fifty of the Lithuanian stock remained in various zoos and game preserves (including Woburn), and in spite of losses in the Nazi War the survival of the wisent now seems assured.

In 1851 the Z.S.L. suffered a considerable loss by the death of Lord Derby—a staunch supporter of the Society and its President since 1832. His successor was Prince Albert; and we may surely find it surprising that during his nearly ten years of office we did not get a *Royal* Zoological Society, as had Ireland (Dublin). The Queen and the Prince had always patronised the Zoo, and this stronger bond with the Society led to their visits becoming more frequent. On one occasion the Queen mentions the 'unpleasant smell' of the big cats, which so distressed her lady-in-waiting that she kept on repeating, 'I don't like it! I don't like it!' A new and more salubrious Lion House, now in its turn about to be replaced, was not built until 1876.

1. Pronounced 'weezants'. The name aurochs, that of an extinct European ox, is sometimes wrongly applied to them. An interesting attempt, made about forty years ago, to reconstruct the aurochs by cross-breeding Scottish park cattle with Spanish fighting bulls produced animals not accepted as such by zoologists.

In 1850 the Queen presented to the Society a giant tortoise which had been sent to her by a family living at the Cape of Good Hope. It was alleged to be 179 years old; but though tortoises are almost certainly the longest-lived vertebrates—fully authenticated centenarians are not uncommon, and it is well established that a male Marion's Tortoise met an accidental death when over the age of 152—all figures in excess of this must be considered suspect.

Formerly these monstrous reptiles, survivors of the remotest past, were to be found in enormous quantities in the Galápagos Islands, and in Mauritius and other islands of the western Indian Ocean; the traveller François Leguat, writing of the Island of Rodriguez in 1691, asserted that it was possible there to walk a hundred yards on their backs without ever putting foot to ground. But giant tortoises are sadly vulnerable: their flesh is delicious, and since they can be kept alive for months without food or water they constitute the ideal 'iron rations' for a long voyage. A large adult will also provide about three gallons of purest oil. Worse still, they are friendly, trusting, and deaf—fearing no attack from before, hearing

Giant Tortoises at Regent's Park. The *Field*, 4 September 1875

no approach from behind, and in any case incapable, with a maximum speed of only five yards a minute over even the shortest distance, of making their escape. Preservation came just in time to save them from extinction.

While the royal tortoise was still at Buckingham Palace, Professor Owen was summoned by Prince Albert to inspect it and record its vital statistics. In the Palace gardens the Prince watched with amusement as Owen, precariously balanced astride the ambling animal, established with his tape-measure that its girth was twelve feet. Owen appears to have been a better tortoiseman than Darwin, who confessed that he could not long keep his seat on the tortoises of the Galápagos.

But the Queen's tortoise, if really 179 years old, was never to become a centen-octo-genarian; for it died at the Zoo that same winter.

It was very convenient for the Society to have so royal a President. For example, when it wished to acquire a breeding stock of Himalaya pheasants, the Prince had only to breathe the word to Lord Canning, the Governor-General of India, and the birds were as good as in the bag.

The common pheasant—a native of south-eastern Europe, Asia Minor and beyond—had probably been in this country since Roman times; at all events, by the regulations of King Harold in 1059, *unus phasianus*—one pheasant—was listed as an item in the rations of the canons of Waltham Abbey, and it is unlikely that either the Anglo-Saxons or the Danes would have introduced it. But handsome as is our polygamous and much-massacred bird, it pales before the splendours of Far Eastern species. The Society had long wanted to increase the quantity and variety of its holdings of Himalaya pheasants, and in 1857 a large collection of more than six different genera was brought down to Calcutta, where one of the Zoo's head keepers was waiting.

The intention had been to keep the birds in confinement in India until they had become reasonably tame, or alternatively to breed from them there and send home young pheasants reared under domestic fowls; but then came the Mutiny, and they had to be speeded on their way. The voyage took a heavy toll of them: of eight pairs of both Impeyan Pheasants (Monals) and Tragopans (Horned Pheasants) not a single bird survived the journey; enough, however, of the collection reached Regent's Park to justify the fairly heavy out-lay, a part of which had been borne by private individuals who received in return a share of the spoil.[1] There was also a shower of Silver Medals which descended upon Lord Canning, the Rajah of Bahadur, and those others who had helped to form the collection.

Most of the birds bred well in captivity. But the Impeyan Pheasant, inhabitant of the highest forest regions of the Himalaya, is a shy breeder, and although it was already represented in the Gardens the loss of this new consignment was much regretted. The magnificent

---

1. Among those that reached England safely were Black-backed, White-crested and Purple Kalijes, Cheer Pheasants, and Hill Partridges.

Bower Birds at Regent's Park. Z.S.L.'s Press-Cuttings, vol. 2

male of the species was chosen by Gould for the cover of his *The Birds of Asia* (1850–83), and of it A. O. Hume wrote: 'There are few sights more striking where birds are concerned than that of a grand old cock shooting out horizontally from the hillside just below one, glittering and flashing in the golden sunlight, a gigantic rainbow-tinted gem, and then dropping stone-like, with closed wings, into the abyss below.'

Another remarkable bird made its European debut at this time—the Satin Bower-bird, denizen of the leafy bush country of New South Wales. Gould, when in Australia in 1840, had observed its strange passion for building and decorating, and eight years later a pair of Bower-birds, despatched by a Mr Aspinwell of Sydney, was safely received at Regent's Park.

The male, which is almost as large as a jackdaw, wears deepest mourning—the body being of black satin, the wing feathers and tail of black velvet; there is colour only in the tip of the beak, the legs, and the gentian-blue eyes. The female, in half mourning only, looks less chic. But it was of course the Bower-bird's behaviour, not its appearance, that excited Gould. For reasons as yet not fully understood, it constructs a kind of tunnel of

'Happy Jerry'.
Zoological Keepsake, 1830

woven twigs, which this 'snapper-up of unconsidered trifles' then proceeds to decorate with bright feathers, shells, berries, bones, scraps of cloth, and any other gaily-coloured or oddly-shaped bric-à-brac it can lay beak on. A forecourt is similarly decorated, and no owner of a collection of curios could devote more time and loving attention to the arrangement of his treasures than does this painstaking, sombre bird. It moves a shell here, shifts a petal there—perpetually fussing, adding, subtracting, adjusting, improving; aiming at a perfection which appears always to elude it. Both the male and the female bird take part in this.

Now many birds decorate their nests with fancy objects. But what the Bower-birds are here building is *not* a nest: it is rather a courtship pavilion and play-pen, a temple of love, a folly—a Petit Trianon even. Like Persepolis it is designed as a ceremonial palace to be occupied only at certain seasons and for certain purposes, not as a fixed abode; and to it the birds repair in the months immediately preceding nidification. No sooner had the newcomers to Regent's Park settled in than they began to build their bower, where, in the intervals of house-painting and decorating, they could be seen 'chasing each other through it, saluting each other with grotesque movements, and uttering varied notes of love, anger and reconciliation'. Sadly, this promising start did not lead to nest-building, and it was not until 1876 that the first nest—a relatively dull affair—was discovered in Australia.

*   *   *

As a tail-piece to this chapter we may perhaps briefly mention a fine Mandrill received from Angola in 1849 and believed to be the only specimen at that time in England. 'Tail-piece' is the operative word, for the sunset splendour of this great West African baboon's posterior outshines even the azure of its corrugated cheeks and the sealing-wax red of its long and rigid nose.

The mandrill had been known for centuries in Europe, though often under other names. Zoologists agree that it was undoubtedly the 'Ape-Wolf' mentioned by Gesner as having 'aroused great wonder when brought to Augsburg and shown there in the year 1551. . . . On his feet he has fingers like a man's, and if one points at him, he presents his arse. He is by nature frolicsome, especially towards women.' Given the chance, mandrills take to the bottle, showing a preference for beer and whisky-and-water. According to Broderip, in the 1820s there was one named 'Happy Jerry' at the Exeter 'Change which drank grog, smoked a short clay pipe, and on one occasion dined (off hashed venison) with George IV at Windsor Castle. Even the King's beloved giraffe was not thus honoured.

9

Bartlett and Buckland

I think I could turn and live with animals, they are so placid and self-contained.

Walt Whitman, *Song of Myself*

FOR nearly forty years—from his appointment in 1859 as Superintendent of the Gardens to his death in 1897—one man, Abraham Dee Bartlett, personified the Zoo. His years of office almost exactly coincided with those of Philip Lutley Sclater as Secretary to the Zoological Society (1859–1903), and for much of the time he was also intimately associated with a man whose connection with the Zoo, though unofficial, was very close: Francis (Frank) Buckland.

Bartlett, who was born in 1812, came of humble stock: his father, John Bartlett, was employed by a barber named Turner, now remembered only because his son was to become one of England's greatest artists. Mr Turner's shop was in Exeter Street, off the Strand and within a stone's-throw of Cross's Exeter 'Change Menagerie. Cross was a friend of John Bartlett, and almost from infancy Abraham had had the entrée of those cages in the 'beast-room' (as it was called) that housed the more amiable animals. Noticing that the boy was particularly fond of birds, Cross gave him the bodies of any that died; this led to Abraham becoming a skilled amateur taxidermist.

At the age of fourteen Abraham was apprenticed to his father, who in the meanwhile had established himself independently as 'hairdresser and brush-maker' at premises in Drury Lane. Seven or eight unhappy and largely wasted years followed, till the time came when the young man could no longer bear this uncongenial drudgery: he had continued to work at taxidermy in his spare time; he now resolved to make it his profession. By good luck and perseverance he soon got to know a number of Fellows of the Zoological Society and leading naturalists of the day, who brought commissions his way and kept him solvent in the first difficult years. In 1848 he made a brilliant reconstruction of the long-extinct dodo,[1] which was included among a number of mounted specimens that won for him the

---

1. The dodo, a Mauritian bird, became extinct in 1681. The unique specimen in John Tradescant the Younger's 'Closet of Curiosities' (Ashmolean Museum, Oxford), being found in 1775 to be looking shabby, was burnt, only its head and left foot being rescued from the flames. These were transferred in 1861 to Oxford's new Natural History Museum.

Abraham D. Bartlett,
Superintendent of the Zoo,
1859–97

first prize at the 1851 Exhibition. His entry consisted of:

> Eagle under glass shade, diver under glass shade (the property of her Majesty the Queen), snowy owl, Mandarin duck, Japanese teal, pair of Impeyan pheasants, sleeping ourang-utang, sun bittern, musk deer, cockatoo, foxes; carved giraffe; two bronze medals from the Zoological Society; model of dodo; dog and deer; crowned pigeons; leopard and wolf.

The dodo was taken to Sydenham when the Crystal Palace was moved there, but only to be destroyed in the great fire of 1866.

Abraham Bartlett prospered beyond all his expectations in his new profession. Already by 1846 he had found himself in a position to move into a large house in Camden Town, which was soon to be frequented by many distinguished zoologists and collectors. He carried out work for the Queen, stuffing her pets and supplying her with canaries and piping bullfinches which he tended when they were ill and housed for her when she was away. He was further employed by the Zoological Society, and on the death in 1859 of the Superintendent of the Gardens, John Thompson, Bartlett was appointed his successor, with a salary of £200 a year, a house, and various 'perks' such as the receipts from the public lavatories.

From now on, wrote his son Edward, he became 'a walking Zoological Encyclopaedia', impressively bound on all occasions in top hat and morning coat. As early as 1839 he had published a paper on 'The Pink-Footed Goose' in the *Proceedings* of the Society, and over the years he made no less than fifty-six further contributions. He also, of course, had arduous duties in supervising the keepers, the animals, the buildings and the gardens, and a considerable, and on occasions an abusive, correspondence to deal with—for in his time the Zoo (as we shall see) came in for a good deal of attack from the public as well as from a number of dissident Fellows. Bartlett was 'the man on the spot'; Sclater was principally to be found at the Society's offices in Hanover Square. He was an Oxford graduate and a barrister with a deep interest in ornithology, a widely-travelled man, and a friend of explorers and collectors.

Bartlett's two books—*Wild Animals in Captivity* (1898) and *Life among Wild Beasts in 'the Zoo'* (1900), both issued by Chapman and Hall—were posthumous publications consisting principally of miscellaneous articles on a wide range of zoological subjects which had appeared in Buckland's paper, *Land and Water*, and other periodicals and journals. The selection and editing of them was carried out by his son Edward, who inherited his father's papers and provided an introduction to the earlier of the two volumes. In a foreword to the later volume, Edward wrote: 'It was not my father's intention that his work should be of the serious order, nor did he wish it to be wholly scientific, but that it should be acceptable to both the naturalist and the non-scientific reader; he gave no thought to the captious critic.'

The books, though Edward had no literary expertise, are still pleasant to dip into. They tell of a man who had nothing to learn about the handling of animals, though perhaps a good deal to learn about the handling of people. Not everyone would care to take a half-frozen alligator on his knees and massage its belly until its circulation was restored; not everyone would have thought of persuading a reluctant aardwolf—the first to reach Regent's Park—to eat by pouring a basinful of tripe over it which it swallowed as it licked itself clean. Bartlett had many splendid qualities; but in his later years his stubbornness, and his reluctance ever to listen to criticism, made him his own worst enemy.

*   *   *

Frank Buckland was a more flamboyant character.[1] To judge from a photograph in which he looks like the bully who torments Charlie Chaplin in some of his early films, one would hardly place him as the product of Winchester and Christ Church, a member of the Athenaeum, or the son of a future Dean of Westminster. Yet such he was.

In 1826, at the time of Frank's birth, Dr William Buckland was a Canon of Christ Church, Oxford, the University's first Professor of Geology, and a Fellow of the Royal Society. Darwin, though admitting his ability[2] and amiability, much disliked him personally and

1. In what follows I have made much use of G. H. O. Burgess's entertaining biography, *The Curious World of Frank Buckland*.
2. His paper on the megalosaurus, read before the Geographical Society of London on 20 February 1824, made palaeontological history.

Frank Buckland in
working clothes,
holding an oyster-
breeding tile.
Photograph, *c.* 1875

described him as 'vulgar and almost coarse'. He was also a notable eccentric, and the infant was early subjected to a sample of the parental whimsicality when, to settle an argument, it found itself snatched from its cradle and weighed against a leg of mutton on the kitchen scales. The Canonry was always full of improbable animals, alive and dead, in improbable places or put to improbable uses, and guests who came to luncheon were not usually so fortunate as to be offered mutton. Ruskin wisely refused an invitation on a day when 'mice on toast' had been pre-announced as the savoury; the Owens were subjected to ostrich, which Mrs Owen thought 'very much like a bit of coarse turkey' but which made her husband ill; and crocodile stew was not unknown. From a man who had once eaten a small but reputedly authentic portion of the embalmed heart of Louis XIV, anything might be expected.

This royal tit-bit is said to have been swallowed accidentally by the Doctor when visiting Frances Lady Waldegrave, and the curious episode has provided the theme for a no less curious poem by William Plomer—'The Heart of a King'.[1] According to Plomer, Dr Buckland had in his time eaten his way 'through more than half the animal creation'—

> . . . . not out of gluttony,
> But in a spirit of enquiry.
> The buzzard, I may say, tastes muttony,
> The texture of its flesh is wiry.

Dr Buckland's whimsicality affected all his doings; he even labelled his umbrella 'STOLEN FROM DR BUCKLAND'. Sir Roderick Murchison, the distinguished Scots geologist, wrote after attending the meetings of the British Association at Bristol that the 'fun of one of the evenings' was provided by Buckland:

> In that part of his discourse which treated of ichnolites, or fossil footprints, the Doctor exhibited himself as a cock or a hen on the edge of a muddy pond, making impressions by lifting one leg after another. Many of the grave people thought our science was altered to buffoonery by an Oxford Don.

In this bizarre atmosphere young Frank grew up, and it would have been surprising indeed had it not left its mark on him.

In October 1845, when Samuel Wilberforce (later known as 'Soapy Sam') was promoted from the Westminster Deanery to the Bishopric of Oxford, Dr Buckland was appointed his successor. One day in the following January Bartlett was invited to the Deanery on a matter of business, and it was doubtless then or soon after that he first met Frank, at that

1. *Collected Poems*, Cape, 1960. See also Augustus Hare, *The Story of my Life*. Dr Buckland was a great 'debunker', on one occasion scandalising the verger in a continental cathedral by establishing, on bended knees and with a lick of the tongue, that the ineradicable spot of martyr's blood on the floor was bats' urine.

BROWN, JONES, AND ROBINSON GO TO THE ZOOLOGICAL GARDENS.

THEY INSPECT THE BEARS.

ROBINSON FEEDS THE WATER-FOWL.

BROWN HAVING RASHLY STRAYED INTO A ROOM FULL OF MACAWS,
WE SEE THE CONSEQUENCE.

JONES VOLUNTEERS TO RIDE THE CAMEL, AND, TO A CERTAIN EXTENT,
HE DOES IT.

IN A LONELY PATHWAY THEY SEE SOMETHING COMING.

THEY ARE PERSUADED TO MOUNT THE ELEPHANT.

THEY GO IN QUEST OF THE HIPPOPOTAMUS.

THEY SEE THE HIPPOPOTAMUS!

time twenty years old and a Student[1] of Christ Church, Oxford. A grinning maidservant ushered Bartlett into the hall of the Deanery 'and pointed to an object on the floor, apparently a man on his knees, cleaning out what I afterwards understood to be a Dr Arnit's [Arnott's] stove.' The man, his face as black as a chimney-sweep's, rose to his feet and greeted his astonished guest.

The Dean had sent for Bartlett to discuss the stuffing and mounting of 'Billy', his late lamented hyena. There was a history attached to this animal. In 1821, when the Doctor was working on the famous bone cavern of Kirkdale in Yorkshire, he had found a portion of a skull which he believed to be that of a young hyena; but wishing to be certain, he had asked the explorer, William Burchell, to send him a live specimen from the Cape. In due course Billy arrived at the Exeter 'Change, where Cross, who was negotiating the trans-action, was so charmed by its 'good temper and playful manners' that he begged for its life. This was conceded, but with the proviso that Cross should find him another skull—one which was, in fact, to prove that the Dean had been right. So Billy lived on for twenty-five years, first at the 'Change and subsequently at the Surrey Zoological Gardens when Cross took them over. As a child Frank had often gone with his father to feed Billy, and he continued to do so until the hyena's death.

Billy had been enormously popular at the Surrey Gardens, entertaining the visitors at feeding time 'by the gesticulations of delight he manifested at the moment, and by his curious imitations of the human voice resembling laughter. This animal suffers himself to be caressed, and is so familiar with the keepers, that when any repairs are wanting in his cage they have no hesitation in going in with him.' But old age and an enormous goitre had finally put an end to this patriarchal animal. At the sale of the Dean's property after his death, both the mounted animal and its skeleton were purchased for the College of Surgeons.

Frank was very much his father's son. The keeping of dogs at Christ Church was strictly forbidden; but apparently the interdict had not been worded so as to cover more exotic pets, and his rooms in College soon became not only a natural history museum but also a menagerie. The animals were always escaping. His marmot found its way to the Chapter House just as the Chapter was about to meet; his baby bear, Tiglath-Pilesar ('Tig' for short), who had been dressed in cap and gown to enliven a scientific meeting, broke loose and entered the Chapel during the reading of the first lesson.[2] 'Either you, Sir, or that animal must leave the College,' stormed Dean Gaisford—the greatest Greek scholar of his day; but Frank had an influential father, and both he and Tig remained.

Tig, now usually to be seen in academic dress, continued to hit the headlines. He was introduced to the Prince of Canino (a nephew of the great Napoleon) and to Florence

1. Scholar. As a Student he received an annual grant which ceased only upon marriage.
2. It is hard to believe what is alleged—namely, that the lesson happened to be about this Assyrian monarch (1 Chron. V).

Nightingale; he was hypnotised by Monckton Milnes (Lord Houghton). But in the end his behaviour became impossibly outrageous, and in November 1847 he was presented to the London Zoo, where he did not long survive such close captivity. After his death he was mounted by Bartlett and accorded a place of honour on the staircase at the Deanery.

After graduating at Oxford Frank studied medicine, and in 1852, on taking his M.R.C.S., spent a year as House Surgeon at St George's. One of his great qualities (and in those days an unusual one) was that he was totally without class-consciousness. Though he knew many distinguished people, he was equally (or even more) at ease in the company of his 'social inferiors': of animal dealers, taxidermists, showmen, trapeze artists, sailors, sword-giants, dwarfs, and working-class men of all kinds. Among the last-named was a coachman by whose daughter he had in 1851 a natural son, but whom he married as soon as he could afford to sacrifice his Oxford grant.

In 1854 Frank was gazetted Assistant Surgeon to the Second Life Guards, who were stationed for half the year at the Regent's Park Barracks in Albany Street. Two years later his father, who had been off his head for a long time, died, leaving Frank, his elder son, enough money to make his immediate future secure. It was now that Frank began to discover his talent as a popular lecturer and writer on natural history subjects, and it was very convenient for him that when he was at the Regent's Park Barracks his friend Bartlett was near at hand, and the Zoo even nearer. Then Bartlett became Superintendent, and thereafter the two men were constantly together when circumstances allowed.

At first Buckland wrote principally, but by no means exclusively, for the *Field*; in 1866, however, he started his own rival *Land and Water*, to which he contributed regularly until his death. Many of his articles dealt with recent arrivals at the Zoo or with animal behaviour in general; but, says Burgess, 'he also wrote about giants and dwarfs, about scientific ballooning, about Charles Jamrach the animal dealer, indeed about anything odd or strange that came to the notice of his observant eye.' Between 1857 and 1872 he published the four highly successful volumes of *Curiosities of Natural History*, which were frequently reprinted in the latter part of the nineteenth century.[1]

In 1860 Buckland founded an Acclimatisation Society, whose principal object was the introduction of exotic animals thought likely to accept our wayward climate and, by multiplying in the parks of stately homes, enrich our tables; at one time the future King Edward VII was its President. A memorable dinner was held at Willis's Rooms in July 1862, when a company of more than a hundred distinguished guests sat down to eat their way for nearly three hours through such improbable dishes as Japanese sea-slugs, kangaroo steamer, Syrian pig, botargo and Chinese yams—some of which were found to be 'interesting' rather than enjoyable.

1. A selection of the four volumes, edited and illustrated by L. R. Brightwell, came from the Batchworth Press in 1948.

Many of the Society's projects bordered on the ridiculous, and did not always escape the ridicule of the Press; but one—the improvement of Britain's freshwater fisheries—flourished and became Buckland's major interest for the rest of his life. This led to the publication of his *Fish Hatching*, *Familiar History of British Fishes* and other piscatory works; to the founding of his Museum of Economic Fish Culture at South Kensington, and to his appointment in 1867 as Inspector of Salmon Fisheries. He was a pioneer of anti-pollution.

In 1863, Buckland resigned from the Army, married, and established himself with his wife (the boy had died) in a house in Albany Street.[1] This soon became a kind of unofficial sanatorium for small and ailing mammals from the Zoo, and to open unguardedly any package that arrived was almost as dangerous as opening a letter-bomb. It was, too, a cabinet of curios which ranged from Kaffir skulls and a piece of mammoth skin to a few hairs from the head of King Henry IV which old Buckland had managed to appropriate when Dean of Westminister. Human visitors to the house were no less assorted and improbable, and were one and all treated with strict impartiality: 'A fish salesman would receive equal courtesy with a royal duke from the unconventional naturalist in *déshabillé*, and as he talked with the visitor his hands would be employed in the dissection of some interesting "specimen".' A young girl who went with her father to deliver an enormous salmon for Buckland to cast, was to recall her experiences more than sixty years later:

> Buckland greeted us. He was coatless and bare-armed. In the middle of a long table was a tray with a dissected animal on it. At the end of the table a large bowl of Irish stew. Buckland was running up and down, now taking a cut at the dissection and now gobbling a spoonful of the stew. 'Have some?' he asked, hospitably waving towards the stew.
>
> On each side of the fireplace was a tethered monkey, their leashes cleverly arranged so that they could not touch the fire, but could just touch each other's finger-tips, and were not near enough to fight.
>
> Buckland seized a stick and poked behind a bookcase and out rushed a hare—a wild one, said Buckland, but he would soon get it tamed. I mentioned my love for white rats, and he at once produced from somewhere a large white rat and put it on my shoulder. He showed us the original pot of curari poison brought by Bates from the Amazon, put it in my hand, and said I was holding enough to poison half London. . . .[2]

Buckland had worked ceaselessly all his life and without any regard for his health, often spending hours on end wading in icy streams. In 1879 he suffered a severe lung haemorrhage, and though he was soon on his feet again it was clear that he would never make a full recovery. Other and various troubles followed, and on 19 December 1880, at the age of fifty-four, he died. The death certificate gave as the cause of death, hepatic disease of about

1. Subsequently No. 37 but now demolished. The commemorative plaque is now inside the building that stands on the site.
2. *Sunday Times*, 1937, quoted by Burgess.

two years' standing, and bronchitis. 'He was at work . . . to the last full of mental energy and vigour as ever, and said he only wished to publish the masses of information he had acquired in his note books to refute the theories of Darwin and Huxley, which greatly troubled him. . . .' As the end approached, he said, 'God is so good, so very good to the little fishes. I do not believe he would let their inspector suffer shipwreck at last. I am going a long journey where I think I shall see a great many curious animals. This journey I must go alone.'

Sclater, Bartlett and Buckland we shall often meet again in later chapters of this book.

10

Hippopotamus

The animals went in four by four,
The big hippopotamus stuck in the door.

'One more river' (*Oxford Song Book*)

IN the Natural History Museum at South Kensington are three montage pictures showing some of the more spectacular pre-historic British mammals in a modern setting. In one, a polar bear stands upon an ice-flow beneath the Chiswick fly-over; in a second a woolly mammoth and a reindeer are about to visit the Natural History Museum, while in a third we see a hippopotamus,[1] a cave lion and other beasts at the foot of Nelson's monument in Trafalgar Square. On 25 May 1850 there arrived at Regent's Park the first hippopotamus to be seen in England for half a million years, the first in Europe since Roman times. Of all the 'firsts' achieved by the London Zoo in the nineteenth century none was to create greater public excitement than 'Obaysch' (as he was called), and the number of visitors to the Gardens that year was nearly double what it had been in 1849.

I suppose it would be true to say that, taken all in all, people do not much like the hippopotamus, though Theo Johnson rather overstated the case against it when he wrote in his *Personal Recollections of the Zoo*: 'I consider the Hippopotamus simply to be among large animals what the Hog is among small ones: stupid, violent and brutal; without intelligence, courage or affection: altogether *unnecessary* in the scheme of creation, and uninteresting alike to the zoologist and the observer.' Perhaps he had unpleasant personal recollections of a brush with an ill-tempered one.

It was Herodotus who in the fifth century B.C. first called this great beast *hippos potamios*, 'river horse'. He should have known better, for the animal is no close relation of the horse; 'river *hog*' would have made more sense. Indeed, it may well seem doubtful whether he ever actually saw one; for though several of its features are correctly described, his references to 'hoofs like an ox . . . the mane and tail of a horse . . . and a voice like a horse's neigh' are woefully wide of the mark. Pliny, who later made much use of Herodotus's

---

1. Bones of a hippopotamus have been found at Charing Cross.

account, added that when the hippopotamus leaves the river for its daily pasturage it walks backwards so as to mislead possible pursuers!

In the temple of Horus at Edfu, in Upper Egypt, there are some splendid reliefs, dating from the second century B.C., showing Horus attacking his enemies, who are portrayed as hippopotamuses and crocodiles. 'The court sculptor,' wrote Jennison, 'represented importance by size, and the King made fast to a hippo is ludicrously like a very tall lady in a very wide-brimmed hat (and unusually short skirts) leading a particularly small pug down Bond Street.' The Hippopotamus was worshipped locally by the Egyptians, who called it *p-ehe-mau* ('water-ox'). This may be the origin of the Hebrew 'behemoth' ('great beast'); for the biblical animal is almost certainly the hippopotamus, which may possibly have inhabited Palestine at that time. The description of behemoth in the fortieth chapter of the Book of Job fits the hippopotamus so perfectly that Linnaeus, in his *Systema Naturae*, named the animal 'Behemet Jobi':

> He eateth grass as an ox. . . . He lieth under the shady trees, in the covert of the reed, and fens. The shady trees cover him with their shadow; the willows of the brook compass him about. Behold he drinketh up a river, and hasteth not . . .

It is said that in 58 B.C. Aemilius Scaurus, while aedile, brought the first hippopotamus to Rome, and that a canal was specially constructed to receive it and a handful of crocodiles.[1] Augustus (29–14 B.C.) had an enormous zoo whose inmates, which included a hippopotamus, were of course mainly destined for combats in the arena; but there seem to have been among his keepers some who took a genuine scientific interest in their charges. Hippos are several times mentioned during the two following centuries, but almost always in connection with the arena. After the time of Commodus (murdered A.D. 192), however, we hear nothing more of them in captivity in Europe until the nineteenth century, beyond an obscure reference to the dissection of one by Fabio Colonna in Italy in the year 1616.

On 14 April, 1849, Caroline Owen noted in her diary: 'Mr Duncan here. He is our Chargé d'Affaires at Dahomey. It seems a present of peacocks is to be given to the King there, in order to induce him to make us a present of a hippopotamus.' Whether or not the King got his peacocks, we do not know; but he certainly failed to produce the hippo, and Obaysch, like our first giraffe, came from Egypt.

According to Caroline Owen, Obaysch was sent to Regent's Park 'on approval', the purchasing price (£350) being in due course found acceptable. But in fact it seems that some kind of an exchange took place, the new Viceroy, Abbas Pasha, sending a varied collection of animals and receiving in return a stud of greyhounds and deerhounds together with an experienced trainer. The British Consul-General in Cairo, (Sir) Charles Murray,[2] took charge of the negotiations. When today we deal with Oriental potentates we barter arms for oil.

1. The Leviathan of the Bible.   2. For his subsequent career see the *D.N.B.*, Suppl. I.

It was in the spring of 1849 that Abbas had despatched a posse of hunters to the White Nile, where on the island of Obaysch they came upon, and mortally wounded, a large female hippopotamus. The dying animal was observed to be struggling with her last gasp towards some bushes that grew beside the river bank. This heroic gesture defeated its object, which was to rescue her infant; for one of the hunters, following in her tracks, soon caused the youngster to break cover and then gaffed it with a boat-hook as it was about to enter the water.

Obaysch was brought down the Nile to Cairo in a specially constructed boat which also carried cows to provide milk for the still unweaned animal. Indeed in Cairo, where it arrived in November and passed the winter, its daily consumption of seven or eight gallons was jokingly alleged by Murray to have created a shortage throughout the city.

The Consul-General was enchanted by what he called his 'little monster':

> The hippopotamus [he reported] is quite well, and the delight of everyone who sees him. He is as tame and playful as a Newfoundland puppy; knows his keepers, and follows them all over the courtyard; in short, if he continues gentle and intelligent as he promises to be, he will be the most attractive object ever seen in our Garden, and may be taught all the tricks usually performed by the elephant.

His keeper, Hamet, slept on the floor beside his charge, having given up the attempt to use a hammock after Obaysch had twice playfully pitched him out of it in the middle of the night.

With the coming of spring, Obaysch was placed in a padded cart and taken by Hamet and two amateur assistants—they were by profession snake-charmers—to Alexandria, from where they sailed to Southampton in a P & O steamer which had been provided with a pool and other amenities for its distinguished passenger. The journey to London was made in a 'special', 'every station yielding up its wondering crowd to look upon the monster as he passed'—but fruitlessly, for all that was visible was the head of its ever-watchful keeper, who 'for want of air was constrained to put it out through the roof'.

A van deposited the 'great overgrown dropsical baby' at the gates of the Zoo that same evening. Here Hamet, 'followed by the unwieldy creature, trotting along, and sniffing grotesquely at the bag of dates which his keeper carried', saw his charge enter his cage willingly, receive his reward, and proceed to examine his pool (which was kept at a suitable temperature by 'Mr W. Hill's improved Flue Boiler and Furnace'). Richard Owen, who was soon on the spot, wrote later an excellent account of the new arrival, which was already seven feet in length and almost as much in girth:

> When I saw the hippopotamus it was lying on its side on the straw, with its head resting against the chair on which its swarthy attendant sat. It now and then uttered a soft complacent grunt, and, lazily opening its thick smooth eyelids, leered at its keeper with a singular protruding movement of the eyeball from the prominent socket, showing

The Hippopotamus
arrives by balloon.
Punch, 12 October
1850

an unusual proportion of the white . . . It had just left its bath, and a minute drop of glistening secretion was exuding from each of the conspicuous mucosebaceous pores . . . This gave the hide, as it glistened in the sunshine, a very peculiar aspect. When the animal was younger, the secretion had a reddish colour . . . After lying quietly about an hour, now and then raising its head, and swivelling its eyeballs towards its keeper, or playfully opening its huge mouth and threatening to bite the leg of the chair on which the keeper sat, the hippopotamus rose, and walked slowly about its room, and then uttered a loud and short harsh snort four or five times in quick succession, reminding one of the snort of a horse, and ending with an explosive sound like a bark.

The keeper understood the language, and told us the animal was expressing its desire to return to the bath.[1]

Hamet then led the way, the animal following close to his heels like a dog:

On arriving at the bath-room, it descended with some deliberation the flight of low steps leading into the water, stooped and drank a little, dipped its head under, and then plunged forwards. It was no sooner in its favourite element than its whole aspect changed, and it seemed inspired with new life and activity: sinking down to the bottom, and moving about submerged awhile, it would suddenly rise with a bound, almost bodily out of the water, and splashing back, commenced swimming and plunging in a cetaceous or porpoise-like style, rolling from side to side, and taking in mouthfuls of water, and spurting them out again, raising every now and then its huge grotesque head, and biting the woodwork of the bath. . . .

After half an hour spent in this amusement, it quitted the water at the call of its keeper, and followed him back to the sleeping-room, which is well bedded with straw, and where a stuffed sack is provided for its pillow, of which the animal, having a very short neck, thicker than the head, duly avails itself when it composes itself to sleep. When awake, it is very impatient of any absence of its favourite attendant, rising on its hind-legs, and threatens to break down the wooden fence by butting and pushing against it in a way very strongly significative of its great muscular force.

Caroline Owen, who considered that Obaysch was 'just like a spoilt child, and showed a spirit of obstinacy very pig-like', mentions a visit she made with her husband to see the great attraction of the London season:

There was an immense crowd of visitors to the Gardens. R. and I got through the crowd to the giraffe paddock, in the hope of getting some friends into the house, but soon found it out of the question. There was a dense mass of people waiting their turn to get inside, and the whole road leading to that part of the Gardens was full of a continuous stream of people. Mr. Mitchell said that there were more than 6,000 last Saturday, and that there were about 10,000 today.

1. *The Times*, 6 June 1850.

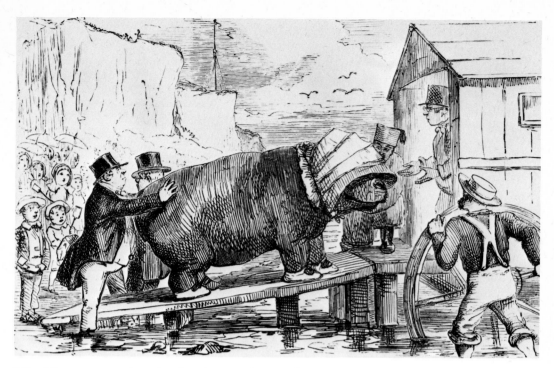

'The Hippopotamus is ordered a change of air, and a little sea-bathing,' by John Leech, *Punch*, 27 July 1850.

The only disappointed visitors were those who had expected to see a kind of water-horse such as might have served to draw a 'sea-captain's gig', and Macaulay, who wrote, 'I have seen the Hippo both asleep and awake, and I can assure you that, asleep or awake, he is the ugliest of the works of God.'

The Zoo could not have found a better advertisement—and for financial reasons it has never been averse to its exhibits receiving favourable publicity. Obaysch became a god—worshipped 'in a manner which one indignant divine compared with the Israelites and the golden calf'. The Press, who dubbed it 'H.R.H.' ('His Rolling Hulk'), could not leave it alone, and *Punch*, in particular, was constantly returning to it:

One of the great peculiarities of the Hippopotamus is its extreme sensibility, which is found very inconvenient to the Arab in attendance, who cannot go away from his young charge for half an hour, without its beginning to whine after him like a young baby just put out of the nurse's arms, and refusing to be dandled by a stranger. It is in vain that the ordinary *employés* at the gardens attempt the soothing system, and utter such endearments as 'Pretty little Hippy Pippy', or sing songs about 'Hush-aby Potty on the tree-top'; or warble an invitation to 'Ride a Sea-horse to Banbury Cross'; for, in spite of all these little attentions, that usually tell so well on the infant mind, the

Hippopotamus only replies with a melancholy whine for its Arab nurse, who is compelled to return and 'sit a bit' with the sentimental juvenile . . .

Hamet (alleged *Household Words* facetiously), feeling that he owed to Obaysch his spectacular emergence from total obscurity to undreamed-of fame, proposed to start a fund for the erection of a public monument to his benefactor, whom he now dubbed the 'Good' Hippopotamus:

> He had thought of a number of adjectives, as, the oily Hippopotamus, the bland Hippopotamus, the bathing Hippopotamus, the expensive Hippopotamus, the valiant Hippopotamus, the sleepy Hippopotamus, when, in a moment, as it were in the space of a flash of lightning, he found he had written down, without knowing why or wherefore, and without being able to account for it, those enduring words, the 'Good' Hippopotamus. . . .
>
> He never howled, like the Hyena; he never roared, like the Lion; he never screeched, like the Parrot; he never damaged the tops of high trees, like the Giraffe; he never put a trunk in people's way, like the Elephant; he never hugged anybody, like the Bear; he never projected a forked tongue, like the Serpent. He was an easy, basking, jolly, slow, inoffensive, eating and drinking Hippopotamus. Therefore he was supremely the 'Good' Hippopotamus. . . .

The fictitious subscription list was headed by the milkman and his family, who out of gratitude to so excellent a customer contributed the sum of twenty pounds.

There was, of course, a 'hippo craze' in London that season, though it did not involve excesses such as had accompanied the arrival of the first giraffe in Paris. There were no hair styles '*à la hippo*', and if there were 'hippo waists' they resulted from self-indulgence rather than from adoration. But models of Obaysch in silver were on sale in the Strand, a Guards' officer was observed sporting a hippo breast-pin, and a 'Hippopotamus Polka' was immensely popular in London drawing-rooms. In July the Queen drove to the Zoo with 'the girls' and others to see the new arrival:

> We were received by Mr Mitchell, the Sec^y & went straight to the house where the hippopotamus is kept. We had an excellent sight of this truly extraordinary animal. It is only 10 months old & its teeth are only just coming through. Its eyes are very intelligent. It was in the water, rolling about like a porpoise, occasionally disappearing entirely. The little Egyptian serpent charmer enticed it out by grunting to it, & holding out a piece of bread.
>
> We next went to the Giraffe House, to which the serpents were brought. The boy, who is 15 & was taught by his old Uncle, for years a snake charmer, did wonderful things with these snakes, pinching their tails & making them sit up & hiss, they absolutely obeying him. When he wishes them to be quiet, he opens their mouths, spits into them

THE HIPPOPOTAMUS POLKA.

'The Hippopotamus Polka'. Cover of composition for piano, *c.* 1850

'A "charming" day at the Zoological Gardens'. *The Ladies' Companion*, 1850.
These two Egyptian snake-charmers, uncle and nephew, accompanied Hamet to London to help
him look after Obaysch

& lays them down; there they remain, like dead, till he again takes them up. One, he put round his neck & it crawled into his dress, the regular Egyptian one. . . .

This was the first of five royal visits which included an inspection of the hippopotamus and a report on its progress.

The arrival at the Zoo, in April of the following year, of a female elephant and young calf provided a formidable counter-attraction to Obaysch, and a *Punch* cartoon showed 'The Nose of the Hippopotamus put out of joint' by the engaging new youngster. But a worse humiliation was to come with the advent of the great ant-eater, which provoked the same periodical to a poem entitled *A Howl from the Hippopotamus* (to be sung to the air of 'I'm a broken-hearted Gardener'). The first verse ran as follows:

I'm a hippish Hippopotamus and don't known what to do,
For the public is inconstant and a fickle one too.
It smiled once upon me, and now I'm quite forgot,
Neglected in my bath, and left to go to pot.
    And it's oh! oh! out of joint is my nose,
    It's a nasty Ant-eater to whom everyone goes.[1]

However, when a year later the Viceroy, only a few days before he died, provided for Obaysch a young female named 'Adhela' (or 'Dil' for short),[2] the fallen idol recovered some of his lost ground. He would no doubt have recovered yet more had he and Dil produced a calf; but seventeen years were to pass before a 'happy event' took place. Meanwhile there was to occur one of those mishaps to which all zoos are periodically liable: on a summer morning in 1860 Obaysch escaped from his cage.

Jennison was perfectly right in declaring that the hippopotamus, though timid by nature and relatively easy to keep in captivity, is not usually an amiable or a reliable animal when it reaches maturity,[3] and certainly not one to be welcomed running loose in the Gardens. It has a nasty temper, and when intentionally or accidentally provoked in the great African rivers where it lives it can easily snap a man or a canoe in half or capsize a stouter craft; yet probably more natives have been flogged to death by whips made from hippopotamus hide than were ever killed by the live animal—which is not, of course, carnivorous. As the

1. *Punch*, 22 October 1853. And see p. 126.
2. Nott (*op. cit.*) tells us that Dil was very sensitive to music; she certainly had the figure for an Isolde.
3. See Oliver Graham-Jones's account of sedating 'a pregnant, nervous and thoroughly truculent hippo' (*Zoo Doctor*, pp. 108 ff.).

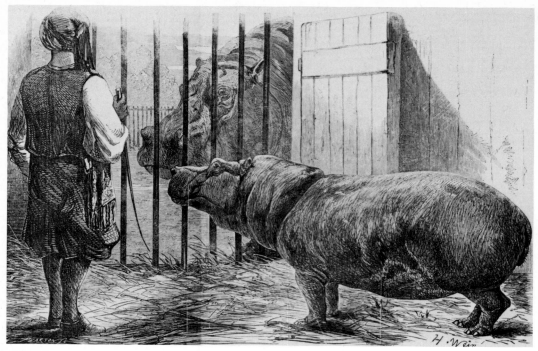

The Female Hippopotamus at Regent's Park. *Illustrated London News*, 12 August 1854

Encyclopaedia Britannica says, 'Old bulls which have become soured in solitude are at all times dangerous', and only a hero, or a man with a passion for publicity, would attempt to ride one. Firmes the Seleucian is said to have done so when in A.D. 273 he assumed the purple in Alexandria, and more recently Gerald Iles, of the Belle Vue Zoo at Manchester, made his television debut astride an adult beast considered to be absolutely reliable.

But it was no such rash enterprise that led to Obaysch temporarily regaining his freedom. On that morning of 1860, Hunt, now Obaysch's keeper,[1] had reported to Bartlett that his charge seemed restless and was attempting to dislodge the block of wood that had been put to prevent the sliding door of his cage from opening. Having ordered a carpenter to investigate the matter, Bartlett went to his office to attend to his morning's post. An hour later a terrified office boy burst into the room crying, 'Master, master, the hippopotamus is out!' Bartlett ran to the window, from where he saw Obaysch, apparently in a very nasty temper, 'moving slowly and with cautious steps, his eyes protruding from their sockets, his head raised and his back set up.'

There appears to have been no alarm bell for such a contingency, so the boy was despatched by a back way to alert the staff and to fetch Scott, the elephant keeper, who was Obaysch's *bête noire*. Bartlett knew that Obaysch would charge Scott the moment he saw him; his swiftly improvised plan was therefore for Scott to act as a decoy: to show himself

1. Perhaps Hamet and his snake-charming assistants had by now returned to Egypt.

and then to beat the animal to the open door of its cage where, once inside, he could make his escape up a flight of stairs that had been constructed for the use of any keeper who got into difficulties. A hippopotamus, for all its ungainly bulk, can run faster than a man, so that Scott was exposing himself to some danger; but he made his appearance at a spot from where he had a good start, and the ruse worked perfectly. Five minutes later Obaysch was back in his cage, and Scott safely out of it through the emergency exit.[1]

One very hot August night Hunt had an alarming adventure. Returning late from the pub to the hippopotamus house, where he slept, and remembering that the pool had just been cleaned and refilled with fresh water, he decided to have a bathe. He knew he had left his charge locked up in his den (which he should not have done); what he did not know was that, acting on a report from one of the nightwatchmen that Obaysch seemed to be suffering from the heat, Bartlett had ordered the door between the den and the pool to be opened. Hunt dived in, to find himself under the submerged Obaysch! It is hard to say which of the two was the more surprised; but Hunt was the quicker to recover from the shock, and so managed to make his escape.

Bartlett also describes how on one occasion he successfully extracted a tooth which Obaysch had fractured. Having had a stout oak fence erected between the animal's pond and the iron railings, he armed himself with a powerful pair of forceps more than two feet long:

> With these I grasped his fractured incisor, thinking that, with a firm and determined twist, I should gain possession of the fine piece of ivory.[2] This, however, was not so easily done, for the brute, astonished at my impudence, rushed back, tearing the instrument from my hands, and, looking as wild as a hippopotamus can look, charged at me just as I had recovered my forceps. I made another attempt, and this time held on long enough to cause the loose tooth to shift its position, but was again obliged to relinquish my hold. I had, however, no occasion to say, 'Open your mouth', for this he did to the fullest extent; therefore I had no difficulty in again seizing the coveted morsel, and this time drew it forth, with a good sharp pull and a twist, out from his monstrous jaws.
>
> One of the most remarkable circumstances appeared to me to be the enormous force of air when blown from the dilated nostrils of the great beast while enraged. It came against me with such a force as quite surprised me. . . .

The mating calls of a pair of hippos (though not their antics) remind one of two irate clubmen in postprandial altercation. These calls must have been audible at the Zoo some time in the summer of 1870, for on 21 February 1871, seventeen years after Obaysch had

1. In the summer of 1870 a hippopotamus at the Jardin des Plantes, conducted chained into the Seine because his pool had dried up, broke loose and scattered terrified bathers until his recapture near the Pont d'Austerlitz.
2. Formerly hippopotamus ivory, which is hard and keeps its whiteness, was used for the manufacture of false teeth.

THE BABY HIPPOPOTAMUS.

Art and Literature were largely represented at the post-mortem

But these were the real Mourners.

been given a mate, Dil astonished the world by producing a calf. (Surprisingly, the gestation period of the hippopotamus is only eight months, whereas that of the elephant and the rhinoceros is more than a year and a half.) The infant died after two days; but Obaysch had presumably now got the hang of things, for the following January a second calf was born.

The first calf had died from maternal neglect; when, therefore, the new infant failed to locate its mother's extremely obvious teats (vainly sucking at her ear, mouth and paws), Bartlett decided to remove it and rear it by hand. The hazardous undertaking of extracting it from the cage was accomplished by the use of a powerful hose to keep Dil at bay. It was difficult as well as dangerous, for the infant, which weighed about a hundred pounds, was slippery as an eel and struggled furiously in Bartlett's arms. 'Placed in a warm room on a soft bed of hay,' wrote Bartlett, 'and covered with a blanket, it seemed to revive. Two goats supplied it with plenty of warm milk, which it readily sucked from a large feeding bottle in sufficient quantity, which caused me to think that I should be able to save its life.' But in spite of every attention it died after four days. It had been named 'Umzivooboo'—a syllable for each day of its short life.

Before the year was out came a third calf—a sturdy little creature which was the first ever to be successfully reared by its mother[1] in captivity and which was to live to the ripe age of thirty-six. This time Bartlett did not interfere but let nature take her course; possibly, therefore, Dil rather than Bartlett should have been the recipient of the Society's silver medal. But Theo Johnson approved the award: 'For great is the virtue of letting things alone.[2] Is it not a matter of common knowledge that "pins have been the means of saving many lives, through people NOT swallowing them"?'

The calf had been born—in the water, as is always the case—on the morning of 5 November, and that same evening Buckland wrote in *Land and Water*:

> The little animal has discovered, and readily made use of, its mother's milk. The little thing generally lies sleeping by the side of its gigantic mamma, but sometimes it gets up and takes a tour of inspection round its den, when its family likeness can immediately be perceived. Every now and then the mother rolls her great eyes, listens attentively with her horse-like ears, and grunts loudly with a deep organ-like note; the young one instantly answers in the same note, but in an infantine key. Its colour appears to be that of a polished mahogany table, it is about 3 ft. 6 in. long and its weight about 100 lbs.

In spite of an anonymous letter to the Secretary of the Society begging that the young hippo should not be named 'Guy Fawkes'—'thereby reminding your visitors and the public generally of a sad event in history, which Protestants and Catholics alike should

1. One had been successfully hand-reared in the Amsterdam Zoo.
2. Cf. 'Admirals, extoll'd for standing still,
       Or doing nothing with a deal of skill'.
                    William Cowper, *Table Talk*

Guy Fawkes. Photograph by J. F. Nott in *Wild Animals Described*, 1886. That intrepid Victorian explorer, Mary Kingsley, said she could never decide whether the hippo was Nature's first and botched attempt at creation, or her last exhausted fling: 'Here just put these other viscera into big bags—I can't bother any more'

wish to be buried in oblivion'—this was in fact the name chosen. Whatever the religious objection, a more valid one became apparent when it was discovered that the calf was in fact a female; but the name was retained.

At the age of eight months the young lady, chaperoned by her mother, was introduced to her father:

Obaysch was peacefully eating his breakfast of fresh grass when the sliding door of the female's den was quietly raised, and the mother and young one peered out with a most comical expression. On seeing the female the old male left off eating, and loudly trumpeted. Guy Fawkes cautiously went up to her father, and their noses all but touched, when the mother, fearing danger to the younger one, immediately rushed forward and challenged her husband. Obaysch retreated a little distance, while she pretended to be feeding, at the same time keeping her eyes steadfastly fixed on him . . .

At last Dil made a rush at Obaysch. They raised themselves on their hinder legs and, clashing their teeth together, bit and struck at each other in a most savage manner, Guy Fawkes keeping at a most respectful distance behind or at the side of her mother. When Obaysch and his wife got on to their forefeet again the female, by a dexterous lunge with her head, pushed Obaysch into the pond, and after driving him up into a corner kept guard over him and held him a safe prisoner. While this state of things continued Guy Fawkes was safely perched on her mother's back looking impudently at her disgraced father.[1]

1. A. D. Bartlett, *Wild Animals in Captivity*.

There were one or two further skirmishes, but within a short time the three had settled down happily together.

Obaysch's death in 1878, recorded by the ever-faithful *Punch* in a poem, was attributed by Bartlett to old age. But Obaysch was only twenty-nine—no exceptional age for a hippopotamus, for Guy Fawkes lived longer, and Pete in New York reached his fiftieth year. Guy Fawkes grew to be even plumper then her mother; and just as the over-tall may be cheered by the sight of a giraffe, so may the obese take comfort from the thought that three or four tons of adiposity seem to present no obstacle to the leading of a long, healthy and active life.

In the rivers of Liberia, and formerly elsewhere in Western Africa, there is found a pygmy hippopotamus, no larger than a pig and weighing when full-grown only about as much as an all-in wrestler. It appears that the Dublin Zoo acquired one—I mean a pygmy hippo— as early as 1870, but it died within a few minutes of its arrival. Theo Johnson, writing in 1905, believed the species to be extinct 'or nearly so'; but another specimen reached London in 1913, and more recently Basel, Washington and Whipsnade are among zoos which have successfully bred and so preserved a seriously endangered species from extinction. This is perhaps the most important function of zoos all over the world.[1]

It would seem that the big hippopotamus, though no longer found in vast territories where it once roamed, is not now in any immediate danger of extinction. It was once, of course, and very understandably, much trapped and killed by natives for food, its flesh being considered by one African explorer 'a good substitute for beef' and that of a calf like 'poor veal'. But with the arrival in the nineteenth century of the big game hunters armed with powerful rifles and 'bullets made of platinum', the survival of the hippopotamus must for a while have seemed in doubt; for many of these 'sportsmen' killed for the mere joy of killing, and the bigger the bag the bigger the fun and the glory. Mr Gordon Cumming, said the writer of an article in *Chambers's Edinburgh Journal*, 'talks of "bagging" fifteen first-rate hippopotamuses as coolly as if they were so many snipes; he, however, destroys the interest of his tales by the cold-blooded and life-wasting tone which he throughout assumes.' It is pleasant to find such a comment at a time when these butchers, on their return to Europe, were fêted by society as heroes.[2]

---

1. For an interesting account of the pygmy hippopotamus, or *nigbwe*, see Wendt, *op. cit.*, pp. 423–7.
2. And see pp. 159–60.

❦ 11 ❦

'A Brazilian in Bloomsbury'

IF anyone still doubts that the Almighty has a sense of humour, or at all events a sense of the ridiculous, he has only to look at some of the more bizarre members of the animal kingdom: at the mandrill for example, the proboscis monkey, the pelican, the duck-billed platypus—and why omit man himself? From any such list it would be hard to exclude the great ant-eater, *Myrmecophaga jubata*.

Linnaeus placed the ant-eaters in an Order he christened Edentata, 'the toothless ones': an ill-chosen name since many of these animals—though not in fact the four species of ant-eater—have teeth of a kind. Their heyday was in the pleistocene age, when the mighty megatherium—a giant terrestrial sloth the size of an elephant—struck terror into the inhabitants of the swampy forests of tropical South America. What little survives of the Order today is a strange rag-bag of smaller mammals. In the New World, in addition to the ant-eaters, there are the armour-plated armadillos, and the tree-climbing sloths (which have six more ribs than the elephant and, according to Sydney Smith, pass their lives in suspense 'like a young clergyman distantly related to a bishop'); in the Old, the aardvarks (or 'earth-pigs') of South Africa, and the Asian and African pangolins—described by someone as 'animated spruce fir-cones furnished with head and legs'. The most remarkable of the extant Edentata is the great ant-eater.

When asleep or sheltering from a storm, the great ant-eater assumes the form of a nondescript hairy grey mound, having no apparent end or beginning. But rouse the animal and, like those magical Japanese paper flowers that as children we used so eagerly to immerse in water, it slowly unfolds into something wholly unexpected, wholly fascinating. Before, there emerges a long, tapering snout (Buffon compared it to the head of a pike), terminating in a mouth like the end of a hose-pipe from which an eighteen-inch-long, thread-like, sticky tongue can dart at lightning speed to capture its prey. So stupendous a nose must surely have a fine sense of smell? It has; but good zoologists conscientiously check the apparently obvious, and only after extensive tests made with camphor blanketed by eucalyptus (success in identification being rewarded with food) was it definitely established that an ant-eater can detect camphor in solutions forty times weaker than can man.

Before, then, the snout; behind, no less remarkable, a huge plumed tail, like a wave

Great Ant-eater. Joseph Wolf, *Zoological Sketches*, first series, 1861

drawn by Hokusai, expands in greatest glory. The shaggy legs show terrifying claws which, curling inwards and upwards, make it walk on its knuckles. Long wedge-like strips of black, stretching from the head along the sides of the neck and body, play such tricks with the overall appearance of the animal that there are times when a foreleg can easily be mistaken for the head; and when a young one rides its mother jockeyback—which it continues to do until it is at least half her size—confusion is worse confounded.

Waterton, in his *Wanderings in South America* (1825), describes the great ant-eater as 'the most inoffensive of all animals', never injuring man's property but ferocious, indeed invincible, if attacked:

He is chiefly found in the inmost recesses of the forest. . . . There he goes up and down in quest of ants, of which there is never the least scarcity, so that he soon obtains a sufficient supply of food with very little trouble. He cannot travel fast; man is superior to him in speed. Without swiftness to enable him to escape from his enemies; without teeth, the possession of which would assist him in self-defence; and without the power of burrowing in the ground, by which he might conceal himself from his pursuers, he is still capable of ranging through these wilds in perfect safety. Nor does he fear the fatal pressure of the serpent's fold, or the teeth of the famished jaguar. . . .

One September day of the year 1853, David Mitchell was walking through the more squalid parts of Bloomsbury when he observed in a window a notice inviting him to 'step inside and see the great ANTITA heat a hegg'; admission was sixpence, 'with the usual tenderness in the allowance of half-price to children'.[1]

The Secretary may of course have passed that way by chance, as Scherren implies; but it must seem more likely that news of the arrival of this wonder had reached the Society on its bush telegraph. If he did in fact tumble accidentally on this notice he must have been amazed indeed, for he believed that the great ant-eater had never before been seen alive in Europe. We now know, however, that in this he was mistaken, Buffon having been shown one in 1778 in the prince de Condé's menagerie at Chantilly-Vineuil, near Paris. At all events, when he paid his sixpence and entered, Mitchell must have expected to see either a very great rarity or a very great fraud. He was not to be disappointed: the animal before him was indeed a great ant-eater, and though rather emaciated it was indubitably alive.

The circumstances in which this ant-eater came to England were as follows. Some impoverished Germans, travelling for an unspecified reason along the Rio Negro in the interior of Brazil, succeeded in acquiring four young ant-eaters. Thinking that there might be good money to be made out of these extraordinary creatures, they decided to sail to Europe and display two of them in London, the other two in Paris. One of the four, however, died before reaching Rio, where it was badly stuffed by a local taxidermist, and two more did not survive the voyage; the Germans, therefore, found themselves in London with a single live specimen and a mounted one, with little cash, and with even less English. It was not without some difficulty that they eventually succeeded in renting a small shop for themselves and their improbable infant in 'that perverted and degenerate thoroughfare, Broad Street, Bloomsbury'; and it was here, a week after their arrival, that they were visited by the writer of the above-mentioned article in *Household Words*:

On opening the shop door we found ourselves, in proper showman fashion, shut from the sight of the inner mystery by a check curtain. Passing that we came into the shop, which was divided by a little wooden barrier into a small space for the spectators, and a small space for the proprietors of the animal himself, whose den was a deal box standing on its side, with a small lair of straw inside, and the stuffed Anteater on the top of it. On the straw was a rough grey hair mat, of a circular form, or a heap of hair, which presently unrolled itself into the form of a magnificent tail, from under which the long

1. 'A Brazilian in Bloomsbury', *Household Words*, 1853.

nose of the living Ant-bear[1] was aimed at us like a musket. Then the whole curiosity came out to eat an egg, which it heard cracked against the wall. . . .

Being now five months old, he[2] stands about as high as a Newfoundland dog. As there were no other visitors present, we had an opportunity of becoming pretty sociable with him and with his owners, and could feel his long nose and shaggy coat with the same hand that had been called upon to feel the small heads of the Aztecs. Here however was a fit object upon which to spend our wonder—not a deformed fellow-being, but a work of creation hitherto unseen among us, an example not of defect, but of perfection in the adaptation of means to an end—from mouth to tail an Anteater.

It is now healthy, but thin and languid, as most exotic animals become when they are brought among us. . . . The Ant-bear that crawled lazily out of its box under the shadow of St Giles's steeple, would at this time have been fishing and leaping with fierce vigour if left to the shelter of the forest of Brazil. At home, when rendered fierce by hunger, it will make a bound of ten feet to spring on the back of a horse, tear open the horse's shoulder with its huge claws, and then suck the blood of the wound. Here it comes, lean as it is, very lazily out of its box at the crackling of an egg-shell to follow its master about, licking the yolk out of an egg with its long tongue. It does that very cleverly. Like most of the tame Ant-bears in Brazil, this one in Bloomsbury, though not an infant, eats fifty in a day, with a little milk, and meat chopped finely, or in soup. . . .

We remained for some time with our young Brazilian, during which there arrived only one visitor. . . . He saw the Ant-bear eat an egg and scratch itself, then went away. It scratches and pulls its hair about with its hard fore-claws, precisely as it would if they were horny fingers, and turning its head round always when it does so to bring one bright eye to bear upon its work; its mouth is brought at the same time into the neighbourhood of its hind feet or of its tail. We heard two little sons of St Giles, asking outside whether that was where the show was and what was the charge of seeing it, but they demurred at threepence and retired. An object of attraction that in proper hands would draw half London was of no account in Bloomsbury.

When the young Brazilian had in a leisurely way refreshed himself with eggs and milk, properly scratched himself with each of his four legs, and made inspection of our trousers, he determined to lie down. Not, however, till he had made his bed. When he had arranged the straw to his satisfaction, he lay down on one side, and holding out an arm for his long head, took it to his breast and cuddled it as though it were a baby that he had [taken] to bed with him. Then he drew over his long tail in the fashion of a counterpane, and remained thereunder as quiet as death.

Mitchell, on seeing the ant-eater, had immediately decided that it must be shown at Regent's Park. He hesitated to pay heavily for an animal that might not live long; he there-

1. Strictly speaking, the ant-bear is a name for the aardvark.
2. The animal was later found to be a female.

Aardvark, or Cape Ant-eater, at Regent's Park. *Illustrated London News*, 3 July 1869

fore offered the Germans a handsome sum weekly—far more than they could have hoped to collect by casual display in a Bloomsbury back street—for the possession of the ant-eater for so long as it survived. But its owners, either pressed for ready money or doubtful also of the state of the animal's health, shrewdly insisted upon an outright purchase; Mitchell was therefore obliged to buy his pig-in-a-poke for two hundred pounds. In the first week of October it was placed on show in Regent's Park where it became a nine-days' wonder, *The Times* venturing so far as to describe it as 'by far the most important addition, in a scientific point of view, which has been made to the collection since its commencement'. Indeed, although it made little attempt to ingratiate itself with the public, it created such a stir that, as has already been told, it continued to draw the crowds away from the current idols—a female elephant and her young calf, and Obaysch the hippopotamus—until its death in the following July.

In 1866 a fine large adult male great ant-eater arrived at Southampton and was given its freedom in a large kitchen garden there. Bartlett visited it and found it 'amazingly strong, active, and somewhat dangerous, as he would suddenly strike with his front claws any one who ventured to approach him', uttering as he did so 'a loud, savage, and half choking, roaring bark'. Bartlett rashly entered the enclosure and was 'much astonished by the suddenness of his attack', which obliged him to 'beat a retreat in double quick time to save my clothes and, probably, my skin from being torn off'.[1] He learned that the animal throve on thin worm-like strips of raw beef with, occasionally, arrowroot, milk, and the yolks of eggs. It was eventually sent to the Hamburg Zoo, where it survived on this diet for a considerable time.

A year later the London Zoo received a young female great ant-eater in rather poor shape. It had previously been fed only on milk and eggs, but as soon as it was given meat it began to put on weight. 'Improbable as it may appear,' wrote Bartlett, 'I found this animal somewhat partial to ripe fruit, particularly soft pears and apples, which she would eat with apparent relish if mashed up into pulp; and I have no doubt that she would have inserted her long snout into a ripe melon and eaten out the contents.' Indeed, he believed that the 'woodpecker-like' tongue had misled earlier zoologists into thinking that it was designed solely for the capture of small insects. He himself was never to persuade an ant-eater to eat that most succulent of all insects, the meal-worm, though occasionally a common worm was found acceptable. Perhaps the Brazilian ant, which in its native land must form a substantial part of an ant-eater's diet, is more nutritious than any that it can be given in captivity.

The first recorded birth of a great ant-eater in captivity occurred in 1896 in the Stuttgart Zoological Garden, and at a meeting of the Z.S.L. on 17 January of the following year Sclater exhibited a photograph of the two-days-old infant. No birth has ever occurred at Regent's Park.

The aardvark or ant-bear, though sometimes referred to as the 'Cape ant-eater', belongs to a different family of the Edentata, of which it is the sole representative; unlike the true ant-eaters it has teeth. The first specimen of this hardly less strange nocturnal South African mammal to reach Europe was acquired by the Society in 1869, and though its arrival created a good deal of interest in scientific circles it made small impact on the public. For this it had no one but itself to blame, since it slept the long day through and displayed to visitors no more than its porcine posterior protruding from the burrow it had made in the sand.

The ant-bear is not excessively rare; but it is difficult and laborious to take alive, because to do this often involves days of digging during which it may easily be injured. Though smaller and less formidable than the great ant-eater, it is savage enough, often killing or maiming the dogs used in its capture. Moreover, even when taken unharmed it is liable to sulk and, refusing all food, starve itself to death. 'The head is long,' wrote Buckland, 'and reminds one of the kangaroo; the jaws are prolonged so as somewhat to resemble one of the bottles in which light wines are served at table.'

In May 1876, when the Prince of Wales went to Regent's Park to see the menagerie he had brought back from his Indian tour,[2] he and his party 'visited the Ant-eater's House,

1. This would appear to contradict Waterton's description of the great ant-eater as 'the most inoffensive of all animals' unless attacked.
2. See chapter 17.

Echidna, or Spiny Ant-eater. John Gould, *Mammals of Australia*, vol. 1, 1845

where they examined with much interest those curious animals the South American ant-eater, and the ant-bear, from the Cape of Good Hope'; there had, in fact, been an edentate—a pangolin—in the Prince's collection, but it had died during the voyage. Ant-eaters and ant-bears come and go at the Zoo, and at the moment of writing neither is to be seen there. However, by the time this book appears, it may well be that either or both will have been added once more to the collection.

*　　*　　*

At the Annual General Meeting of the Zoological Society of London in 1845 it was triumphantly announced that Regent's Park had just acquired 'an echidna, or porcupine ant-eater—the first specimen of that animal which has been exhibited alive in Europe, and one of the very greatest interest to naturalists.' The triumph was short-lived; it died after four days.

These extraordinary Australian and New Guinea marsupials, which are not in fact related to the true ant-eaters (the edentates), perplexed zoologists for much of the nine-teenth century. Together with their next of kin, the yet stranger web-footed, aquatic duck-billed platypus (*Ornithorhynchus*), they refused to fit into any accepted zoological pigeon-hole. First, the female of each, though she has no teats, oozes milk through slits in her abdomen which the infant licks—so she was a mammal; yet it was reported that she behaved in a most un-mammalian manner by *laying eggs*. Second, unlike all other mammals these animals were 'monotremes'—or, more plainly if more vulgarly, 'one-holers': that is to say, like birds and reptiles they have only a single, multi-purposed orifice ('cloaca') for the passage of excrement, urine, semen and offspring. Morus says, 'In this particular department nature has its own aesthetic laws, which are not like those of man',[1] though really our own confused sex-and-sewerage system is hardly more tasteful.

A naturalist named George Bennett, who spent several years in New South Wales in the early 1830s, made a special study of the platypus and cross-examined the Yas natives about it. Was it ovoviviparous, or was it viviparous?[2] Their answers were quaint and con-tradictory: Yes—'Egg tumble down'; No—'No egg tumble down; bye bye, pickaninny tumble down'. On his return to England he gave an interesting lecture on the platypus to the Z.S.L.,[3] but he was not prepared to offer a definite opinion as to its manner of birth.

Bennett was followed by Gould, who came back in 1840 from his four years in the southern hemisphere denying that the platypus was oviparous. 'On my return from Australia,' he wrote, 'the venerable Geoffroy St.-Hilaire put the following question to me, "Does the Ornithorhynchus lay eggs?" and when I answered in the negative, that fine old gentleman and eminent naturalist appeared somewhat disconcerted.' In fact, it was not until the autumn of 1884 that, independently and almost simultaneously, two zoologists both working in Queensland—the German Wilhelm Haacke and the Britisher W. H. Caldwell—established beyond all doubt that these two mammals really *were* oviparous. (One is reminded of other remarkable 'doubles' in different scientific fields: for example, the discovery in 1845 by Adams and Leverrier, independently and almost simultaneously, of the planet Neptune.) Haacke reported his findings to the Royal Society of Australia; Caldwell sent his to the British Association, then in session in Montreal, for the sake of economy compressing his information to produce what must surely be the most famous telegram in the history of zoology:

MONOTREMES OVIPAROUS, MEROBLAST OVUM
('One-holers are egg-laying; the egg has only a partial power of germination')

Yet a whole generation of careful observation was still necessary before an Australian

1. *Animals, Men and Myths* by 'Morus'.
2. *Ovoviviparous*, of animals in which the embryo develops within its mother's body, and may obtain nutriment from it, but is still separated from its mother by membranes of the fertilised egg. *Viviparous*, of an animal whose embryo develops within its mother, obtaining nourishment from maternal tissues, e.g. placenta.
3. 27 May 1834, published in the first volume of the *Transactions* of the Z.S.L.

zoologist, Harry Burrell, was able to solve most of the many problems that still remained. As had long been known, birds and mammals both emerged in the remote past from reptilian types, and it is now established that the monotremes are the sole survivors of a race which diverged from the mammals soon after the latter had parted company from the birds.

There are various echidnas, of which the Australian already mentioned—an unglamorous creature that looks very like a large hedgehog or sea-urchin—is the best known. Regent's Park has, of course, a fluctuating population, but as a rule some kind of echidna is to be seen there in the new Charles Clore Pavilion, where, for lack of charisma, it fails to elicit from visitors the attention it deserves. Births have occurred only twice in captivity—in Berlin (1908), where the offspring lived for three months, and at Basel (1955) where it survived only two days. Before giving birth the female develops a temporary pouch in which she deposits her freshly-laid eggs; and from these, a week or ten days later, emerge infants less than half an inch long. What induces the male also to develop a pouch at twenty-eight-day intervals still remains obscure; perhaps it may be seen as a kind of couvade.

Echidnas have long lives. 'Daydream' in the London Zoo survived there, in spite of her ghastly name, for more than thirty years, and another in Philadelphia for nearly fifty (from 1903 to 1953). In fact, with the exception of man the echidna may very well prove to be the terrestrial mammal with the longest life-span; however, to establish this it has yet to beat one old-age pensioner—a sixty-nine-year-old female Asiatic elephant—and one or two quinquagenarian African elephants, hippopotamuses, chimpanzees and horses. Time alone will show.

It was doubtless the platypus which inspired that crazy poet Thomas Beddoes to write the poem entitled *The Oviparous Tailor*, in which a 'wee, wee tailor', bewitched by a sorceress, suddenly finds himself irresistibly impelled to lay eggs. A few lines from it will suffice:

> Tho' he swallowed many a muck's pill
> Yet his mouth grew like a duck's bill,
> Crowed like a hen,—but maler,—
> Wee, wee tailor, . . .

> And all the doctors wondered
> When he layed about a hundred
> Gallinaceous eggs,—but staler,—
> Wee, wee tailor.

For a contemporary poem about the platypus we need look no further than to Ogden Nash:

> I like the duck-billed platypus
> Because it is anomalous.

Duck-billed Platypus. John Gould, *Mammals of Australia*, vol. 1, 1845

I like the way it raises its family,
Partly birdly, partly mammaly,
I like its independent attitude.
Let no-one call it a duck-billed platitude.[1]

It may seem slightly cheating, in a book ostensibly about the London Zoo, to give further space to an animal which has never reached Regent's Park, or indeed any other European zoo, alive. I must plead in extenuation that the platypus was at least discovered by an Englishman, Joseph Banks, and that several Englishmen closely associated with the Z.S.L.—

1. *The Private Dining-room*, Dent, 1953. Mark Twain also addressed a poem, *Invocation*, to the platypus (see *Zoos* by Emily Hahn, p. 165).

among them Richard Owen, Sir Everard Home, and George Shaw of the British Museum—did valuable work on the first carcases that came to London.

There have been occasions when artifacts have been mistaken for real animals, and there have been occasions when the skins or drawings of genuine animals have been summarily dismissed as too good to be true; as Wilde (I think it was) once said, 'Man will believe the impossible, but not the improbable.' It took a Linnaeus to expose the famous counterfeit stuffed hydra at Hamburg; and once at least an artifact has been mistaken for a live animal: when the first aeroplane landed near a village in the interior of New Guinea, half the villagers came out to feed the engine with bananas, while the remainder crawled under the creature's tail to determine its sex. We shall later see how Sir Harry Johnston's drawing of an okapi was derided by the Fellows of the Royal Society.[1] When, in 1798, the first platypus skin reached London, this improbable object—a sort of otter, it seemed, but with a bill like a duck's and a poisonous spur on the heels of the hind feet—was pronounced an ingenious fake. Then, several years later, some complete carcases arrived, and the mockers mocked no more. Shaw dubbed it *Platypus anatinus*, the 'duck-like flat-foot'; then a German renamed it (as Germans will) *Ornithorhynchus paradoxus*, the 'paradoxical duck-bill'. After bitter dispute a compromise was reached and the name *Ornithorhynchus anatinus*, the 'duck-like bird-bill', agreed. But you and I will (I hope) continue to call it the 'duck-billed platypus'.

The platypus, though of a retiring disposition, is by no means a rarity on the banks and in the sluggish waters of Australia's gently-flowing rivers; like the echidna, it has escaped the hostility of man through its good fortune in having neither fur that is commercially valuable, nor the slightest urge to kill lambs or destroy crops. But the difficulties involved in keeping one in captivity, even in its native land, are considerable. The chief trouble lies in feeding the brute; for the platypus is at once a *gourmand* and a *gourmet*, as voracious as it is choosy. Shortly before the First World War Harry Burrell managed to keep four or five in the Sydney Zoo in a specially designed 'platypusary' equipped with an extensive artificial burrow; but in the end he not unreasonably came to begrudge the six hours that had to be set aside daily for the collection of their supper. 'A platypus weighing three-and-a-half pounds,' says Grzimek,[2] 'can consume over a pound of earthworms a day, twenty to thirty crayfish, two hundred meal-worms, two small frogs, and two eggs'—appreciably more than half its own weight. For its size it must be one of the biggest eaters in the world.

Yet soon after the First War, at the suggestion of an American animal dealer named Ellis S. Joseph, Burrell agreed to attempt to export five live platypuses to the States. A platypus travels with more impedimenta than a film star and requires a thousand times more sustenance *en route*. It will not contemplate embarking on a long journey without its portable

1. See p. 242.
2. Admirable accounts of the monotremes will be found in the works of Grzimek and Wendt already mentioned.

platypusary and well-stocked larder. Even though four of the five did not survive the voyage, Burrell was down to his last earthworm when, forty-nine days later, his ship docked at San Francisco. However, after laying in fresh supplies he took the train to New York, where until its death seven weeks later the platypus held court at the Bronx Zoo for one hour each day for the benefit of those who had the curiosity to attend and the patience to wait their turn in the long queues. Since then, two further attempts at introduction have been made by the Bronx Zoo, one of which resulted in a couple of the animals surviving for more than ten years. But today, once again, there is—so far as I know—no live platypus outside Australia.

Shall we ever see a platypus at Regent's Park? It might be imagined that, thanks to the aeroplane, this was a real possibility. But the venture would still be hazardous, the expense enormous; and at present the export of platypuses from Australia is strictly forbidden. If we cannot visit Australia we shall have, for the foreseeable future, to be satisfied with watching them on television or seeing stuffed specimens in natural history museums.

The Zoo's first live Gorilla. *Illustrated London News*, 12 November 1887

12

Gorilla Warfare

Dialogue
MAN TO GIRAFFE:
You walking Eiffel Tower, tall fantastic shape
GIRAFFE TO MAN:
Go back to the gorilla, little trousered ape.

William Plomer, *Notes for Poems*

IT was not until the autumn of 1887 that Regent's Park acquired its first gorilla, a young male named 'Mumbo'—and a pitiful object it proved to be; but so rare outside Africa at that time was the great ape that zoos had to be thankful for anything they could get. Within a few weeks it was dead, and not for some years yet was any gorilla to be kept alive for more than a matter of months in captivity. No doubt the diet tried out on some of these vegetarians—the daily ration at one zoo consisted of two sausages and a pint of beer in the morning, followed later in the day by cheese sandwiches, boiled potatoes and mutton, and more beer—contributed substantially to the premature decease of several of them. Indeed, as late as 1910 it was stated in an article in the *Encyclopaedia Britannica* that 'fully adult gorillas have never been seen alive in captivity—and perhaps never will be, as the creature is ferocious and morose to a degree.'

The western lowland gorilla—to the zoologists, *Gorilla gorilla gorilla*—inhabits the steaming forests of tropical West Africa, particularly Gabon; the blacker-skinned eastern race, and their rarer, hairier, and more restricted mountain cousin, are only to be found in the north-easternmost part of equatorial Zaire, and just over the Ugandan border.

The word 'gorilla' first occurs in 'that curious fragment of antiquity' called *Periplus*—a supposed translation, from the Punic into Greek, of the travels of a Carthaginian navigator named Hanno, who probably lived around 500 B.C. On an island off the west coast of Africa he came upon a number of 'wild men—but much the greater part of them were women, with hairy bodies, whom the interpreters called gorillas'. It is remarkable that this very dubious 'sighting' (for Hanno's animals may have been baboons) should have provided the word that is now both popularly and scientifically attached to the largest primate.

More than two thousand years were to pass before the existence of the gorilla, this equatorial 'Loch Ness monster', was firmly established. In 1607 an English adventurer,

Andrew Battel, returned home after an absence of eighteen years spent mostly in tropical West Africa, first as a prisoner and later as an agent of the Portuguese. An account of his remarkable experiences was dictated to Purchas, who included it in his *Pilgrimes* (1613). When in the Congo Battel saw and described 'two kinds of Monsters, which are common in these Woods, and very dangerous': the pongo and the engeco. These were undoubtedly the gorilla and the chimpanzee respectively:

> This Pongo is in all proportion like a man, but that he is more like a Giant in stature, than a man; for he is very tall, and hath a mans face, hollow eyed, with long haire upon his browes. His face and eares are without haire, and his hands also. His bodie is full of haire, but not very thicke, and it is of a dunnish colour. He differeth not from a man, but in his legs, for they have no calfe. Hee goeth alwaies upon his legs, and carrieth his hands clasped on the nape of his necke, when he goeth upon the ground. They sleepe in the trees, and build shelters for the raine. They feed upon Fruit that they find in the Woods, and upon Nuts, for they eate no kind of flesh. They cannot speake, and have no understanding more than a beast.
>
> The People of the Countrie, when they travaile in the Woods, make fires where they sleepe in the night; and in the morning, when they are gone, the Pongoes will come and sit about the fire, till it goeth out: for they have no understanding to lay the wood together. They goe many together, and kill many Negroes that travaile in the Woods. Many times they fall upon the Elephants, which come to feed where they be, and so beate them with their clubbed fists, and pieces of wood, that they will run roaring away from them.
>
> Those Pongoes are never taken alive, because they are so strong, that ten men cannot hold one of them; but yet they take many of their young ones with poisoned Arrowes. The young Pongo hangeth on his mothers bellie, with his hands fast clasped about her: so that when the Countrie people kill any of the femals, they take the young one, which hangeth fast upon his mother. When they die among themselves, they cover the dead with great heapes of boughs and wood, which is commonly found in the Forrests.

The same story is repeated soon afterwards by another ship's captain whose name has not come down to us, after which for nearly two-and-a-half centuries the gorilla again vanishes from sight. Then in 1846 an American missionary in Gabon named Dr Thomas Savage became the chance possessor of a skull of the great ape, and the following year a sketch of this and two actual skulls reached London, where some months later Professor Owen read a paper to the Zoological Society on what he inappropriately proposed calling *Troglodytes savagei*.[1] A complete skeleton followed in 1851, and seven years later a complete

---

1. Inappropriately, because *Troglodytes* means 'cave-dweller', and the name had in any case been allotted to the Wren. (The long and tangled story of zoological nomenclature cannot be discussed here.) Owen had in fact been beaten to the post by Geoffroy Saint-Hilaire and the American anatomist Jeffries Wyman—hence the finally accepted name, *Gorilla gorilla*.

specimen, tubbed in alcohol, which was mounted by Bartlett.

Now comes the strangest part of the story. In 1855 Wombwell's famous menagerie had briefly displayed a young primate which was then believed to be an unusual kind of chimpanzee; but in 1861, in the light of fuller knowledge by that time available, Dr John Edward Gray, Keeper of the Zoological Department in the British Museum, established from its remains that it had in fact been a young female gorilla. Yet even this may not have been the first live specimen to be seen outside Africa, for Bartlett was of the opinion that priority must go to 'Jenny', an anthropoid ape which Charles Waterton had had in his possession as a young man. Waterton's description of his animal's protuberant abdomen, small ears, and prominent flat nose 'as if some officious midwife had pressed it down with her finger and thumb at the hour of Jenny's birth', certainly fits the gorilla better than the chimpanzee.

Next on the scene, and destined to be the centre of a storm almost as ferocious as that which raged over Darwin's *Origin of Species*, was Paul Du Chaillu (1831–1903), a young American of French origin whose father had traded in the French Congo on behalf of a Paris wine firm. As a boy Paul had been taught there by missionaries, and he had sufficiently impressed the Academy of Natural Sciences at Philadelphia for that body to agree to send him back, when only twenty, to explore the interior of Gabon. On his return to America four years later he had written a long and stirring travelogue, *Explorations and Adventures in Equatorial Africa, with Accounts of the Manners and Customs of the People, and of the Chace of the Gorilla, Crocodile, and other Animals*, which John Murray published in London in the spring of 1861. At the same time Du Chaillu arrived in England with a collection of skins and stuffed specimens, including more than twenty gorillas, which was exhibited at the Royal Geographical Society's rooms in Whitehall Place.

Du Chaillu also lectured before the Fellows of the Royal Geographical Society, but soon afterwards Gray launched a savage attack on the unfortunate young man in *The Times* and the *Athenaeum*. Du Chaillu's qualifications as a naturalist were, he claimed, 'of the lowest order'. Not a single one of his exhibited mammals suggested that he had traversed any new region. His narrative was incredible, his map worthless, his illustrations either lifted without acknowledgement from the works of others or hopelessly inaccurate. And so on, in great detail. Finally, had M. Du Chaillu entitled his book *The Adventures of the Gorilla Slayer*, Gray would have recognised it as the *oeuvre de vulgarisation* that it was, and ignored it.

Men of science are apt to look with suspicion on books that a layman can enjoy, but it must be admitted that much of the *Explorations* reads like something out of the *Boy's Own Annual*; indeed, R. M. Ballantyne was soon to help himself liberally from Du Chaillu when writing his schoolboys' best-seller, *The Gorilla Hunters*. Here is Du Chaillu shooting his first gorilla:

His eyes began to flash fiercer fire as we stood motionless on the defensive, and the crest of short hair which stands on his forehead began to twitch rapidly up and down,

'My first Gorilla'. P. Du Chaillu, *Explorations and Adventures in Equatorial Africa*, 1861

while his powerful fangs were shown as he again sent forth a thunderous roar. And now truly he reminded me of nothing but some hellish dream creature—a being of that hideous order, half-man half-beast, which we find pictured by old artists in some representations of the infernal regions. He advanced a few steps—advanced again, and finally stopped when at a distance of about six yards from us. And here, just as he began another of his roars, beating his breast in rage, we fired, and killed him.

With a groan which had something terribly human in it, and yet was full of brutishness, he fell forward on his face. The body shook convulsively for a few minutes, the limbs moved about in a struggling way, and then all was quiet. . . .

Gray certainly had grounds for suspicion. But writing may be purple yet basically factual, and in addition to this travelogue material there were plenty of scientific (or allegedly scientific) observations.

Du Chaillu immediately set about defending himself as best he could. Had Gray not been an officer of the British Museum, he said, he for his part would have treated this attack 'with silent contempt . . . I am not conscious of pretending to high qualifications as a traveller, naturalist, or artist, but I do maintain that my book contains a truthful narrative of what I have done and encountered.' Many of his animals were indeed new, he repeated, and he challenged Gray to produce evidence of earlier specimens in any European museums. He said that he had met Gray once only, and that the Doctor had then given it as his opinion that Dr Livingstone was 'a great humbug'; he was, therefore, 'consoled by being placed on a par with that illustrious explorer'.

Soon came another powerful attack, this time from Charles Waterton; it concluded, 'In a word, I condemn, unhesitatingly, the entire account which the American has given us of his encounters with gorillas; and I here call upon him to defend them. I am quite ready for him.' But Du Chaillu does not seem to have accepted the challenge, for a week later Waterton struck again: 'If the book is to go into a second edition,' he wrote, 'I would advise the compilers to sweep away with unsparing hand nearly all those parts of natural history which have already appeared in the first. They are a disgrace to zoology. Were I to hazard a conjecture, I would presume that by the descriptions and figures which Mr. Du Chaillu has given us of the Gorilla—he has never seen a live one.'

The Z.S.L. seems to have steered fairly clear of the great gorilla controversy; but Bartlett became involved, and he has an instructive story to tell of his conversation with Du Chaillu when he came to inspect one of the skins that the latter had brought him for mounting:

> I called M. Du Chaillu's attention to the face of the animal, which, I told him, was not in a perfect condition, having lost a great part of the epidermis [outer skin]. In reply he assured me that it was quite perfect, remarking at the same time, that the epidermis on the face was quite black, and that the face of the skin being black was a proof of its perfectness.
>
> I, however, then and there convinced him that the blackness of the face was due to its having been painted black. Finding that I had detected what had been done, he at once admitted that he did paint it at the time he exhibited it in New York.
>
> The question that arose in my mind upon making this discovery was, did M. Du Chaillu kill the Gorilla and skin and preserve it? If so, he must recollect that the epidermis came off. Supposing he did forget this, he must have been afterwards reminded of the fact when he had to paint the face to represent its natural condition. These facts (to which I had a witness) led me to doubt the truthfulness of M. Du Chaillu's statement, and it occurred to me that he was not aware of the state of the skin, and probably had not prepared it himself.[1]

But Du Chaillu was not without his champions in high places, among them being Professor Owen and the renowned explorer Richard Burton; and at a meeting of the Ethnological Society on 2 July 1861 the latter read a paper on Du Chaillu's explorations, during the course of which he declared his work to be 'as authentic as it was interesting'. The Secretary of the Society also quoted from letters from his brother-in-law in Gabon, who had met Du

1. *Wild Beasts at the Zoo.*

Chaillu on his return from the interior and seen his trophies.

Meanwhile it had not escaped the notice of the audience that in the hall was a man whose pent-up indignation could not much longer be contained. Suddenly

> Mr. Malone, a gentleman who had frequently made loud exclamations during the proceedings, rose in a very excited manner to make some objections to M. Du Chaillu's work. He said that, as a scientific man, he denied the correctness of the statement that a negro harp was made of fibres from the roots of trees, for it was impossible to obtain a musical note from such a substance . . .
>
> M. Du Chaillu rose evidently much excited. He said he should not, in the presence of ladies, make such an answer to the abusive remarks of the speaker as they deserved. There were many persons who dared to vilify an author who were afraid of pistols (cries of 'Order'). . . .
>
> At the close of the meeting, when many of the audience had withdrawn, but whilst the room was nearly half full, M. Du Chaillu stepped over the benches and chairs to where Mr. Malone was standing, and after touching him on the shoulder, held his fist in a menacing manner to his face, and, after asking him how he dare speak of him in the manner he had done, he spat in his face. Mr. Malone, in great astonishment, said he must call for protection from the chairman from such outrage, and was retiring for that purpose when M. Du Chaillu called out, 'Coward, coward!' There were several ladies and gentlemen close to them, but no one interfered, and M. Du Chaillu then left the room.[1]

To Du Chaillu's credit it should be mentioned that in a letter to *The Times* he expressed his 'deep and sincere apology' to the Society for his behaviour.

For months to come, the Press was full of what it now called 'The Great Gorilla Controversy'. The *Literary Gazette*, which attacked Du Chaillu, could not accept the many undeniable contradictions in his book, doubting even whether he had written it himself; the *Critic*, on the other hand, supported him throughout, considering that small discrepancies in his chronology served only to strengthen belief in his veracity. One of the many points of dispute was whether Du Chaillu had, as he claimed, shot his largest gorilla from *in front*. Owen, generally accepted as the greatest living comparative anatomist, after careful examination confirmed Du Chaillu's story, and Sir Philip Egerton, a distinguished scientist, agreed with his verdict; Gray, needless to say, was convinced that the gorilla had been shot from behind. And so, all through a long summer, the battle raged. On 25 September the *Daily Telegraph* took stock of the situation and pronounced itself bored with the whole affair:

> Two questions of stupendous importance are just now before the world. Is M. DU CHAILLU the modern MUNCHAUSEN? and is the gorilla allied or not allied to the

1. Press-cuttings albums; name of paper not given.

Gorilla. Joseph Wolf, 1872

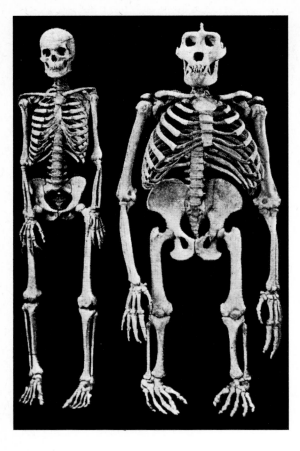

Skeletons of a Man and a Gorilla

human species? These are the problems which are now agitating certain classes of society and, unless they are speedily solved, the most disastrous consequences to the national peace will, it is to be feared, ensue. For it has now become pretty obvious that we cannot get on at all until our minds are made up upon these important points.

It was true, the writer continued, that there were one or two other topics that claimed attention. There was the 'melancholy conflict' in America (the American Civil War), the crisis in the Lancashire cotton mills and in the shipping industry; Rome was occupied, Venice still enslaved, Hungary in revolt; the Poles were restless, and in the East Christians and Moslems were once again preparing for mortal conflict. 'All these topics, however, to judge by the ardour of certain correspondents, are of secondary importance, if not of utter insignificance, compared with the two great questions upon which the fate of England evidently hangs . . . In sober earnestness, however, have we not heard enough about this subject in all its phases?' The article concluded:

Even if Mr DARWIN and his friends could persuade us that our distant ancestors were guinea pigs or caterpillars, people would not, we are inclined to think, found a new system of ethics on the discovery.[1] We should still be more interested in our present and our future than in our past. But human dignity and human feeling both revolt against the absurdities of the would-be scientific men. GOD made man in his own image, says the Book of Books; and though this is ancient testimony to the divinity of our origin, it has not yet been upset by modern conjecture or modern assumption.

Yet, bored though the *Daily Telegraph* might be, it could not resist devoting an enormous amount of space in October to Mr Spurgeon's lecture (with 'dissolving views') on Gorillas in his brand-new Metropolitan Tabernacle at Newington. Spurgeon was the most popular preacher in England, and with him on the platform were Du Chaillu, Layard of Nineveh fame, and the great Gorilla itself. Every seat in the building—and it held six thousand people—had been sold in advance, and the proceedings opened with the singing, by five hundred children of the Band of Hope, of 'some hymns in a very pleasing style':

> We do not entertain the slightest doubt [said the *Daily Telegraph*] that the myriad admirers of Mr SPURGEON are firmly persuaded that he can do anything and everything that is within the power of man to accomplish;—that in addition to being a preacher of funny sermons, he is a universal linguist, an accomplished musician, a brilliant artist, a profound mathematician, and a skilful engineer;—that he can square the circle, dance on the tight rope, balance cheese-plates on his chin, presage winds and tides, model flowers in wax, swallow red-hot pokers, decipher the Rosetta inscription, settle the National Debt, and 'play the fiddle like an angel'. . . .

And so on. The 'pseudo-Reverend C. H. Spurgeon', the writer continued, had in this instance only to procure Du Chaillu's book and thus acquire all the 'monkey lore' he needed for his purpose. The reason given by this 'egregious Gospeller' for lecturing on the Gorilla was his belief that 'the human animal needs amusement of some kind or other, and that if the right kind were not supplied he would certainly seek the wrong':

> We shall not follow Mr SPURGEON into his spasmodically humorous description of the married gorillas, and the bachelor gorillas who were 'cross and grumpy'. To say the truth, we are growing very sick of the gorilla, and would prefer, by way of change, a few lectures about the griffin, or the ibis, or the dragon, or the dodo, . . . although, bearing Mr SPURGEON's style of pulpit eloquence in mind, we cannot help thinking that he has been wasting very valuable materials. The gorilla should have been kept for a sermon. . . . If Mr SPURGEON lectures too often, he will soon exhaust his theology; and when he ceases to be funny in the pulpit he will, we are afraid, cease to be anything at all.

We have almost disposed of Du Chaillu—but not quite. The great gorilla controversy

1. Darwin's *On the Origin of Species* had appeared two years earlier, in 1859.

provoked Winwood Reade, a young nephew of the novelist Charles Reade, to raise money on his inheritance in order to enable him to go to Gabon to investigate Du Chaillu's claims on the spot. In the preface to his *Savage Africa* (1863) he gives his terms of reference:

> I make, of course, no pretensions to the title of Explorer. If I have any merit, it is that of having been the first young man about town to make a *bona fide* tour in Western Africa; to travel in that agreeable and salubrious country with no special object, and at his own expense; to *flâner* in the virgin forest; to flirt with pretty savages; and to smoke his cigar among cannibals.[1]

In saying that his journey had 'no special object' he is being somewhat ingenuous: it was a fact-finding expedition, and in *Savage Africa* he gave his considered opinion of Du Chaillu: 'He has unhappily been induced to sacrifice truth to effect, and the esteem of scientific men for a short-lived popularity . . . He has written much of the gorilla which is true, but which is not new; and a little which is new, but which is very far from being true . . .'

Though widely dismissed at first as a Münchhausen, Du Chaillu came in time to be accepted by most zoologists as a basically truthful reporter; and no one has ever disputed his discovery of several other West African animals, including the extremely interesting Giant Otter-shrew. 'Never were we more in the right,' wrote Sir Roderick Murchison to Owen in October 1864, 'than when we stood up for this fine little fellow.' But it could not be denied that Du Chaillu had embroidered fact with fantasy and even, on occasions, resorted to deliberate deception. It has never been established for certain whether he himself shot (as he claimed) the gorillas whose skins he brought back, or whether he merely bought them from natives. But Burton believed him, and on his return in 1862 from a visit to West Africa, he wrote to *The Times*: 'No one, save the jealous European, doubts his having shot the great anthropoid (mind, I modestly disbelieve in the danger), and surely it is something for this French sportsman to have succeeded where three Englishmen—Mr Levison, Mr Winwood Reade, and myself—have failed.'

In 1903, at the time of his death, Du Chaillu was everywhere described as the 'discoverer' of the gorilla. But this, as Theo Johnson pointed out in his *Personal Recollections of the Zoo*, was untrue: 'Du Chaillu did not discover the Gorilla: the Gorilla discovered *him*.'

The London Zoo's first gorilla did not come straight to Regent's Park but was passed on from Cross in Liverpool. In *Land and Water* (22 October 1887) Bartlett wrote:

> On arrival the poor beast appeared to be completely exhausted and almost lifeless— no doubt partly from exposure to the cold and the shaking and noise of the railway journey. In this condition no one could be expected to offer to purchase the animal;

---

1. This dandyish tone is misleading. Reade was in fact a daring explorer and formidably gifted, author of *The Martyrdom of Man* (1872)—a dazzling survey of the history of religions and societies culminating in a fearless statement of the atheist-humanist position. He died when only thirty-six.

in fact, the owner could not ask any one to take it, however low the price he might ask; all he asked was that it might be attended to, and that whatever could be done to save it should be done.

And everything possible was indeed done. Fed on fruit and bread it seemed for a while to grow stronger; but it spent much of its time dozing in its travelling-box (to which it had grown attached), and though making friends with Bartlett, it ignored a young macaque monkey put in its cage for company. Two months later it died, and its body was sold to the Royal College of Surgeons. It was probably about three years old.

In March 1896 came Jenny, a young female who broke the existing record for a captive gorilla by remaining alive for five months; but the following year the Breslau Zoo obtained a female, Pussi, who lived for seven more years. With a better understanding of the gorilla's needs there soon came a marked improvement, till finally, in December 1956, the first birth in captivity of a (lowland) gorilla took place at the little-known Zoo of Columbus, Ohio; so far none of the mountain race has followed suit. James Fisher[1] also mentions 'Bamboo', who died at Philadelphia in 1961 after more than thirty-three years in the Zoo there. The survival of neither the lowland nor the mountain race is as yet very seriously threatened; the former is still fairly abundant in the Cameroons, while there may perhaps be fifteen or twenty thousand of the latter in eastern Zaire and south-west Uganda.

Today, thanks to the devoted labours of one or two enthusiasts, we know a great deal about the life and habits of the gorilla in the wild. The pioneer in this field was George Schaller, whose two books, *The Mountain Gorilla* (1963) and *The Year of the Gorilla* (1964), achieved great and deserved popularity on their first appearance. Now Dian Fossey is doing for the gorilla what Jane Goodall did for the chimpanzee and the baboon: that is to say, establishing herself among them and entering into the life of the troop, chewing leaves alongside of them (though unable to bring herself to swallow them), and even finding herself allowed by some of the females to play with their infants. The picture that emerges from these recent studies is very different from that painted by Du Chaillu:

> The gorilla leads an unhurried, uncluttered existence. His family around him, the male wanders peacefully through the forest, building a nest to sleep in at night and feeding, resting and moving around all day. He does not attack his neighbours, and they normally do not attack him. He is confident in his giant strength that he will not be molested; he announces his presence, 'here am I, king of the jungle', by resoundingly beating his chest. Olden-day explorers would quake at the sound, and clutch their guns; the newer type of explorer walks unarmed into the gorilla's domain, and emerges unscathed to prove that a gun is not merely unnecessary, but actually an encumbrance.[2]

*   *   *

1. *Zoos of the World.*
2. Colin P. Groves, *Gorillas.*

It has taken a century for the true character of the gorilla to be better understood, and it may still be some time yet before the public accepts the new image. 'Give a dog a bad name . . .'; and King Kong[1] has not helped its cause.

Basel Zoo, which has always had the highest reputation, was the first European zoo to breed the gorilla (1959). When a pair of gorillas in the Sacramento Zoo (California) had failed to breed after nine years together, its director, believing that ignorance of the facts of life might be responsible, recently commissioned Basel to provide what has been described as a 'gorilla blue film' to arouse them. The results of this interesting experiment are not yet known.

But it is Cincinnati which is at present scoring the greatest successes in breeding gorillas. In the spring of 1974 King Tut and Penelope gave birth to their fourth child in four years, and there is a second breeding pair, Hatari and Mamari. So pleased, indeed, is Cincinnati with its record that it is spending two million dollars on building a tropical rain forest for its gorillas' greater happiness. Such luxuries are beyond the purse of Regent's Park; but at the time of writing the visitor can see a fine adult male, Guy, received as a youngster of two-and-a-half in 1947, and his mate Lomie, in the new Michael Sobell pavilions for apes and monkeys.[2]

1. The first Hollywood version appeared in 1933.
2. Since this paragraph was written, the following has appeared in *The Daily Telegraph* (8 October 1975):

A 320-lb gorilla, on extended loan to Mr John Aspinall, the zoo owner, from Chicago, has set a world record by fathering his fourth baby in six months. The gorilla, Kisoro, and his four wives, now have a family of fifteen—the largest gorilla collection in Britain.

13

Sixteen Porpoises and some Dolphins

'A young porpesse,[1] the whiche kynde of fysshe is nother praysed in the olde testament nor in physycke.'

Andrew Boorde, *Dyetary, c.* 1542

'It is an offence to the Gods to hunt dolphins . . . because the Gods hold the massacre of the monarchs of the deep to be as execrable as the murder of a human.'

Oppian, *Halieutica,* 2nd century A.D.

THE porpoise, like its close relative the dolphin (with which it is sometimes confused), is a pocket whale. Both are members of the Odontoceti or toothed whales, as opposed to those unlucky whalebone whales which were hunted with particular viciousness in the age of the crinoline. In the eighteen-sixties, Bartlett and Buckland made some sixteen valiant and historic but abortive attempts to introduce into Regent's Park this difficult mammal, which had rarely been seen in captivity. All but one of these animals were common porpoises, *Phocaena phocaena.*

The only three recorded cases of a porpoise apparently kept with some measure of success under restraint at an early date stem from France at the time of the Renaissance. The most interesting, and perhaps the most reliable, account is that of the animal in the splendid menagerie attached to the Hôtel Saint-Pol, a royal palace built in what is now almost the heart of Paris by Charles V ('the Wise') when Dauphin.[2] On 13 March 1417 his son Charles VI, in one of his moments of lucidity, sent from Normandy to his wife Isabeau at Saint-Pol a '*marsouin*'[3]—or porpoise. No doubt it travelled almost from door to door up the Seine and was thus spared an awkward overland journey; but it was still a remarkable achieve-

---

1. Innumerable spellings are recorded: porpess, porpus, porposs, porpass, porpas, porpese, porpaise, porpice, purpose, purpease, porcpisce. The last of these gives the clue to the derivation: porcus + piscis — 'hog-fish'. It is hardly necessary to point out that the porpoise is not a 'fysshe' but a mammal, the vestigial traces of its hind legs being concealed within its streamlined form.
2. Which of course is the French for 'dolphin'. The origin of this curious title is obscure, but it was probably once a proper name. Loisel, *op. cit.* i, pp. 171–6 gives an interesting account of Saint-Pol.
3. A corruption of the German '*Meerschwein*''—'sea-pig'.

Buckland reviving a Porpoise.
Buckland's *Curiosities of Natural
History*, third series, vol. 2, 1866

ment of which one would like to know more, and especially to be told how long this and the two other French porpoises survived in captivity. But here the chroniclers are silent.

About 1860 the Americans managed to keep a beluga, or white whale, alive for two years in the Aquarial Garden at Boston; and inspired by their success with this outsize dolphin— its length is some sixteen feet—Bartlett and Buckland resolved to attempt to get a live porpoise to Regent's Park.

The story of the Zoo's porpoises begins on the morning of 4 December, 1862, when Buckland received from Bartlett an urgent summons to the Gardens: there had just arrived from Brighton a live porpoise, much the worse for wear after a train journey followed by several undignified hours on a fishmonger's slab in Bond Street, and he needed help and advice.

A porpoise needs to be kept wet and cool, and when out of water supported to prevent its weight crushing its lungs; Buckland therefore found the animal, which had been put in a small tank of sea-water behind the aquarium, in a critical condition. It had been 'drowning in air' for half a day, and was breathing slowly and laboriously through its blow-hole. He recommended, and waded into the icy pool personally to administer, a 'good dose of sal volatile and water', which seemed to afford some relief. Two hours later he followed this up with a stiff brandy-and-water and, after staunching a wound in its tail, transferred the animal to the seals' pond to give it room to swim about.

Kate and Tom, the rightful owners of the pond, did not take kindly to their new lodger. 'It was most absurd,' wrote Buckland, 'to see them cut away in the greatest alarm to the further end of the pond, turn suddenly round, and stare up at the poor sick porpoise with their huge eyes distended to twice their size; and then down again they went in an instant under their house, shortly to reappear and have another long and frightened stare at the intruder.' An hour later the porpoise appeared to be better, for without any prompting it swam twice across the pond; it seemed, however, very blind and stupid, after each crossing hitting its nose against the edge of the pond. Next day it died.

Buckland carried out an autopsy. He found that the animal had been hit on the side of the head by its captors, who had also callously blinded it with a sharp instrument. 'I have since learned,' he wrote, 'that it is the custom of fishermen, in some parts of England, when they catch a shark or porpoise, or other enemy of their nets, to put the poor beast's eyes out, whether they bring him up to the market or not.' No Greek ever did this to a dolphin.

The experiment had failed; but it had at least established that it was possible to get a porpoise to the Zoo alive, and Buckland expressed the hope that 'should any gentleman residing at Dover, Folkestone, Brighton, Southampton, or any place within easy reach of London, be kindly willing to aid in procuring a live and uninjured specimen (I should say tie him by the tail in the sea when caught), Mr Bartlett, or myself, if telegraphed for, will be [only] too happy to run down and see if we cannot bring him up alive to London. . . .' This appeal brought a reply from a Mr Hyde Briscoe, a Southsea artist, who said that he had placed the following notice on the beach near Portsmouth:

NOTICE TO SICK PORPOISES
If visiting this beach
their carriage to London will be paid.
A DOCTOR will be in attendance, and MEDICINE,
in the shape of
No end of Grog, will be found.
Please land early.
Apply to

Regent's-park   FRANK T. BUCKLAND, 2nd L.G.

Three months later Brighton produced a second porpoise, but it had died by the time Buckland arrived there. Then in October 1863 another reached the Zoo from Lincolnshire, alive after nearly eight hours out of water through being kept all the time wrapped in a wet blanket, surrounded with wet grass, and periodically douched. It was placed in a pool with a recently acquired sturgeon, which demonstrated its jealousy by swimming about at the bottom and 'looking as savage as a fish can look'. But this porpoise too had been blinded and, like its predecessor, died almost immediately. *Punch*[1] recorded its demise in a long *Elegy on the Porpoise* by 'the Sturgeon' (alias Thackeray), which begins:

> Dead, is he? Yes, and wasn't I glad when they carried away his corpus?
> A great, black, oily, wallowing, wallopping, plunging, ponderous porpus.
> What call had Mr Buckland, while I don't deny his kindness,
> To take and shove into my basin a porpoise troubled with blindness?
> I think it was like his impudence, and praps a little beyond,
> To poke a blundering brute like that in a gentlefish's private pond. . . .

Then one morning, while Buckland was at breakfast, Bartlett burst into his room brandishing a telegram from Blackpool which read, 'How much will you give for a young, live spouting whale, uninjured?' An hour later the two men were on their way to Blackpool, eagerly discussing what kind of whale it might be and how large a vessel they might need to bring it by sea to London. That afternoon they found themselves confronted with—a thirty-inch moribund porpoise!

Of another porpoise, little seems to be recorded beyond the fact that it drank a pint of cow's milk from a baby's feeding-bottle and forthwith died. However, Bartlett and Buckland were not yet beaten, and in December the latter raced down to Folkestone to collect yet another which had been taken in a sprat-net. He found that the animal had grazed its chin, which was bleeding 'just like a man's chin bleeds when he has cut himself shaving'; but a pennyworth of styptic soon dealt with the trouble.

The journey to London in a guard's van with doors open was chilly, and Buckland was kept constantly busy sponging the blow-hole of the animal, which sneezed alarmingly whenever the train passed through a tunnel. In the cart which carried them from London Bridge Station to Regent's Park, Buckland, an inveterate pipe-smoker, accidentally dropped a vesuvian (an explosive match) on the porpoise's back, which 'made him jump up and roll around in his wooden cage like a "jack-in-the-box".'

'He is a-going, Sir; he is a-going!' cried the driver.

'No, he is *not* a-going,' said Buckland. 'You cut along with the cart and attend to the horse; leave the porpoise to me.'

To avoid the risk of another 'poetical jobation' in the Press, the new arrival was placed in the big reservoir. Its condition was declared 'very bad'; but next morning it seemed to rally, and both Bartlett and Buckland thought it should be fed. The problem was how to do this. Bartlett suggested a fresh herring tied by a string to a pole—without a hook, of course. The porpoise took the fish; but though it 'chumped and gnawed at it, it was too weak to swallow it and let it fall to the bottom'. They had no better success with scraps of herring and whiting, or with a little live carp—the scraps probably being rejected because a porpoise has to *learn* to eat dead fish, and the carp as being a freshwater fish. It was therefore

1. Reprinted in *The Times*.

decided that the porpoise must be 'helped':

> So I got down by a ladder into the reservoir [wrote Buckland] and, catching the porpoise by the fin as he passed, watched my opportunity and pushed a herring with my hand right down into his stomach; he scored my hand with his teeth, but I did not care about that. For a minute or two after I had given him the herring, he seemed better, but he very soon began to show that his supper did not agree with him, for he began to flutter his tail and dance in the water. After sundry efforts he made a spring, spat up the herring, and then—ungrateful wretch! after all the trouble and labour I had bestowed upon him—turned up his fins and died right off.[1]

Three further porpoises came from Deal, Liverpool and Aldeburgh, none of which lived for more than a few days. But at last, in December 1864, there arrived another from Deal which actually survived for just over a month. Though 'much bruised about the face and eyes, probably from attempts to escape during capture,' and though refusing for the first eleven days to feed, it finally decided to co-operate—and Bartlett and Buckland were jubilant. Its sex was unknown, and it was named 'Ceta'. Buckland wrote to *The Times* on 18 January:

> The beast apparently recognises the whistle (the signal for dinner) of the keeper; we are going to erect a proper dinner bell. It is highly interesting to see the quiet and velvet-like motion with which our new friend dives about in his pond, occasionally showing his snow-white sides as he turns to catch a fugitive and much frightened eel. It now seems pretty certain that the porpoise will do well in the gardens, and it is only after making many attempts and meeting with many failures that our knowledge of the mode of conveyance and treatment of these creatures has at last enabled us to place before the world the first living cetacean ever seen in captivity in London.

Buckland spoke too soon: before January was out, Ceta too was dead. As he said later, 'My porpoises always died as soon as I wrote them up in *The Times*.'

Records also tell of a porpoise which came from Dungeness in October 1865 but which lived for only four days, and there were probably four or five other attempts. However, before the decade drew to its close, Bartlett and Buckland must have been forced to admit that as yet there was not enough known about air-breathing marine animals to justify further experiments, and more than a century was to pass before the Society finally succeeded in establishing some bottle-nosed dolphins in its new Water Mammals Exhibit at Whipsnade (May 1972).[2]

*   *   *

1. A verse current at the time ran:

> Who stuffed me with his bits of fat?
>   And, standing where the eider duck land,
> Who tantalised me with a sprat?
>   Who cut me open, eh? Frank Buckland.

2. A beluga reached the Westminster Aquarium in 1877, and another in the following year. Both soon died. The Brighton Aquarium, founded in 1869, had more success with porpoises and a beluga.

Porpoises rarely enter the Mediterranean, which is apparently too salt for their liking; it is therefore the dolphin, rather than the porpoise, which plays so important and charming a role in Classical mythology. The Nereids sported with them. Greek sailors, who saw their appearance as a good omen and their disappearance as a storm warning, would release them from their drag-nets. Delphi bore their name, and it was dolphins that conducted spirits to the Islands of the Blessed. Aristotle alleges that they were 'passionately attached' to boys, taking pleasure (like Henry Scott Tuke) in watching them bathe; and the elder Pliny writes of a dolphin which daily transported a boy across the Bay of Naples to his school at Pozzuoli. Pliny also mentions a tame and affectionate dolphin at Hippo, on the Numidian coast, which became such a tourist attraction that the inhabitants, to regain their lost peace, had it secretly killed. Today such a potential money-spinner would of course immediately be commercialised; and indeed this is just what happened in 1955 with a bottle-nosed dolphin at Opononi, in New Zealand.

Aristotle has other pleasant stories of this marine charmer which invented the Habsburg jaw long before the first Habsburg came on the scene:

> After a dolphin had been caught and wounded off the Carian coast, a shoal of them entered the harbour and would not leave until the fisherman had freed his captive. . . . A shoal of youngsters is always escorted by an adult which protects it. On one occasion a shoal of large and small dolphins was sighted, and a little way off two more appeared, swimming in under a little dead dolphin and, out of compassion, supporting it on their backs to prevent it sinking and falling a prey to some predator. . . .[1]

Those who have heard a dolphin's odd assortment of grunts, creaks, barks, whistles and wails might reasonably maintain that—by human standards, at all events—dolphins are not musical; yet it was Arion's sweet playing on the cithera, just before he was thrown overboard by a thieving crew of Corinthian sailors, that moved a dolphin to carry the bard on his back to the nearest port. 'Arion on the dolphin' and 'Boy on a dolphin' are recurrent themes in Classical art.

Aristotle certainly appears to strain our credulity (and seemingly, too, his own) when he reports that the dolphin is said to be the swiftest and most athletic of all animals, marine and terrestrial, and able to 'leap over the masts of a big ship'; but of recent years the belief has been growing in many circles that some at least of these ancient fables may well be founded on fact.[2] What now follows is no more than the briefest sketch of a vast subject of inquiry which over the last thirty or forty years has opened up for us dazzling vistas; it may, however, perhaps serve to send the reader to the works of Dr John C. Lilly, Robert Stenuit, and those other researchers who are dedicating their lives to one of the most fascinating fields of modern zoology—the study of the behaviour and intelligence of the

---

1. But also perhaps, not realising that it was already dead, to allow it to breathe.
2. A dolphin has been recorded as jumping to a height of 35 feet out of deep water.

Dolphins: TOP White-beaked Dolphin   CENTRE Bottle-nosed Dolphin   BOTTOM Common Dolphin. A. Thorburn, *British Mammals*, vol. 2, 1920–21

dolphin and other toothed whales. It has, I freely admit, nothing whatever to do with the Zoo in the nineteenth century; but surely an author may be excused an occasional digression!

For centuries it was assumed that the anthropoid apes afforded the best hope of establishing communication between man and animal; now (so many delphinologists inform us) it has been shown that the brain of some cetaceans is at least as large and as complex as that of man, and far superior to that of any ape. Heini Hediger wrote in 1965:

It is possible that on the subject of the relationship of man and animal we are now facing the beginning of a breakthrough such as has never been known in the history of science. In any event G. Pilleri, a research worker on the brain in Bern, stated in 1962 that the degree of centralisation in the brain forms of certain toothed whales goes far beyond that of man; this throws doubt on the previously held view that the brain of *Homo sapiens* occupies the highest position in the scale of mammals.[1]

Indeed, Dr Lilly dared to prophesy (in 1962) that 'within the next decade or two the human species will establish communication with another species: non-human, alien, possibly extraterritorial, more probably marine; but definitely highly intelligent, perhaps even intellectual. An optimistic prediction, I admit. . . .' Optimistic indeed! Yet who, in 1960, really believed that a man would be placed on the moon before the decade drew to its close?

The first substantial step forward in the study of toothed whales was taken in 1938 with the opening of the great new tanks of Marineland, on the east coast of Florida, in which they could be kept successfully in captivity. After the War came Florida's Sea Zoo at South Daytona, and in 1954 the yet larger Marineland of the Pacific at Palos Verdes in California, which has a tank with a capacity of more than half a million (Imperial) gallons. In 1956 the first 'seaquarium' (dreadful word!) outside the United States was opened at Enoshima, in Japan, and was soon attracting nearly two-and-a-half million visitors annually. England's 'Marineland Morecambe' followed in 1964, and other 'oceanaria' are constantly springing up all over the world—even so far inland as Chicago (1961). Indeed, our Queen has only to step down from her Castle to see her loyal British dolphins at play in the Windsor Safari Park. Thanks to television and films (even fatuous ones like 'The Day of the Dolphin'), there can now be few people who have not seen and marvelled at the almost unbelievable performances of these amazing animals.

The dolphin, as preferring a higher water temperature (80°–85°F.) than the porpoise, was found a more acceptable 'guinea-pig' by those who foresaw the necessity of spending many hours fraternising with whales in their own element; and for a variety of reasons the bottle-nosed dolphin (*Tursiops truncatus*)[2] is the species most frequently chosen for practical experiment. But as research widened and pools grew in size, even an eighteen-foot pilot whale, Bimbo, could be made comfortable at Marineland of the Pacific; and that at Windsor is hardly smaller. Bartlett and Buckland's primitive methods of transport have of course long since been superseded by air transport in fibreglass tanks padded with polystyrene foam, and for the most part the dolphins reach their destinations in good condition. That at first a number of them died during experimental operations—for example, electrodes planted deep in the brain to localise motor zones—is highly regrettable; how much nicer than man is the dolphin, which, though capable of tearing or biting off an arm

1. *Man and Animal in the Zoo*, English translation by Gwynne Vevers and Winwood Reade.
2. Known to Americans as the common porpoise.

or a leg, has never been known deliberately to harm a human—not even one who had maltreated it!

It would seem that there are two main schools of delphinologists—what Stenuit, in his *Dolphin, Cousin to Man*, calls the 'Pros' and the 'Cons'; it goes without saying that all these zoologists, neurophysiologists, psychologists, linguists, and scientists of every kind are perpetually at one another's throats.

We may leave the Cons in their ivory-tower laboratories, high and safe and dry as they feed their slices of the nerve tissues of the Delphinidae into their microscopes, and turn to the Pros, who are chiefly to be found among the practical investigators. These believe that the dolphin and its relatives possess 'a complex language and also a complex social organisation', and that they can relate cause to effect:

> Dolphins [writes Stenuit] can isolate, interpret and analyse simultaneously several signals of varied frequencies; deduce from them geographical information and the respective positions of the other dolphins in the group, in order to work out appropriate hunting tactics; discuss plans with the other hunters and select the choicest fish, all the while avoiding nets. To do all this, and dolphins do it as the most natural thing in the world, takes a brain which surpasses the most complicated electronic computers, and which in this regard surpasses the human brain. It even surpasses our capacity to conceive it.

Armed with every kind of modern scientific apparatus—hydrophones, microphones, tape-recorders, electric oscillographs and acoustic spectrographs, computers, unscramblers, and spectrons (optic-acoustic-electronic machines)—these Pros, in America and elsewhere, work tirelessly and ceaselessly in close contact with the live dolphin. Margaret Howe, one of Lilly's young assistants, spent more than a week in a half-flooded room with Pamela, teaching her English (or perhaps American?) and table manners and never being parted from her day or night. Miles of tape-recordings have been made, but since the range of frequencies employed by the dolphin extends far beyond man's into the ultra-sonic, the results have to be played back at a reduced speed. Like the fond mother who understands, or claims to understand, the incoherent babblings of her beloved infant, so the Pros find, in this Donald-Duck chatter of the dolphin, sense and meaning where the Cons find nothing but gibberish and wishful thinking. Yet those who have heard the dolphins at the Brighton Aquarium 'sing' 'Happy birthday to you!' can, with the ears of faith and if duly forewarned, at all events recognise the rhythm of the greeting. André Gide once wrote, 'The less intelligent the white man, the more stupid he finds the black'; similarly the Pros would maintain, 'The less intelligent the man, the more stupid he finds the dolphin'.

As for the Cons, Dr Lawrence Kruger, Professor of Anatomy at the Institute for Brain Research of the University of California, though not yet prepared definitely to put the intelligence of the dolphin below that of the rabbit, considers that the spectacular performances of dolphin stars must be classed with those of performing dogs: 'excellent examples of the trainer's skill in reinforcing some variant in normal behaviour and building it into an act'. Mrs Ekaterina Chichkova, of the Hydro-Aquatic Laboratory of the Oceanographic Institute of the U.S.S.R., has, we are told, taught a Black Sea dolphin to say 'Mama' in Russian. Well—what of that? Thousands of parrots and budgerigars and mynahs can do far better without help from Mrs Chichkova. Was there not once, in pre-dialling days, a budgerigar that learned to ring up Harrods on the telephone? And who can doubt that a dolphin might be taught to dial a number?

How, we may ask, does all this experimentation appear to the dolphin, which—strangely enough—seems to like us, to welcome our companionship, and to be ready to offer us what Plutarch has called its 'disinterested friendship'? Does it, for example, *want* to learn English? Might it not prefer to meet us half way with half-remembered Greek or Latin or with what Stenuit terms 'inter-species Esperanto'? What is really needed might be a Ventris, or, as one delphinologist has suggested, 'a Rosetta stone' for dolphins. Or should we meet it the whole way by learning Dolphinese? More important still, does the dolphin yet realise the great dangers lying ahead in the possible unethical extension of its exploitation by man? What, in fact, are the demands we shall make of it and the advantages we may try to take of its good nature in the future?

Some of these demands may be harmless enough. The United States Navy is investigating the dolphin's sonar in the hopes of improving its own instruments. Psychiatrists believe that a study of Dolphinese might help them to 'penetrate the barriers of the esoteric language used by schizophrenics'. Medical men wonder whether they could learn for mankind's benefit from an examination of the ulcers and coronaries to which dolphins too are prone. Much useful knowledge might also be gained if we could discover why dolphins are largely immune from the 'bends', or how it is that they can move in water at a speed[1] described by Stenuit as 'three times faster than is mathematically possible'. In all these matters we might, if we proceed humanely, gain much from the dolphin without damaging or degrading it.

Some of the circus turns that dolphins have been trained to take part in are no more than faintly absurd:

At Sea World in San Diego, California, the dolphins perform a short morality play in partnership with four pretty mermaids. The first act is a graceful ballet about the innocence and beauty of Eden-under-Sea. The second act introduces a fisherman of vandalistic propensities; in the third act the dolphins tidy up his refuse—beer cans and dirty wrappings; in the fourth, shamed by their behaviour, the wicked tourist realises the error of his ways and is converted to love of, and respect for, nature.[2]

1. Up to about 30 knots, with only some 2 horse-power at their disposal.
2. Stenuit, *op. cit.*

Others, however, are degrading to all concerned:

The Follies' opening night [at the Whitehall Theatre, London] should see the climax of [Paul] Raymond's theatrical career, with what he calls 'the most imaginative and expensive act I have ever staged.' Specially trained dolphins will deprive Miss Nude International of her bikini. ('You put a piece of fish on the bra hooks.') The onstage swimming pool has cost him £45,000, the dolphins' offstage dressing-room pool £7,000, and the lift to move them about, £15,000.[1]

But there could be even worse in store for the dolphin. Certain American officers, Stenuit tells us, 'are now talking of training dolphins to kill hostile frogmen'. They could also, it is suggested, learn to place mines in foreign harbours or on shipping lanes. There might at first sight appear to be nothing very novel in this: in World War Two, the Russians taught dogs loaded with explosives to run under enemy tanks, where they and their burdens were blown up by remote control. Attempts, too, were then made to parachute behind the enemy lines bats carrying phosphorus, but they escaped from their keepers and burned down their own barracks. The dolphin, however, would act *knowingly*; and if it is really more intelligent than man, then surely it would never allow itself to be made a party to mass murder?

Meanwhile, as this decade rolls on, I watch with growing interest Dr Lilly's neck. Has he stretched it out too far? Well, he may in a sense be said to have dodged the axe that seemed about to fall, for in 1967—in his second book, *The Mind of the Dolphin*—he wisely added to his original prophecy a brilliant codicil which would appear to cover every contingency: 'I would suspect,' he wrote, 'this estimate will be either too long or too short.' However, the time may yet come when dolphins give interviews to the Press, dictate their autobiographies, or at all events add valuably to our knowledge of marine and submarine matters. By their choice, many millions of years ago, of water as their environment they have—and it would seem for ever—ruled out the possibility of their living, like the dog, permanently with us in our homes, of walking abroad at our heels, of frightening away our burglars, or of learning (though no doubt with some reluctance) to bite our postmen. Do they perhaps here show their greater wisdom? The dog has become the slave of man; the dolphin is his friend, and might resent servitude.

However, there is certainly a porpoise very close behind us, and sooner than we think he may be treading on our tails.

1. From an article entitled 'Erotic Dolphins help Raymond grow richer', by Anthony Holden, in the *Sunday Times*, 24 February 1974. Something seems to have gone wrong, because, according to the *Financial Times* (26 March 1974), on the night there were no dolphins: 'they seem to have swum off somewhere else'.

❧ 14 ❧

'Nature's Great Master-peece, an Elephant'[1]

The human race has, with the exception of Mr Bernard Shaw, no rival among its vegetarian teetotallers to compare for wisdom and longevity with elephants. . . .

The Times, 31 May 1949

FOR those who admire lions and tigers, yet are reluctantly forced to admit that these magnificent carnivores are not really suitable pets in most homes, the Almighty, with man's assistance, has produced a perfect substitute: the domestic cat. This handsome, lap-sized animal is affectionate (though not servile), clean, healthy, relatively odourless, easy to acquire, cheap to feed, little trouble about the house, and to be had in colours and hair-styles to suit all tastes. It is much to be regretted that few if any of our other big mammals are available in miniature, domesticated versions. A house-trained, eighteen-inch-tall giraffe? A pocket bear or pandalet? A pygmy hippo that was truly pygmy? What charming pets they would make! But as things are, all that most of us can (or should) have is a cat, a dog or a budgerigar; only the skilled, or the foolish, attempt to keep such animals as monkeys in the sitting-room.

Our greatest desideratum, however, is surely a tiny household elephant, for the elephant holds a very special place in our affections: it is, to the best of my knowledge, in one respect unique. Whereas the names of innumerable genera and species of animals have passed, adjectivally or otherwise, into our language, the only *particular* animal to have achieved this distinction is an elephant: Regent's Park's immortal Jumbo.[2] Now we have everything from 'jumbo' jets which dwarf the largest elephant, to those 'jumbo-sized' lily bulbs which on arrival prove to be a great deal smaller than we expected.

The elephant in captivity is a subject for a book (and indeed there are several), not for a brief chapter or two; on elephant-*hunting* there are a hundred books already—and most

1. John Donne, *The Progress of the Soul*.
2. The story of Jumbo is told in chapter 16.

of them make repetitive and repulsive reading.[1] No doubt it is very necessary at times to reduce numbers or to shoot a 'rogue' which has become destructive or dangerous; but one could wish that the killing of so magnificent an animal did not seem to afford such pleasure to the killer. No hunter has ever been heard to murmur, 'This hurts me more than it hurts you'; if only it did, and (as Saki wrote) that more often the animal won! 'It is a pity,' lamented Richard Meinertzhagen, 'that an intelligent creature like the elephant should be shot in order that creatures not much more intelligent may play billiards with balls made from its teeth.'

Nearly fifty years ago William Plomer wrote some memorable lines[2] on an erstwhile big-game-hunter showing off to fellow passengers on a liner bound for the Cape:

> A big-game-hunter opens fire once more,
> Raconteur, roué, sportsman, millionaire and bore:
> 'A Brownie in this hand, a Browning in the other,
> Some gruff gorillas took me for their brother,
> And introduced me to the family kraal,
> Where I took snapshots and then shot them all.
> Here is a photograph I took in Tanganyika,
> Here, marked with X, you may observe the speaker,
> That is one morning's bag not far from Ruwenzori,
> Ten lions and a ladybird, quite rare—the story
> Is told in all my books—I'm such a lad—
> An author too—you make me feel quite coy—
> As fond of good clean sport as any boy.
> Here are some titles which can usually be had—
> "WITH CAMEL AND CHAMELEON IN
>   OUBANGI-TCHARI-CHAD",
> "A DASH ACROSS THE DESERT ON A
>   MOTOR-SCOOTER",
> "AMONG THE APES AND PEACOCKS MYSELF
>   WITH A PEA-SHOOTER",'
> His blood boils up again, remembering how
> He's safer on a sofa than on far safari now.

But this beastliness is not merely a thing of the past, as those who saw Hugh Burnett's

---

1. See, for example, R. G. Gordon-Cumming's *Five Years of a Hunter's Life in the Far Interior of South Africa*, 1850—a book which (says the D.N.B.) 'made him the lion of the [London] season'. A pity the lion-hunters who pursued him carried no guns! In the popular edition of 1904 the text has been 'edited' to make him appear less callous and bloodthirsty than he actually was. With what Sclater and Thomas in their *Book of Antelopes* call 'characteristic audacity', Gordon-Cumming named an East African bushbuck after himself.
2. 'A Passage to Africa', *Notes for Poems* by William Plomer, Hogarth Press, 1927.

BBC documentary *The Killing Game* (18 March 1969) will know—and can hardly have forgotten. It followed the fortunes of an American on £60-a-day safari in Kenya, said not a word in condemnation of its subject (wrote John Holmstrom when reviewing it in the *New Statesman*), 'and didn't need to:

> The sickening poverty of imagination of men whose idea of bliss is to kill anything— let alone wild creatures of a beauty and power that shame the killer—can seldom have been displayed with such cold contempt. One blenched at the endless inventory of delicatessen and home comforts that travelled with the pampered hunter, the manic giggling that rewarded his hilarious tag-line 'well—let's go out and shoot sompn else', the crowing over the felled elephant which, even after repeated *coups de grâce*, continued to groan and rattle.
>
>   Our brave little marksman (who had never been within sniff of danger), asked how he felt after bagging his first elephant, sighed happily: 'I'm just fulfilled. It's the most gratifying experience of my whole life . . .'

Incidentally, it is sad to recall that less than twenty-five years ago seven hundred black bears were slaughtered in British Columbia in order to provide bearskins for the Brigade of Guards.[1]

*   *   *

Taking now a swift and bird's-eye view of the past, we remember Hannibal's fifty (presumably African) elephants, only one of which survived the rigours of the Alpine crossing to reach the plains of Italy alive. Elephants, in spite of their intelligence in other ways, were never very reliable battle-animals, having a regrettable lack of ability to differentiate between friend and foe—a defect which sometimes led them to score an 'own goal'; and Semiramis's dummy elephants, propelled by camel power, were not a success. We think of Thutmose III, who brought the first elephant to Egypt; of Alexander the Great, and of the bloody combats in Roman arenas; of the Indian (or, more accurately, Asiatic) elephants of Kubilai Khan, Tamerlane, Babur and Akbar. These were elephants in the plural;[2] but a handful of historical animals deserve individual mention.

It was in the year 797 that Charlemagne received, at his special request, an elephant named Aboul-Abbas from Harun al-Rashid of Arabian Nights fame. Shipped to Pisa, it joined its new master in Lombardy and dutifully followed him around, as did Mary's little lamb its mistress, until its death in Germany thirteen years later. Then in 1254, as has already been told, the first elephant reached England. Another famous beast was Hanno, presented in 1514 by King Manoel I of Portugal to the newly-elected Medici Pope, Leo X,

---

1. *Purnell's Encyclopedia of Animal Life*, p. 221.
2. Though we do in fact know the names of sixty-six of Akbar's elephants, e.g.: Earth-shaker, Heart-ravisher, Always Drunk, Enemy-treader, Valiant with the Cut Ear, and Victor Victorious. Sillar and Meyler (see Bibliography) give the full list.

Humming Birds (Docimastes).
Hand-coloured lithograph from John Gould's
Monograph of the Trochilidae, 1849–1887

Impeyan Pheasant.
Hand-coloured lithograph from John Gould's *Birds of Asia*, 1850–83

for his fine menagerie in the Vatican gardens. At an audience, and in obedience to a barely visible sign from its mahout, the pious animal knelt three times at the feet of the Pontiff; then, observing a holy-water stoup conveniently to hand, it plunged its trunk into it and deliberately sprayed all within range—not even excepting Leo, who took this *lèse-majesté* in good part. But Hanno is best remembered for having been drawn by Raphael.

There is record of the chivalry of an elephant which reached Vienna in the middle of the sixteenth century. So great was the crowd that collected to see it pass through the streets that a little girl of five was thrown to the ground just in front of the oncoming animal. 'But the elephant, without taking another step, made a wide sweep with its trunk to give itself room, then gently lifted the child and, with the air of a gentleman, handed her to her weeping mother, Frau Marie Gniger.'

The gift of an elephant, though always generous, could be untimely or even unwelcome, 'Interfauna' being always a less satisfactory service than 'Interflora'. One sent to Henri IV of France by sea from India arrived at Dieppe just when the King was busy besieging Noyon, and a year later, on learning what it cost to feed, he had it forwarded to 'madame ma bonne seur' Queen Elizabeth of England. Incidentally, we know the daily rations of an elephant sent to Louis XIV by the King of Portugal in 1668: eighty pounds of bread, twelve pints of wine and two bucketfuls of gruel—in addition to the tit-bits fed to it by the court.

In spite of such an improbable diet, this witty, intelligent, and in the main amiable French elephant survived at Versailles for thirteen years. It loved children, learned how to untie a knotted cord, and when given a small sheaf of corn used it as a fly-whisk. One night, without waking the keeper who slept beside it, it broke out, and after calling on its neighbours proceeded to explore the remotest corners of the park before it was recaptured. Very sensibly it objected to being teased, twice nastily wounding courtiers who tormented it. Less severe was the revenge it took on an artist who resorted to deception to get it to pose as he wished—with mouth wide open and trunk held high. To effect this, he had got his servant to keep it fed with fruit; but often the man only pretended to throw something, so that the elephant found itself performing without reward. However, it bided its time, and when the picture was finished soused both the artist (*not*, it should be noted, the servant) and the canvas with water. Perrault[1] adds the information that only on dissection was this supposedly male animal found to be a female; but the sex of an elephant is far from obvious.

Hannibal had managed to get one elephant alive across the Alps; more than two thousand years were to pass before this achievement was repeated, though under very different conditions. In the 1930s an American journalist, Richard Halliburton,[2] succeeded, after a number of false starts, in travelling from Paris to Turin over the Great St Bernard on his whimsically-named elephant, Elysabethe Dalrymple—or 'Dally' for short. Dally came from the Jardin d'Acclimatation in the Bois de Boulogne; but at the Porte Maillot the

---

1. Perrault, C., *Mémoires pour servir à l' Histoire Naturelle des Animaux*, Paris, 1733–4.
2. *Seven League Boots*, Bles, 1936. Photographs in the book confirm a seemingly improbable story.

Echelle de · 5 · 10 · 15. Toises

Profil de l'Edifice sur la longueur.

'L'Eléphant triomphal. Grand Kiosque à la gloire du Roi'
by C. F. Ribart, *Architecture Singulière*, 1758. Not surprisingly, this pavilion, intended for the
Avenue des Champs-Elysées in Paris, was never erected

unfamiliar and aggressive hooting of a Parisian taxi-driver caused her to bolt up the Avenue de la Grande Armée, thus bringing the first attempt to an inglorious conclusion a little short of the Arc de Triomphe. A year later, however, Dally having meanwhile been conditioned to traffic, Halliburton set out again and this time reached Turin—though not, as he had hoped, Rome. His ambition reasonably satisfied, admittedly in circumstances easier than Hannibal's, Hally (if we may so call him for short) returned Dally to the Bois, leaving her in possession of an outsize harmonica as a reward for her loyalty and cooperation.

*   *   *

Regent's Park had an Indian elephant from the first, and a picture in the *Mirror* of 6 September 1828 shows him 'in his bath'. Then in 1831 came Jack, purchased that year from a Captain Smith for £420 and said to have been twenty-four years old at the time. He was a tremendous tusker who achieved immortality through receiving mention in the lighter pages of Thackeray, Dickens and Charles Lamb, and notoriety by killing in 1849 the Indian rhinoceros which had been at Regent's Park for more than fifteen years. Broderip wrote that the rhino

> was constantly forced upon his belly by a pugnacious elephant, who pressed his tusks upon the back of his neighbour when he came near the palings which separated their enclosures. This rough treatment appears to have led to his death, as Professor Owen found, on dissecting the massive brute, which weighed upwards of two tons, that the seventh rib had been fractured at the bend near the vertebral end, and had wounded the left lung.[1]

Jack was thoroughly spoilt. He had his own special supplementary catering arrangements, a woman being given permission to sell cakes and buns for him alone and thereby disposing daily of goods worth up to thirty-six shillings. Soon after his arrival, a visitor wrote to the Assistant Secretary suggesting that his keeper should be dressed 'in something of an Asiatic costume', cheap to make and quick to slip on and off. 'The elephant thus attended . . . will fancy himself at home, and visitors suppose themselves transported into Asia.' But this idea was not adopted; nor did the London Zoo ever indulge, for its more exotic species, in houses imitating mosques or Hindu temples, as was sometimes attempted on the Continent. (This practice irritated Orientals, who very reasonably asked how *we* would like to find British animals housed in the East in gothic churches.)

Jack, 'this monster attraction' of the Zoo, 'expired on Sunday morning, June 6th, 1847,

---

1. According to Joshua Sylvester (1563–1618), an elephant usually loses when pitted against a rhinoceros:

> But, his huge strength, or subtile Wit, cannot
> Defend him from the sly *Rhinocerot*.

Death of Jack by George Landseer, *Illustrated London News*, 19 June 1847

at his residence, in Regent's park', said the *Illustrated London News*, which also graphically described his last hours:

Shortly before his death, the symptoms of his malady (which began with an affection of the left knee) became more distressing, and it was thought desirable that visitors should be no longer admitted to see him; he survived his seclusion but two days. On Sunday morning, (the 6th instant), at four o'clock, he was in his usual posture, leaning upon the partition in front of his apartment; at five o'clock, he had sunk back to the ground, and lay with his hind legs stretched forwards, his fore-legs extended in front, his trunk resting on the left fore-leg. Thus he remained, perfectly quiet, until seven, when his trunk relaxed, and sank to the ground, and his eyes closed; he was dead! There was no movement—no shudder—not a sigh! his head did not fall—he lay upright, in nothing death-like but the perfect stillness and repose. The doors were all closed; and the morning sun, which could struggle but dimly through a high window, rested gloomily on the dark, mighty form, which had lost none of its dignity in death.

Bartlett was invited to skin the animal and prepare his skeleton; but while he was doing this the tackle broke and the great breast fell and almost crushed him. Owen, who assisted in the removal of the brain, also had a narrow escape: as a result of lacerating his hands against the ragged edges of the skull bones he developed septicaemia, which in those pre-penicillin days nearly proved fatal.

In April 1851 the Zoo acquired for £800 a female Indian elephant and a very young calf. The dam, Katimeh, which had been bought by a dealer in August of the previous year at a fair in Cawnpore, had given birth on the journey down to Calcutta to a healthy little calf. After mother and child had rested for three weeks they continued on their way to the coast, the calf being fed with zebu's milk since the fatigue of the march had diminished the mother's supply. The infant caused quite a stir in the villages through which they passed, elephants seldom breeding in the state of semi-domestication in which they are kept in India.

From Calcutta Katimeh (now regrettably renamed Betsey) and her infant (oddly named

Butcher, and later found to be a female) were shipped for England, together with another adult female destined for Jamrach. During the five-months' voyage Betsey's jealousy was aroused by the excessive affection shown by little Butcher for Jamrach's elephant. In mid-ocean there was a pitched battle—a fight to the death which ended only when Betsey succeeded in pushing her rival overboard.

At Regent's Park Obaysch, the recently acquired hippopotamus, was reigning favourite; but Butcher soon became a serious rival, for so young an elephant had never before been seen in England. She sucked daily until 1854, when Betsey, her services being no longer

An Indian Elephant carrying Children. *Illustrated London News*, 20 October 1866

Young Jumbo.
Illustrated London News,
15 July 1865

required, was sold to the Brussels Zoo. Butcher lived on at Regent's Park until 1875, by which time she was just eight feet high at the withers. Partial paralysis left her for the last four years of her life unable to extend her trunk, and for the last two she suffered in addition from some kind of rheumatoid arthritis which made kneeling very painful; but she battled on gamely, and within thirty-six hours of the end was still carrying her daily quota of children round the Gardens. A post-mortem showed the cause of death to have been tuberculosis.

In July 1855 a female elephant who had been at the Zoo for twenty years, and who had 'upon many occasions manifested great fear in storms of thunder and lighting', was subjected to a thunderstorm of exceptional severity. All attempts to soothe her were unavailing; 'excessive looseness' set in, and a fortnight later she died.

Jumbo,[1] that king among elephants, came to the London Zoo on 26 June 1865. People said at the time that he was the first African elephant to set foot in England, but it is probable that one or two others had preceded him without their identity being recognised.

He had been captured by a party of Matabele hunters who had succeeded in separating him from the herd. They brought him to the Cape, where Carl Hagenbeck acquired him and sold him to the Paris Zoo before London had had a chance to make a bid. However, the French were at that moment eager to possess an Indian rhinoceros, which London could provide; an exchange was therefore effected, and although Jumbo was 'in a filthy and miserable condition' it was generally considered, and events were to prove, that London

1. 'Of uncertain origin: possibly the second element in Mumbo Jumbo, a name applied (in English since the 18th c.) to a West African Divinity or bogy.' (O.E.D.)

had got the best of the bargain.

Bartlett put the emaciated youngster in the charge of Matthew Scott, the antelope keeper, under whose constant and loving care he soon became 'very frolicsome'—indeed a considerable nuisance, kicking the woodwork of his den to pieces and breaking off his tusks as fast as they grew. A stop had to be put to his gambols:

> This [wrote Bartlett] we accomplished in a very speedy and effectual manner. Scott and myself, holding him by each ear, administered to him a good thrashing. He quickly re-cognised that he was mastered by lying down and uttering a cry of submission. We coaxed him and fed him with a few tempting morsels, and after this he appeared to recognise that we were his best friends, continuing on the best terms with both of us until about the year before he was sold. He was at that time [1882] about twenty-one years old and had attained the enormous height of nearly eleven feet.

About three months after Jumbo's arrival a female African elephant, Alice, was purchased from a London dealer for £500; she had been obtained in the Sudan by an Italian traveller named Casanova, and had come to London by way of Vienna. So tiny was she that Bartlett first considered taking her across London in a cab, but in the end he decided that she should make the journey under her own steam. To propose walking through London's East End in the company of a baby elephant was asking for trouble, and he and his charge found themselves pursued and pestered by several hundred 'dirty, ragged, noisy boys, and not a few of that nomad, the London rough, the curse to modern travellers about town'. It was already dark by the time they arrived at Bartlett's house in the Gardens, and he was famished; so was Alice, 'who seated herself by my side at the table and evidently enjoyed the bread, apples, etc, with which I supplied her.'

*   *   *

The New Elephant House at Regent's Park. *Illustrated London News*, 26 June 1869

In June 1871 the Duke of Edinburgh arrived at Plymouth in the *Galatea*, bringing with him from India a four-year-old elephant, Tommy, destined for the London Zoo. Young Clarence Bartlett (another of Abraham Bartlett's sons) and a second keeper, a man named Smart, travelled to Plymouth to help Paton, Tommy's mahout, to bring the elephant by rail to London.

No sooner had the train started when Tommy began to behave exactly like a football fan. It would seem that he intended no harm when he began to smash up the van, and it was just a piece of bad luck that in the process he leaned rather heavily against Paton and crushed him to death. Rumour soon had it that both Paton and Tommy had been drunk at the time; but it was stated at the inquest that the former, at any rate, had taken the pledge several years before. Buckland, using information given him by Abraham Bartlett who in turn had received it from Clarence, wrote a long account at third hand of the incident in *Land and Water* (17 June 1871), praising the courage and the exemplary behaviour of Clarence and Smart; but he failed to give satisfactory answers to a number of rather embarrassing questions that had been asked by 'R.G.K.' in a letter to the *Western Daily Mercury* (8 June 1871):

> Sir,—I have always been under the impression that at an inquest every means would be adopted to ascertain what was the cause of death, but at the inquest on the body of the keeper of the well-known elephant 'Tommy' a verdict was returned of 'accidental death'—what killed the poor fellow is not mentioned. Was he crushed by the elephant? If so, were there no marks to show such to have been the case? The weight of the huge beast would have been sufficient one would think to literally smash the man; and in that case a doctor would scarcely say that he could not tell whether the man died from internal injuries or not without a *post mortem* examination.
>
> Why was not a *post mortem* examination made?
>
> This poor fellow was well known in Devonport, and there are many who cannot understand either the evidence or the verdict, and who would gladly be enlightened on various points. . . . For instance, what became of his money—there only being three-halfpence found in his pocket? and this on paying-off day, and he a steady man and a teetotaller. Where were his two gold rings—one a handsome diamond? Both were on his fingers when in Devonport on that fatal Friday.
>
> What became of all his property removed from the dock-yard in a hand-cart and presumed to have accompanied him on the train? No mention is made of either this or his money being claimed by his friends, or being in possession of any authorised person.
>
> How does it come to pass that two men, keepers of wild beasts and elephants in particular, should so lose their presence of mind and become so frightened as to be unable to state how the accident happened? And why did they refuse to speak on the subject when at Newton?
>
> After the accident happened, was assistance asked for at the next station? Why was

the man left to die without medical help? Surely if the two men could not obtain water they might have procured help, and had the poor fellow removed from the train. I cannot see that the slightest effort was made to save his life; and, if his death was really the result of accident, why was not something done to alleviate his sufferings or save his life?

The inquest seems to have been a mere farce, and a verdict returned all in a hurry, without sufficient evidence being given to arrive at a single fact.

As for Tommy, he was safely deposited in the Zoo, and since he did not again strike the headlines it must be presumed that he was not involved in further trouble.

This was to be the first of a succession of unfortunate incidents, in several of which elephants were to figure, and in which Sclater, Bartlett and Buckland were to find themselves under heavy fire, not only from the Press but also from a number of Fellows who disapproved of the dictatorship that controlled the Zoo at that time. To keep things in perspective, however, it must always be borne in mind that an animal that leads a blameless life at the Zoo for thirty years and then dies peacefully in its sleep is not 'news', and does not provide the material for entertaining reading; people prefer to hear about the exception that savages a visitor or kills its keeper. This is a simple fact of life.

❧ **15** ❧

Interlude: 'The Muddle at the Zoo'

On 25 November 1874 the following account appeared in the *Daily Telegraph*;

On Saturday morning last a very serious accident occurred at the Gardens of the Zoological Society in Regent's Park. The elephant house consists of a number of cages, opening into one large paddock, and each cage is provided with double doors. On the above morning, Andrew Thompson and Richard Godfrey, keepers, were sweeping out the cage of the large Indian rhinoceros [Jemmy], when the brute, which is of a most malevolent disposition, rushed in from the paddock, knocked the men down, and tried to trample on them.

Matthew Scott, assistant keeper, who was in the building, came at once to their aid, and hitting the rhinoceros in the eye with his whip, drove it off. Fortunately, there is a corner of the cage which is fenced off with iron, and into this Scott dragged the two men. Godfrey at once fainted, and fell with his head in the cage, and the rhinoceros, seeing him within its reach, rushed back and again attacked him. Scott, with nothing but his whip, once more drove the animal off. Godfrey, however, fell a second time, and the rhinoceros, returning to the charge, tore the flesh off the man's leg from the thigh down to the knee, laying the bone bare. Once again Scott drove the beast away, and finally succeeded in carrying the two other men out of the cage. We need hardly state that all this was done at the risk of his own life. The rhinoceros has no horn, which has been worn down by rubbing against the bars; but it is a most mischievous and spiteful brute, and weighs close upon seven tons.

Godfrey's life is despaired of. Thompson is badly bruised, and it is feared that he has suffered some severe internal injuries. Scott escaped unhurt. He is a small man, by no means remarkable for his strength, but possessed of very great courage and presence of mind. All three of the men have been for several years in the service of the Society, and are well known to visitors to the Gardens . . .

Now the *Daily Telegraph* had for some time past been waging war on the Zoo—and the

'Shocking Occurrence at the Zoological Gardens'. *London Clipper*, 5 December 1874

Zoo at this moment was, for practical purposes, Philip Sclater (the Secretary) behind the scenes, and on the spot Abraham Bartlett, the latter being hand-in-glove with Frank Buckland. The Editor of the *Daily Telegraph* therefore joyfully seized the opportunity to provide his readers with a melodramatic leading article in which the 'facts'[1] as stated above were richly embroidered. Though the Zoo was not directly attacked in it, criticism of the way the institution was run was undoubtedly implied.

A few scraps from this leader will serve to convey its tone: 'Mr MATTHEW SCOTT, the hero, is no ideal GUY LIVINGSTONE, with the strength of a HERCULES and the proportions of an ANTINOUS; he does not even hold Her Majesty's commission.' (This was a dig at Buckland, who did.) He was, said the writer, a plain, straightforward man who for the sake of his comrades pitted his own life 'against odds so terrible that the boldest man alive might well think twice before venturing upon so forlorn a chance'. We are spared nothing—from 'the savage snort of the infuriated monster . . . wild with rage, maddened with the pain of its wounded eye' to 'the piteous cries of its victims'. The article concluded: 'There was no crowd to look on, no encouraging shout, no Victoria Cross to win; there were none watching during those few terrible seconds but Death on the one hand and Fortune on the other. And seldom has Fortune favoured a bolder or a worthier effort.'

At the time of the accident Buckland was away at Worcester inspecting salmon, and Bartlett elsewhere in the Gardens. Having learned the 'facts' from Bartlett, who was not an eye-witness, Buckland immediately wrote to *The Times* to correct alleged inaccuracies

1. How could a hornless animal have ripped the flesh off a man's leg from thigh to knee?

in the 'highly wrought article' in the rival newspaper. The accident, he said, was the result of the carelessness of the two keepers. There were doors which could be used to confine the rhinoceros in the next loosebox, but to save themselves a little trouble Thompson and Godfrey had not bothered to shut them. Scott ought to have been keeping the rhino entertained in the paddock; Thompson and Godfrey ought to have kept their eyes open. Finally:

> Godfrey, instead of having 'the flesh torn off his right leg from the hip to the knee in a ghastly wound that laid the leg bone bare for its entire length', had his leg severely bruised . . . Fortunately there are no bones broken, neither was there any wound, the skin being only grazed. Thompson was less hurt, and both men walked out of the den and were not carried by Scott. Not one drop of 'blood or foam or bloodshot eye' was seen during the whole tableau. The rhinoceros vented most of his rage on a large watering-pot which the men had left in his cage. Both men are shortly expected to resume their duties.

The letter was an unpleasant one: it contained not a word in praise of Scott's heroism or of sympathy for the two injured keepers. If *The Times* received any replies, it did not publish them; but a number of angry letters, mostly pseudonymous, appeared in the *Daily Telegraph*. Some of the writers enclosed money for Scott and—to the great annoyance of Sclater and Bartlett—an appeal was launched on his behalf. Some had visited the two keepers in hospital, tried to talk with Scott (who had evidently been ordered to keep his mouth shut), and examined the scene of the accident; they all declared that the three men were honest and reliable and had been very unfairly treated. 'I think it a mean and unworthy thing in Mr Buckland,' wrote 'Indian Sportsman', 'to try to spoil such a piece of manhood by quibbling as to whether the men were led or carried out.'

For some months there was silence. Then in July of the following year a new misfortune prompted 'An Old F.Z.S.', the writer of a previous letter, to return to the attack. Buckland, he said, had declared in November that 'the men will shortly resume their duties';[1] in fact, 'Thompson has never resumed his duties at all.[2] Godfrey was so terribly injured that he did not resume work until the 24th of May.' As to the chains and pulleys—though the men had constantly asked for these to be provided, this had never been done. Of course they were there *now*; but they had only been installed *after the accident*! There was no point in arguing with Buckland about 'carelessness' since 'facts' did not seem to interest him:

> But, Sir, my complaint is this . . . How does it then happen that Thompson has been discharged altogether, and, after thirty years spent in the service of the Society, has been turned adrift without even a pension? Why is it that Godfrey has been retained,

---

1. Buckland had been misled by a too optimistic report of William Meehan, the doctor retained by the Zoo to look after its keepers. Meehan had asked the eminent surgeon Henry Hancock, a former President of the College of Surgeons, for a second opinion, and he also had underestimated the gravity of Godfrey's injuries.
2. Thompson resumed his duties on 6 January 1875.

but has been degraded to an inferior post?[1]

Thompson, he continued, had looked after an old Indian elephant, Chunee,[2] for nearly twenty years, watching over her 'with a devotion that was almost comical in its intensity:

> After Thompson's dismissal I noticed that day after day poor Chunee grew restless, irritable and melancholy, and so touchy that I was afraid to let my children go near her. She died last week at an age which is, for an elephant, comparatively young. And I am convinced that—although I impute no negligence to her present keepers, who are, I believe, a couple of very expert gardeners, and used to manage a little market-garden down by the deer-sheds before their recent promotion—Chunee has died for want of that care and attention which Thompson used to bestow upon her. . . . Perhaps Mr Buckland can explain all this as satisfactorily as he can the original accident.

A leading article developed the material in the letter, and many a reader must have shed a tear as he read the touching description of dear old Andy Thompson helping 'a little four-year-old mite' to shake hands with his enormous pet. Nor was sarcasm excluded: 'Mr BUCKLAND, no doubt, when he has any time to spare, occasionally looks in on the Regent's Park, and Mr BARTLETT is, we have every reason to believe, a most intelligent and able gentleman'; but it was the Thompsons of this world who bore 'the real labour and heat of the day', and 'all Mr BARTLETT's vast knowledge and all Mr FRANK BUCKLAND's inexhaustible energy would go for very little indeed, were it not for the zealous and devoted assiduity of their subordinates.'

Other letters followed, including one from Thompson himself who, being no longer in the employ of the Society, was now free to speak out. After confirming that in spite of frequent requests the chains and pulleys had never been installed, he continued:

> And now Sir, a word as to the manner in which I have been treated. When I felt I was getting a little strength I went down to the gardens to see if I could do a little work. I was at once told to go to the cattle and deer sheds, the coldest place and the hardest work in the gardens. At this time I was suffering from the shock to the system, and had a bad rheumatic attack. I had even to be dressed and undressed by others, and to go, therefore, to the new work would have been simply to send me back to bed. I will not say anything of being sent away from my old charge, the elephant, lest I may be thought sentimental.
>
> I then spoke to a member of the council, who advised me to report myself to Mr Bartlett, and tell him I was utterly unable to do the new work. At the same time he said he would try and get me my pension, to which I had been long since entitled. I have waited till now, and find myself, after thirty years' faithful service and with a large

---

1. Thompson was not discharged (see p. 174), nor was Godfrey demoted.
2. Not, of course, the Chunee of the Exeter 'Change.

Philip Lutley Sclater, Secretary of the Z.S.L.,
1859–1902. From a photograph

family, thrown on the wide world. All I ask, Sir, is justice. . . .

In view of this letter and of another from 'A Fellow of the Zoological Society of about twenty-eight years', Sclater felt himself obliged to break his silence. Writing to the *Daily Telegraph* he suggested that the 'Fellow' should either visit him at the Society's offices in Hanover Square or raise the matter at the next General Meeting. The former offer was taken up by another correspondent, 'An Old Oxford Man and F.Z.S.', who was informed by Sclater that Thompson, 'by refusing to work in the cattle-sheds where Mr Bartlett sent him, had discharged himself, and had so forfeited his claim to a pension altogether.' Had Bartlett therefore deliberately provoked Thompson to lose his temper and resign, thus putting himself technically in the wrong? 'I then saw at once that the matter was hopeless, and asked, quite frankly, whether I was not wasting time? I received a courteous assurance that I had wasted a good deal of time already; and accordingly the interview came to an end . . .' The 'Fellow', on reading this letter, sensibly decided that no good purpose would be served by his visiting Hanover Square too.

After the death of Chunee, the two 'gardeners' found themselves without an elephant; Bartlett therefore took Alice away from Scott, who had tended her devotedly for a decade, and handed her over to his two inexperienced protégés. These seem to have been accident-prone, for within a matter of weeks disaster had overtaken Alice also: she lost a piece a foot long, and weighing more than two pounds, from the end of her trunk—that wonderful highly-sensitive all-purpose organ by which an elephant eats, drinks and breathes, and which also serves as its fingers.

The story does not make pleasant reading. Indeed, Theo Johnson described Bartlett's account of the accident as 'simply revolting', adding that his whole book (*Wild Animals in Captivity*) was marred 'by the total absence of that nice reticence which those who write about animals should be most careful to observe, lest they wound the susceptibilities of their readers and render distasteful the subject they would recommend.' *Pace* Johnson, we quote Bartlett:

One morning Waterman, one of the keepers, came to me in breathless haste saying that Alice had torn off a part of her trunk. I went of course immediately and found the end of her trunk lying in the middle of the den. Scott and one of the other keepers handed it to me at my request. It was warm and the nerves and muscles were still quivering and in motion; it gave me a most painful shock. The poor beast appeared in great distress and agony, whirling and elevating her trunk and screaming; she would not allow any one near her. I ordered the tank in the house to be filled with cold water, and a tarpaulin to be hung up in front of the den. I was sadly afraid I should have to destroy the poor creature and made the necessary preparation for an emergency; however, I found, after visiting her from time to time, that the bleeding had stopped and that she had availed herself of the cold water into which to thrust the ragged end of the torn trunk.

Surprisingly enough, Alice made a complete recovery, though for a long time she had to be fed by hand and given water from a hose placed in her mouth. What was never satisfactorily explained was how the accident happened. Bartlett does not even hazard a guess, but Johnson does. After very properly dismissing the 'incredibly absurd' explanation offered by the Press, that Alice had *inadvertently* trodden on her own trunk, he quoted the opinions of Waterman and another member of the staff:

> [Waterman's] theory was that 'Alice' was at that time chained[1] by one of her fore-feet; that in her efforts to obtain release she inserted the finger of her proboscis between it and the links of the chain and got it there entangled; that the severance was caused by an impatient tug. The other suggestion was of a startling kind, and although only offered *as* a suggestion I am inclined to accept it as a statement of fact. It was that the elephant was not chained by the leg, but *tied by the trunk* . . .

Whatever the facts may have been, the accident gave the *Daily Telegraph*'s regular zoo-baiters a magnificent opening. A leader-writer, too, revived in every detail the rhinoceros episode and its consequences. It was possible that Mr Sclater might be 'too much occupied to give his full attention to the concerns of the Zoological Society'. He had put 'absolute despotic power' into the hands of the Resident Superintendent, and 'only the most extreme circumstances' could justify the latter's conduct being called into question by the public. Such circumstances had now arisen:

> The Resident Superintendent is a gentleman of ability and experience . . . He will probably upon reflection be disposed to admit that he has acted somewhat hastily, and that his original decision [to dismiss Thompson and demote Godfrey] may with advantage be reconsidered. . . . It is always an unfortunate thing for a body such as the

---

1. 'Of course a leathern band, and not a chain, is the proper thing to use. But I fear the elephant-keepers at the Zoo have much to learn with reference to the management of elephants, and still more as to their character.' (Johnson's note.)

Zoological Society that its internal affairs should be dragged into the fierce light of public criticism, and that matters which ought to be private should be generally and freely discussed. Such a contingency, however, can invariably be averted by judicious management, and it is to be hoped that the recent difficulties at the Zoological Gardens may, upon careful and temperate consideration, be found capable of a final and satisfactory solution.

Towards the end of August the controversy passed from the pages of the *Daily Telegraph* to those of the *Marylebone Mercury*, which dubbed it 'The Muddle at the Zoo' and fanned its flames for another month. Stung by fresh taunts from 'Reformer', Sclater was finally obliged so far to 'sink his dignity' as to reply to his anonymous attacker. The two men in the rhinoceros house were not, he said, gardeners, but keepers. He denied that the statutes entitled a keeper to a pension after twenty-five years' service; he denied that the chains and pulleys had been installed only *after* the accident. He concluded, 'To the personal impertinences with which the "Reformer" interlards his remarks it is unnecessary for me to reply.' The correspondence was brought to a close towards the end of September by a letter signed 'The Rhinoceros "Jim"', who declared that the chains and pulleys had been in his house ever since its erection in 1869.

It is impossible, at this distance of time, to establish the facts of the case. But in particular, where the chains and pulleys were concerned, somebody was lying; and it must seem strange that this matter at least was never cleared up.[1] It is, however, obvious that Sclater, who resented any interference or criticism (even when it came from a Fellow of the Society, whose paid servant he was), behaved with much arrogance, and was abetted in this by Bartlett and Buckland. It was his arrogance which led, on this as on other occasions, to the Society's dirty linen being washed in public: no redress could be obtained by constitutional methods. As 'Reformer' put it:

> The Council of the Society consists of 1st Mr Bartlett, 2nd Mr Sclater; and to appeal from Mr Sclater as Secretary to Mr Sclater as Council is to appeal from Lord Eldon, sitting as Chancellor, to Lord Eldon, sitting as Judicial Committee of the House of Lords. Lord Eldon used to boast that he never had a judgment reversed. Mr Sclater can similarly claim that the Council has never overruled his decision. Here, Sir, is another aspect of 'The Muddle at the Zoo'.

But the seventies were not to close without a further elephant disaster. Over the Easter week-end of 1879 a small Indian elephant, presented three years earlier by the Prince of

---

1. That the keepers may have been guilty is certainly suggested by the fact that an article in the *Illustrated London News* of 26 June 1869 mentions the safety apparatus; yet it is not unknown for a reporter to describe what he is told is soon to be carried out. Or possibly Thompson was saying that there should have been ropes and pulleys on the *outside* doors, whereas Sclater and Bartlett were referring to those on the *inside* doors.

The Camelopard or a New Hobby (King George IV and
Lady Conyngham).
Hand-coloured etching attributed to William Heath, 1827

The Nubian giraffe, its native keepers and Mr. Cross.
Oil painting by J. L. Agasse, 1827

Wales, trampled on an elderly man named Goss, the keeper of the parrot house,[1] who had been left in charge of it while its regular keeper was absent for a few minutes. (Goss, it should in fairness be mentioned, had at one time also worked with elephants.) 'Zoologist' was once again ready to pounce, and in a letter to *The Times* expressed surprise that the incident had not been mentioned in the Press. Goss, he said, had sustained 'very severe injuries' and was in hospital 'in a critical state'.

Sclater replied admitting that there had been an accident but gave his opinion that this 'good-tempered and most docile animal' had probably acted 'more in play than in earnest'. Goss, he added, was by no means in a 'very critical state' and 'was going on very favourably'. When, three weeks later, Goss died of his injuries, Sclater offered no reply to a withering letter from 'Zoologist'. At the inquest Bartlett came forward with the suggestion that 'possibly some mischievous person had prodded the elephant from behind with a stick or umbrella, or else pulled his tail, thus making him suddenly start forwards.'

From much of what has been said above, it might perhaps be assumed that Sclater was not a fit person to act as secretary to the Z.S.L. So far as his scientific qualifications are concerned, nothing could be further from the truth. But admittedly he was too autocratic, too impatient of criticism; admittedly the distance that separated the Society's offices in Hanover Square from the Gardens made it inevitable that he should leave too much power and all the routine management of the Gardens in the hands of Bartlett. However, as can readily be seen from the *Proceedings* and *Transactions* of the Society, he was a tireless worker in the scientific field. In the words of a columnist of *Scientific Opinion* (30 June 1869):

> In Dr. P. L. Sclater, the Society possesses an officer who unites a wide practical zoological experience with a love of scientific research, and a thorough appreciation of the commercial aspects of the Zoological Gardens. A secretary is always the working representative of the body or society to which he belongs, and we believe we are not exceeding the bare facts when we attribute the success of the Zoological Society to the enterprising and indefatigable labours of its secretary. He has in a great measure made the Society what it is. . . .[2]

---

1. Nearly forty years earlier, Goss, then a very young assistant, had held up the parrots that Lear wished to draw.
2. Other excerpts from the same article will be found on pp. 198 and 199 and p. 212.

❧ 16 ☙

Jumbo

Elephants are always drawn smaller than life, but a flea always larger.

Swift, *Thoughts on Various Subjects*

JUMBO had soon accepted that it was to be a part of his job to give children rides in the Gardens. The 'riding money' came in those days in the form of tips and went straight into the pocket of the keeper. Scott never let it be known how much he earned, and certainly not what proportion of his earnings he spent in the pub he much frequented; but when, after the departure of Jumbo and Scott, the ticket system was introduced, it was discovered that even a far less celebrated elephant and keeper were able to earn the very handsome sum of more than £600 a year. Jumbo must have been a gold mine.

According to Johnson, Scott was an awkward chap who gloried in being as rude as possible, 'especially to those who appeared to be at all fashionable or distinguished'. Important visitors began to complain; but Bartlett was in a fix, because no one but Scott could control Jumbo. 'He'll do everything I ask him, bad or good,' Scott would say. 'We're *one*—and woe betide anybody who tries to come between us.' When Jumbo had a terrible attack of enteric fever which reduced him to 'a mere mountain of skin and bone', it was Scott who, rejecting any interference by a professional vet, undoubtedly saved his life—though whether by 'pailfuls of Scotch' (his own panacea), as some asserted, or by a course of faith-healing, as Johnson believed, can never now be known. Attempts were made to force on Scott an assistant who might one day be able to replace him, but none stayed the course for very long: Scott saw to that. In short, it was clear that the only way to get rid of Scott was to get rid of Jumbo; and to do this would create a public outcry that the Society simply dared not face.

At one point it looked as though Jumbo might resolve the problem without human help. As is well known, male elephants, however docile as teenagers, become undependable on reaching maturity and extremely dangerous when in the condition called *must*, which lasts for four or five weeks at a time.[1] The day came when Jumbo, in a fit of frenzy, once

---

1. The 'must' gland, situated between the eye and the ear, becomes enlarged and a black, oily fluid is discharged. It has not yet been established whether 'must' is of sexual origin. (See L. S. Crandall, *The Management of Wild Mammals in Captivity*, p. 459.)

more broke his tusks by trying to pierce the iron plates on the door of his cage. The tusks began to grow again, but in so doing pushed forward the broken jagged ends and, forcing their way through the skin not far below the eyes, produced abscesses on each side of his face. Bartlett decided that these abscesses, which were obviously very painful, must be drained. Armed with a long hooked steel rod, and accompanied by Scott whose rôle was of course to persuade Jumbo that what was to take place had his approval, Bartlett entered the cage:

> Standing under his lower jaw and passing the instrument above the swollen part, I, with a sharp pull, hooking fast into the skin, cut it through, causing a most frightful discharge of very offensive matter; the poor beast uttered a loud shriek and rushed from us, bleeding, shaking and trembling, but without exhibiting any anger. After a little coaxing and talking to he allowed us to wash out the wound by syringing it with water.
>
> On the following morning we determined to operate upon the other abscess. We had, however, some misgiving as to the result of our second attempt to operate upon him, but, to our intense surprise, the beast stood perfectly still until the sudden cut caused him to start and give another cry like the one he uttered the day before. The improvement in the animal's condition after these two operations was most remarkable; the

Lancing Jumbo's face. A. Bartlett, *Wild Animals in Captivity*, 1899

tusks soon made their appearance growing through the apertures that had been cut for the discharge of the abscesses instead of coming out under the upper lip. . . .

By the end of 1881, however, Jumbo had become a serious problem, and it was no doubt with the fate of Goss in mind that Bartlett decided that he must take certain safety precautions.

The elephant was now eleven feet high (and could barely get through the tunnel), weighed nearly five tons, and was increasingly liable to 'fits of insanity'. Since Scott alone could handle him, Bartlett was very naturally alarmed as to what might happen if the great beast went berserk when his keeper was absent; he therefore asked the Council to allow him to have a rifle powerful enough to deal with an emergency, and his request was granted. It chanced that about the same time Phineas Barnum, the famous American showman, wrote to enquire whether the Society would be prepared to sell Jumbo. The Council promptly agreed, fixing the price of £2,000 but wisely stipulating that it was for Jumbo 'as he stood', and did not include his removal from the Gardens. Barnum (who later admitted that he had been ready to pay £3,000) replied by telegram, 'I accept your offer; my agents will be with you in a few days'. The Council was delighted; Scott would probably go with his elephant; if not, then he could simply be got rid of as being no longer indispensable.

Now though Jumbo and Alice had in fact never even shared a den, the ever-sentimental public had long since decided that Alice was 'Jumbo's little wife'; news of the callous separation of this loving pair was therefore greeted with dismay, and when a rumour began to circulate that an 'interesting announcement' about Alice was momentarily expected, indignation reached fever pitch. Angry letters and leading articles, fanning the flames, appeared in the Press, and anonymous abuse was showered upon the unfortunate Sclater. One writer compared the scene to that of Mr Selby disposing of Uncle Tom, while another (Sir George Bowyer, Bt., F.Z.S.) considered the transaction as disgraceful as would be the sale by the British Museum of the *Codex Alexandrinus*. A third, who dwelt on the 'almost human distress of the poor animal at the attempted separation of him from his home and his family,' can hardly have found much consolation in the assurance of W. B. Tegetmeier, a knowledgeable zoologist, in the *Field* (25 February 1882) that those who sought to endow an elephant with human attributes were mistaken: 'The wrong existed only in their imagination—the danger was real.'

Punch of course joined in, publishing a cartoon by Linley Sambourne which showed Jumbo, his howdah filled to bursting point with joyful children, being dragged away by that brute Barnum. The famous cartoonist was killing two birds with one stone, for in the foreground of his drawing stood Head Keeper Punch, tugging at the tail of another villain of the day, the wicked agnostic Bradlaugh (in the guise of a wart-hog), and crying: 'Hail Columbia! an elephant's house is his castle! Leave Jumbo alone, and Three Thousand Million British children, not to mention Billions of British babes unborn, will bless the

'Arcades Jumbo; or, Br.dl.gh and the Elephant'. *Punch*, 4 March 1882

name of Barnum. Take t'other instead and you will earn the gratitude of all parties. . . .'

There were popular songs about Jumbo and Alice, the most famous of which contained lines remembered even today:

> Jumbo said to Alice, 'I love you';
> Alice said to Jumbo, 'I don't believe you do,
> For if you really loved me, as you say you do,
> You wouldn't got to Yankeeland and leave me in the Zoo.'

To this, it was later suggested, 'Poor Jumbo, as a patriotic pachyderm, should have hit back with "I could not love thee half so much, loved I not dollars more."'

A fund was started, to collect 'blood money' and so 'save Jumbo for the Nation'. Crowds flocked to the Gardens bearing gifts of food for the long journey and 'such less practical offerings as dolls, books and sewing-machines'. Children, even adults, wept openly, and it was alleged that Jumbo himself was so moved that tears had been seen coursing down his vast cheeks. Even the Queen asked that he might remain in England.[1]

The Editor of the *Daily Telegraph*, delighted to have another chance to snipe at the

1. For a fictionalised account of this drama see Gillian Avery, *The Elephant War*, Collins, 1960.

Zoological Society, sent Barnum the following telegram:

> F. T. Barnum, New York.—Editor's compliments. All British children distressed at elephant's departure. Hundreds of correspondents beg us to inquire on what terms you will kindly return Jumbo. Answer prepaid, unlimited. *Le Sage.*

Barnum replied wishing 'long life and prosperity to the British nation' but refusing to call off the deal:

> My compliments to editor *Daily Telegraph* and British nation. Fifty millions of American citizens anxiously awaiting Jumbo's arrival. My forty years' invariable practice of exhibiting best that money could procure, makes Jumbo's presence here imperative. Hundred thousand pounds would be no inducement to cancel purchase. . . .

Then came a sensational development. A number of Fellows, considering that the Council had been high-handed in taking this important and reprehensible step without calling an Extraordinary General Meeting, decided to act. An application was made to the High Court to restrain the Society from completing the sale, and an interim injunction granted pending an investigation. The case—a farce, because the Society's by-laws made it clear that the Council's action, however regrettable, had been perfectly legal—came up before Mr Justice Chitty, described by Johnson as 'an owlet of a judge, who saw little and blinked much'. It lasted a week, was notable for the utter irrelevance of a good deal of the evidence produced, and inevitably ended in victory for the Council. After a fruitless attempt by the dissidents to have the by-laws changed, many resignations followed.

So at last Barnum was free to carry off his elephant to an America which had been thoroughly preconditioned by welcome publicity to receive with open arms this prize packet from the Old World. But permission to remove Jumbo was one thing; persuading Jumbo to leave was quite another matter. An enormous crate had been constructed to transport him—a crate upon which, day after day, sympathisers inscribed their names as 'having called'. In spite, however, of chains and tackle, and much coaxing by Barnum's men, the elephant could not be persuaded to enter it, very possibly because (as some alleged) Scott had secretly signed to him not to cooperate; and certainly one might have expected Scott, in view of his passionate feelings about Jumbo, to have been taking some very definite obstructive measures even if not making public statements. It was then suggested that the elephant might perhaps be prevailed upon to walk to Millwall, where a crane could be used to lower him into his box and then hoist him on board the *Persian Monarch*. Jumbo walked politely enough to the gate of the gardens, but would go no further. The passage in the *Persian Monarch* was cancelled.

The *Daily Telegraph*, continuing its championship of Jumbo's cause, movingly reported the great beast's last-ditch stand:

> Then came one of the most pathetic scenes in which a 'dumb animal' was ever the chief

actor. The poor brute moaned sadly, and appealed in all but human words to his keeper, embracing the man with his trunk, and actually kneeling before him. Jumbo's cries were soon heard in the elephant house, where poor Alice was again seized with alarm and grief, so that every note of sorrow from the kneeling elephant in the road had its response within the gardens. At the sound of Alice's increasing lamentations, Jumbo became almost frantic, and flung himself down on his side . . .

Most of the men employed in the gardens had turned out, in their Sunday clothes, to take leave of an old friend; half-expecting, as it seemed, that his departure would yet be delayed. And so it was. Jumbo, having risen from the roadway, accompanied Scott willingly back to the elephant-house; where, on his return, the joy of Alice knew no bounds, her delight being expressed by clumsy gambols round her compartment. Yesterday, when Fellows and their friends were admitted, they found Jumbo somewhat reconciled to his iron bonds, and glad to go through the daily performance of lifting his trunk and presenting his mouth as a target for toothsome delicacies.

Attempt to remove Jumbo from the Zoo. *Illustrated London News*, 25 February 1882

Jumbo's Journey to the Docks. *Illustrated London News*, 1 April 1882

Jingo—Jumbo's successor. *Illustrated London News*, 23 September 1882

So Jumbo went back on the beat, docilely carrying his children by day and after closing-time stubbornly resisting all attempts to inveigle him into entering his cage. At last the time came when Barnum's chief agent, a man named William Newman and known as 'Elephant Bill',[1] finally realised that if he wanted Jumbo he must take Scott too. Scott was therefore offered, and at once accepted, munificent wages, whereupon the miracle happened and on the evening of 23 March Jumbo, no doubt acting on a sign from his keeper, immediately entered his cage.

Next morning at dawn he reached St Katherine's Docks and was taken by barge to Millwall. Here he breakfasted, and was 'treated afterwards to a copious draft of beer by a lady who had followed him all the way from the Zoological Gardens, and now took a mournful farewell of him'. On board the steamship *Assyria Monarch*, which was to carry him and its human passengers (who included seventy Russian refugee Jews) to the nineteenth-century Promised Land, a luncheon was given for a number of distinguished guests. Then, as the trumpetings of the noble emigrant blended with the chugging of the engines, the ship sailed with the tide down the Thames estuary. The great drama was at an end, and before the year was out the *Illustrated London News* was able to figure his diminutive successor, Jingo.

In America, Jumbo was soon to learn that wiliness, so effective in England, cut no ice with the Yankees, who employed more rough-and-ready methods of dealing with stubbornness:

You know old Jumbo was so pleased with himself over that piece of business that he must needs try to repeat it when he got to the States. He refused to go into the specially-

1. Not to be confused with a later bearer of that sobriquet, J. H. Williams.

THE GIANT OF GIANTS.

CROSS'S MAMMOTH ELEPHANT,
JUMBO II.,
WEIGHING
FIVE TONS SIX HUNDREDWEIGHT.
The heaviest animal on the face of the earth.
Over a ton heavier than the much-spoken of Jumbo.

CHALLENGE

To all the Zoological Gardens and Menageries in the
World to produce a Larger and Heavier Animal.

HIS POWER

Is equal to the power of Sixty Horses.
It can run quicker and hold out longer than any
racehorse in the world.

IT EATS PER DAY

3 sacks of potatoes, 120lbs. of bread. 1 sack of
Indian corn, 5 scores of bran, and 300lbs. of hay.

IT DRINKS

Daily forty large buckets of water.
And it is able to drink the same quantity of beer
if offered to him.
If it was fed on bread only, his daily supply would
be sufficient for a full-grown workingman
for two years.
If only fed on hay and oats the quantity devoured
daily would be sufficient for over 100 horses.

THIS LIVING MOUNTAIN

Walked from Hull, where it arrived by steamer,
to Liverpool, as it is too large and too
heavy to be sent by rail.

THIS GIGANTIC ELEPHANTINE MONSTER

Is as gentle as a lamb. It lifts its keeper up with
its trunk, and with the same monstrous limb
it is able to pick up the smallest coin.
The estimated Age of this Marvellous Colossus is

OVER 200 YEARS.

DAILY ON VIEW, from 9 a.m. to 7 p.m., in

WILLIAM CROSS'S

ZOOLOGICAL ESTABLISHMENT,
18, EARLE-STREET, OFF OLDHALL STREET,
LIVERPOOL.

Also on View Now, the Largest SERPENT that
has ever been in captivity.

THE MISSING LINK.

The WILD MAN OF THE FOREST, a Monkey
of the size of a Man and the Power and
Strength of a Lion.

HOST OF OTHER STOCK.

Admission 6d. Children half-price.

Cross's Mammoth Elephant, Jumbo II.
Z.S.L.'s Press-Cuttings, vol. 8

constructed railway car we had made for him—wouldn't be coaxed in. There was Wood,[1] his English keeper, saying, 'Now, come along, Jumbo!' (patting his trunk); 'come along in, old man!' Not he. But he was a fine elephant, the tallest I ever saw. Wouldn't budge. So at last Arstingstall, who was looking on, got tired. 'Oh, blame all this British coaxing,' says he; 'he's in America now.' And Arstingstall, he passes a chain round Jumbo's buttocks, and takes the two ends through the car, and through the opening on the opposite side, where they were fastened on to an old she-elephant.

Still old Jumbo cocks his old head up, he was a tall elephant, and won't go in. So Arstingstall puts two elephants behind him and a man on top of the car. Then he gave the word. The old she-elephant started to pull, and the two other elephants to butt Jumbo from behind. The man on the top of the car fetched him a blow over the head

1. A misprint for 'Scott'. The account is from the *Graphic*, 14 October 1893.

with a crowbar. Jumbo ducked, and he shot into the car like a sack of coals. He never wanted any more coaxing.

Jumbo soon got used to American ways. During a triumphal tour of the States,[1] where he was ludicrously placarded as 'the only surviving mastodon', he found time and opportunity to beget two calves. Then one day three years after his arrival, when crossing the railway line at St Thomas in Canada, he engaged in a trial of strength with an unscheduled freight train. The train won, and he was killed almost instantaneously; but so, too, was the engine-driver, and two of the coaches were derailed and damaged. Jumbo's stuffed body is now in Tufts University in Boston, his skeleton in the American Museum of Natural History in New York.

Scott was invited to stay on in charge of other elephants, but refused when he learnt that he would be expected to wear oriental dress. For a time he escorted the stuffed remains of his old friend round the States, then returned to England where he eked out a living selling a little booklet describing his days with Jumbo.

Alice had soon followed her 'husband' to America, where she died in a fire in 1887. On dissection her body was discovered to contain over three hundred pennies, part of a pocket-knife, four cane ferules, a piece of lead piping and a number of pebbles. The American public must have been either less generous or more sensible, for there is no mention of dimes in the contents of her stomach.

Jingo in his turn grew enormous, but he was always ugly and ungainly. It was probably he who swallowed, 'after a slight mastication', the dropped purse of a certain Mrs Bennett, who had come up from Norwich with her daughter to enjoy a day at the Zoo. Observing the warning notices about pickpockets, she had obediently transferred her purse from her pocket to her bosom; but in mounting the elephant she had naturally leaned forward— with fatal result. Weeping, penniless, return-ticketless, she had been rescued by Bartlett, who 'advanced her a sovereign to convey her home'. Nine days later a half-crown was discovered in the elephant's droppings, and gradually about two pounds—more than half of the missing money—was recovered. The remainder vanished for ever in the litter of the den.[2]

And perhaps Jingo was also 'th'unwieldy Elephant' who

> To make them mirth us'd all his might, and wreath'd
> His lithe proboscis[3]

round the waist of the unfortunate Hon. Mrs Pocklington:

An accident which might have been attended with the most serious consequences has

1. In his first year he earned a million and a half dollars for Barnum.
2. *Chesham Examiner*, 17 August 1892.
3. Milton, *Paradise Lost*.

occurred at the Zoological Gardens. Madame Alice Lili, the well-known Court milliner, of 7, Grafton-street, Piccadilly (she trades under this name, though she really is the Hon. Mrs. Pocklington), had been giving her children a ride on the elephant when, for some reason or other, the brute put his trunk round her waist, held her over his head, and then dashed her violently to the ground. Though very much hurt, no lasting injuries are, at present, apprehended; but Mrs Pocklington will most likely be confined to her bed for some time.[1]

This was all good clean fun. But eventually Jingo in his turn reached the awkward age, and in 1903 he was sold to America—for a mere £200, and with hardly a tear shed. The voyage was exceptionally rough, and Jingo, prone like all elephants to seasickness, died before reaching New York. His enormous carcase was pitched overboard, and not long afterwards a passing ship, the S.S. *Colorado*, observed the corpse floating in mid-Atlantic.

1. *Evening Post*, 22 September 1891.

✣ 17 ✣

Arks Royal

Beautifully he did shoot
Many a royal tiger brute.
Laying on their backs they die,
Shot in the apple of the eye.

An Indian extols the Royal Sportsman

In the nineteenth century, British royalty were constantly receiving splendid gifts of wild animals from miscellaneous Oriental potentates and Indian princes: they were the obvious presents for them to make, costing the giver little and flattering the recipient much. The most spectacular single collection was that brought back by the Prince of Wales (Edward VII) after his four months' tour of India in the winter of 1875–6.

The Prince had included in his party, to take charge of the animals as they were handed over, young Clarence Bartlett;[1] and no doubt the word had already been passed round the Indian courts that gifts of fine or rare animals and birds would not merely be acceptable but were virtually commanded. As to the care of them when they reached England, here there was no problem; a handful were to be presented to the Zoological Society (which duly acknowledged the gift by awarding the Prince its first Gold Medal), the remainder being deposited in the Zoo for as long as it suited the royal convenience. The Prince could keep in touch with them by occasional visits; indeed it might be claimed that he was under some moral obligation to do this, seeing that a number of them had been orphaned at his hand.

The Prince left London on 11 October 1875 and travelled overland to Brindisi, where he boarded H.M.S. *Serapis*, a converted Indian troopship, and a month later reached Bombay. During the winter he saw much of India, including Ceylon; but perhaps his most unforgettable experience was his visit to Sir Jung Bahadour, the virtual ruler of Nepal. Sir Jung, who had been ennobled as a reward for his loyalty to the British at the time of the Mutiny, was a keen sportsman who had 'taken his degree in tiger hunting'; he organised a number of shoots for his royal guest, whom he politely allowed to do all the killing,

---

1. He played his cards well, and in 1901 was awarded the silver medal of the Royal Victorian Order by the new King.

and also gave him a considerable number of live animals.

The *Serapis* sailed from Bombay in mid March, loaded with the loot of India and accompanied by the *Raleigh* and the *Osborne* to carry the overflow. The collection was especially rich in big cats. Two fully grown tigresses, 'Motee' and 'Jahaun', the gift of Sir Jung, occupied spacious cages under the break of the *Raleigh*'s poop. Ignoring the animals' sex, the sailors renamed them 'Moody' and 'Sankey', and attempted to fraternise with them until a midshipman lost a finger (in one account, a hand) by taking too many liberties. Born and bred in captivity, and therefore more amiable, were a young tiger and tigress, Tom and Minnie, who allowed themselves to be led by a couple of natives through the streets of Bombay to the docks, where they boarded the *Serapis* 'just like Christians'—as a sailor put it. Each morning they were exercised on deck, where a few clouts soon cured them of a tendency to spring at the dogs and deer, and even at Georgie, the Himalayan bear; but Minnie, subjected one day to a compulsory bath, could never thereafter overcome an almost pathological antipathy to buckets.

A fifth tiger cub was also carried in the *Serapis*; it rejected all advances—very excusably those of the Prince, the murderer of its mother:

> Its life seems to be mostly spent in a succession of furious springs and hoarse short roars, and when not thus venomously dashing at everybody and everything that comes near it, it lies writhing in a sullen fury of snarls and growling, hissing, and showing its teeth. It made a desperate resistance against the two Nepalese who, after the killing of its mother, were sent into the den to secure it, and it was not captured until, immature as are its claws and teeth, it had inflicted some severe bites and scratches. It is reported to be unaffected by either kind treatment or stronger measures, and most richly deserves its name of 'Vixen'.[1]

There were further big cats in the *Serapis*. P'hool-Jharri, the hunting cheetah, was 'as dangerous and treacherous a beauty as one is likely to meet even in this wicked world'. By contrast, Pompey, a young leopard born in the Calcutta Zoo, was tame and playful as a kitten. 'He is full of antics which the sailors have taught him, and will jump over your arm like a dancing dog, and then put up his beautiful head to be scratched.' A second young leopard, Jacko, was equally kittenish, but 'given to a suspicious and not altogether confidence-inspiring scream, something between the mew of a cat and an incipient roar, accompanied by a display of claws and a very neat assortment of teeth . . . a pretty enough pet just now; but a year hence it may not be quite so pleasant to be within easy reach of his claws'.

Of the two leopards presented to the Prince by Sir Jung, Lizzie was 'bashful and harmless'; but her brother, Sailor, was considered unreliable, a judgment borne out by the state of the face, hands, and arms of the young seaman who had charge of him. 'Sailor'

1. *Daily News*, 13 May 1876.

'Jack v. Jacko'. W. H. Russell, *The Prince of Wales' Tour*, 1877

had a 'festive habit of converting trouser legs into ribbons, and has naughtily deprived sister "Lizzie" of a large portion of one of her ears'. Jamboo, a fully grown leopard presented to the Prince by the sergeants of the 109th Regiment, was also not to be trifled with. But all these big cats were as lambs by comparison with a viverrine cat—'an iron-grey creature studded with dingy black spots' and little larger than the domestic 'pussy':

> This feline demon for the most part lies on his back, with his fore and hind claws close together ready for mischief. He absolutely writhes with devilry when any one approaches, and spits and hisses with indomitable hostility, showing a mouth full of cruel white teeth. It is 'no surrender' with the wild cat, and it is clear his greatest joy would be to be at your throat with teeth and claws. On one occasion he worked himself up into such a fury that it was feared he was going rabid, and his cage was carried into a dark place where he might cool down in seclusion.[1]

The Prince had also been given four young elephants. On board the *Serapis* were Sir Jung's Safar Kulley and Jung Pershad, the latter of whom was taught by the sailors 'an indescribably comic waltz step', and 'to make his bow with the aplomb of a professor of

1. *Daily News*, 13 May 1876.

Jung Pershad. Photograph by J. F. Nott in *Wild Animals Described*, 1886

deportment'. But the pair in the *Osborne*—'two comical black little prodigies of talent' named Omar and Rustom—were still more gifted, even earning their keep by hauling up the ash-buckets from the furnaces. 'They kept watch and watch, and worked in canvas harness. At the words "hoist away", the one on duty would begin to pull, emitting a queer squeak of remonstrance as he felt the weight, and stopping dead at the words "high enough",' The *Osborne* entered Portsmouth harbour with Omar serenely perched on one paddle-box and Rustom on the other.[1]

There were two bears in the Prince's zoo—the already mentioned Georgie, and a young sloth bear named 'Mr Brown'. The latter, whose mother had been shot by the Prince, spent most of his time in the gloomiest corner of his cage; but he did not object to an occasional rough-and-tumble on the deck with his neighbours the young leopards, where it was 'very funny to see all the five rolling about together in a clump'. Georgie, at that time still 'a very playful little fellow', was later to achieve notoriety by breaking out one night from his cage at the Zoo and escaping from the Gardens. He was spotted, heading for the York and Albany public house, by a passing cabby, and eventually enticed back by

1. Omar and Rustom remained at Regent's Park until 1881, when the Prince presented them to the Berlin Zoo.

'A Levée of Pets': The Princess of Wales and her children on board the *Serapis*.
W. H. Russell, *The Prince of Wales' Tour*, 1877

the man who had had charge of him on board the *Serapis*.

Of the remaining mammals—which included deer, goats, wild dogs, monkeys, zebus and sheep—there is space to mention only a few. Two came to untimely ends: the pangolin, which died during the voyage of wounds probably received at the time of its capture, and a magnificent Kashmir deer whose fate will be described in a moment. There was a charming young Axis deer from Ceylon for the Princess of Wales, and a brace of miniature bullocks, Serapis and Tauris, with their tiny crimson-upholstered, silver-wheeled carriage for the use of the Prince's children. A very acceptable rarity was a musk deer, there being no other specimen in England at that time, and the Zoo also warmly welcomed a pair of Thar goats from the higher Himalaya. Among nearly ninety birds were a number of very decorative Nepalese pheasants, and some black partridges which the Prince hoped to acclimatise at Sandringham. Three ostriches were added to the menagerie at Aden; these were particularly acceptable to the Society, since the Zoo's only ostrich had recently died of indigestion after a surfeit of small change.

On 5 May, when the *Serapis* entered Portsmouth harbour, the Prince graciously thanked the ship's company and distributed handsome gifts all round. Then the *Enchantress* drew alongside, bringing the Princess of Wales and their children. The band played 'Home, sweet home', and we are assured that all who witnessed this family reunion 'confessed that

'An incident on the road': the elephants challenged to a race by a dog-cart, and winning.
Illustrated London News, 27 May 1876

they felt a little inclination to gulp down something in their throats'.

After the royal party had disembarked, privileged visitors were allowed on board to inspect the animals, which were 'shown to the greatest advantage. The tame pets, among which was a leopard cub, were fondled to show their perfect harmlessness, while the savage brutes were playfully excited in order that they might display their teeth.' One young sailor demonstrated how a mongoose killed a snake, while another—evidently a Hercules—'made an excursion of the ship with a rather large black bear curled round his neck'. Safar Kulley and Jung Pershad[1] salaamed a dozen times, and were duly rewarded with cake and oranges. But the greatest favourites proved to be the two other elephants, Omar and Rustom, on board the *Osborne*. The *Raleigh* had not yet berthed.

Most of the animals were to travel by train to Willow Walk, the Bermondsey goods station of the London and Brighton Railway, there to be transferred to vans and taken by road to Regent's Park. But Clarence Bartlett had not forgotten the unfortunate accident, five years

1. In 1882 Safar Kulley, sired by Jung Pershad, produced the first elephant to be born in Europe in modern times. Jung Pershad dropped dead in his stall at the Zoo in 1896.

earlier, when one of the keepers had been crushed to death by an elephant in a railway truck. Further, one of his two larger elephants, Jung Pershad, had already wrecked a truck on the way to Bombay. Bartlett therefore decided that this animal and Safar Kulley, together with their native mahouts, a keeper, and a Royal Marine, should make the whole journey to the Zoo on foot. This they successfully accomplished in two days, stopping the night at Godalming[1] *en route*.

It was intended that the 'wild beast train'—consisting of twenty-six trucks, some of which carried the personal luggage of the Prince and his suite—should leave Portsmouth early in the morning, so that the animals could reach Regent's Park before nightfall. But in the event, everything possible went wrong. First, it took far longer than had been expected to load the trucks, the ostriches proving particularly unco-operative, and resort having to be made to fireworks after hoses had failed to persuade two tigers to change cages. Then at Chichester Bartlett was handed a telegram saying that his fine Kashmir deer had broken out and been found dead beside the line. And finally, a mile short of their destination, the engine, which for some time past had been behaving temperamentally, broke down altogether. It was now nearly ten o'clock at night, and the unfortunate passengers, who included some native keepers, were obliged to walk along the tracks in pitch darkness to the station, where a large and inquisitive crowd was impatiently waiting:

> After some delay the train was brought up to the siding, amidst an interest which was scarcely repaid by results. The tigers declined to roar, even the wild cat had temporarily ceased from snarling, and the tail-less dogs were presumably asleep, since when awake they yelp with fiendish persistency. Nothing was to be heard, nothing strange or rare was to be seen, unless in such a category may be mentioned the head of the Barbary donkey on which Lord Charles Beresford distinguished himself at Gibraltar races, and which looked out on the scene with an expression of profoundest wisdom.
>
> The work of shifting the canvas-hooded cages from the trucks to the vans was at once busily commenced—a truck at a time being moved up into the shed, where, by the gaslight, strong and willing arms worked the crane. The quietude of the animals was surprising. The tigress Minnie emitted something between a grunt and a yawn as her cage was run up; the low vindictive gasping of the tiger cub Vixen was audible as a gang of men caught up the cage and carried it across the platform; the demoniacal tiger cat hissed with its chronic venom, and made dabs with its claws at the canvas from the inside while its cage was lifted; and P'hool Jharri, the cheetah, gave a single short sharp growl just as the van carrying it moved on.
>
> That was all; and that it was so little caused much disappointment. It would have been considered much more satisfactory, and a substantial guarantee for the ferocity

---

1. Exactly half way. Probably like Peter the Great and his suite ('a right nasty lot', according to Evelyn), who in 1698 also broke their journey from Portsmouth to London at Godalming, they too lodged at what is now the King's Arms.

of the animals, if the work had been done amidst a medley of roars, growls, hissings, and angry spittings. The want of excitement was obviously depressing, and it was clearly felt that the wild beasts were detracting from their reputation in the eyes of Bermondsey in not eating a small boy or biting off somebody's head with a single crunch.[1]

There was, however, to be a human sacrifice after all; in the crush at Willow Walk a youth fell under one of the vans and was seriously injured.

The animals reached the Zoo safely at 2 a.m., and with the help of a hundred willing workers were soon installed in the temporary quarters that had been prepared for them. These consisted of a large pavilion, canvas-roofed and timber-sided, enclosing a number of iron-barred cages. All the following week the public flocked to Regent's Park, and on the Sunday, when only Fellows and their guests were admitted, the Prince came with innumerable miscellaneous royalty, including a bunch of Hanoverian cousins, to inspect 'his friends in fur and feathers'. Rooms 'tasteful in their combination of elegance and comfort' had been made ready for the Prince's reception, and in the lecture hall he was shown his trophies of the chase, prepared and mounted by Clarence. 'Sixteen tiger skins, with dates affixed to them, bear witness to the Prince's marksmanship, it being noticed that almost every one of these striped tawny hides has a bullet-hole in the shoulder.' There were also the four feet of an elephant shot by the Prince in Ceylon.

The Queen, once so regular a visitor to the Zoo, did not come with the royal party. 'It was strange and painful to me to go there alone, without my dearest Albert,' she had written in her Diary when, eight years after the Prince Consort's death, she had at last summoned up the courage to return. Eventually, however, she decided that Bertie's fine menagerie, of which everyone was talking, must be seen, and on 14 March 1877 she paid what was to prove her last visit to Regent's Park. She was accompanied by Princess Beatrice:

> To the Zoological Gardens, where we got out & saw . . . the splendid new lion house, with the lions, tigers, panthers &c., belonging to Bertie, endless fine pheasants, deer of all kinds, & on the other side Bertie's 4 young elephants, all in a row. They are quite tame, & there were 2 quite little ones, who salaamed & were ridden about at an immense pace. There was also an ostrich belonging to Bertie.

1. *Daily News*, 15 May 1876.

'The Prince of Wales's Menagerie at the Zoological Gardens'.
Penny Illustrated, 27 May 1867

❧ 18 ❧

Sixties and Seventies

Visitor: 'Keeper! Keeper! there's a moose loose!'
Keeper: 'Excuse me, sir, are you Scots or English?'

We have already detailed some of the more spectacular events of the sixties and seventies; but before recording certain other happenings of the period we must make space for a more general survey of the Zoo as it appeared in 1869 to our kindly columnist of *Scientific Opinion*:

The Zoological Society of London is an institution *sui generis*. We know nothing else like it, either in design or success, within the limits, at all events, of the metropolis. It caters for the pleasures and instruction of the public, and it by no means disregards the interests of the scientific world. It is in nearly every respect a model body, though its general popularity might induce fastidious *savants* to imagine that pounds and shillings, more than genera and species, were the especial study of the Council.

But this is certainly not the case. The Zoological Society has a keen eye to those speculations which are likely to advance its funds; but it must also be said for it that it is not chary of these funds in supporting and encouraging scientific research of the highest order. It may provide 'sensations' for its gardens, and it very properly does so; but it does not—like the Botanical Society—confine its attention to this. Its scientific meetings are regularly held, and its *Transactions* contain the *crème de la crème* of the zoological and comparative anatomy of the day. And why are these *Transactions* so full of valuable material? Simply because the Society spares no expense in illustrating such papers and monographs as it deems to be of real interest and importance.

Then, too, unlike the Linnaean [sic] and other societies, whose assistant secretaries seem to slumber in calm repose within the sacred precincts of Burlington House, it sends out early notice of the papers to be read at its meetings, and it circulates freely and extensively an early and well-prepared abstract of its *Proceedings*. It must not be imagined that we have any prejudice in favour of the Zoological Society . . . but when we see a learned body which is not content to exist on the tattered tradition of a former reputation, but is maintained in accordance with the progressive spirit of the

'Visit to the Antediluvian Reptiles at Sydenham—Master Tom
strongly objects to having his mind improved.' John Leech,
Punch Annual, 1855

age, we feel bound as journalists to express our opinion on the matter, and this we do
fearlessly. . . .

Of the Gardens generally we can only say we wish the trees were a little older, and
the seats—we do not mean the chairs—a little more numerous; they are tastefully laid
out and conveniently arranged. Of the houses we can only say that they are invariably
kept scrupulously clean and well ordered; and of the keepers we would observe that they
are without exception remarkable for their kindness to—nay, their very love of—the
animals, and their extreme courtesy to the visitors. . . .

One of the last acts of the Prince Consort as President had been the appointment of Thomas
Huxley—Darwin's bulldog, as he called himself—and Samuel Wilberforce, Bishop of
Oxford, as Vice-Presidents of the Society; on his death in 1861 the Prince was succeeded
by Sir George Clerk. The celebrated verbal duel between Huxley and the oily prelate had
taken place only a year before at the Meeting of the British Association in Oxford,[1] and

1. Wilberforce had offensively asked Huxley whether he was related on his grandfather's or his grandmother's
side to an ape. Huxley replied that he would not be ashamed to have a monkey for his grandfather, but he
would be ashamed to be connected with a man who, like the bishop, 'plunges into scientific questions with
which he has no real acquaintance, only to obscure them by an aimless rhetoric, and distract the attention
of his hearers from the real point at issue by eloquent digressions, and skilled appeals to religious prejudice'.

Dinner in the Iguanodon model at the Crystal Palace, 31 December 1853.
The invitations were sent out on pieces of the wing-bone of a pterodactyl.
Illustrated London News, 7 January 1854

it is hard to imagine that the two men enjoyed the proximity that Committee meetings of
the Z.S.L. must have involved. Richard Owen, another staunch anti-Darwinian, was also
a Vice-President at the time. In the sixties, apes and monkeys were much talked of in
London drawing-rooms and much frequented at Regent's Park.

The interest in evolution stimulated at this time by the writings of Darwin and Huxley,
and in palaeontology by the work of Richard Owen, inspired an architect named Waterhouse
Hawkins to attempt life-sized reconstructions of extinct animals. These cement monsters
delighted the public when they were set up in the geological lake in the grounds of the
Crystal Palace, where on New Year's Eve 1854 Waterhouse entertained to dinner twenty-
one distinguished palaeontologists *in* his iguanodon. Among these was Owen, who showed
his gratitude by savagely attacking his host for giving his monster superfluous toes. But
Hawkins, encouraged by popular acclaim, brushed all criticism aside and had further
casts of his brain-children made for New York's Central Park. Here, however, he came
up against the obscurantism of a certain Judge Hilton, who ordered his work to be des-

troyed—not on account of any minor anatomical inaccuracies, but because he considered that it challenged the authority of the first chapter of Genesis.

In the thirties and forties, post-mortem examinations of animals which died at the Zoo had been fairly regularly carried out; but later the practice seems to have been allowed to lapse. Buckland, however, was always 'in at the death' of any unusual mammal or bird, and ready and eager to dissect it and to enlarge his experience by sampling its flesh; with this in view he had once arranged for the exhumation of a leopard which had inconsiderately chosen to die while he was out of London, and the fire in the giraffe house in 1866 afforded him an even rarer and already roasted delicacy. In 1865, at Huxley's suggestion, the Society decided to provide and equip a room for autopsies and to appoint an official Prosector. Twenty-eight applications for the post were received, and Dr James Murie (1832–1925), dourest of Scots, was unwisely chosen to fill it.

For Murie, though undeniably very able and experienced, was an impossible man. Chalmers Mitchell, who knew him in his old age, agreed that his criticism of the conditions in which many of the animals were kept was justified; 'That he was correct,' he wrote, 'there can be little doubt; that he was offensive, whether deliberately so or not, no doubt whatever.' In 1870, 'genuinely worn out by his own obstinacy', Murie was allowed to resign on the grounds of ill health. Later he became an official of the Linnean Society, where once again his rudeness and incessant bickering brought about his resignation. The Linnean Society possesses a bust of him in which he looks like the most amiable of Greek philosophers. Murie was succeeded at Regent's Park by the equally distinguished but more tractable Alfred Garrod.

One of the most celebrated characters at the Zoo in mid-Victorian days was a French sailor, François Lecomte. Buckland had discovered him and his performing southern sea-lion at Cremorne Gardens[1] in January 1866, and had had no difficulty in persuading Bartlett to acquire his services for Regent's Park; and with him his pet—a welcome addition to the Zoo, for though the species had been known to science since the days of Magellan (1579), this was the first specimen to reach our shores. The animal—a young male which Lecomte had caught near Cape Horn and patiently trained for two years—was an instant success. According to Buckland, one of its acts was to 'enlist as a volunteer in the Mexican army' (how on earth did it do this?), to submit to drilling, and finally to fire a cannon; it would also dance a *pas de deux* with its keeper, the latter dressed as always *en matelot*, and at midday accompany him to the Albany public house just across the bridge. It consumed twenty-five pounds of fish a day, and had a horror of women wearing white ribbons.

The animal survived for only thirteen months, dying from a fish-hook inadvertently

1. In later years Buckland preferred to maintain that he 'found' Lecomte abandoned in a field by the roadside after he and his pet had been evicted from a travelling menagerie.

Lecomte and his Sea-lion.
Beata Francis, *The Child's Zoological Garden*, 1880

left in its food. But so impressed was the Society by Lecomte's handling of aquatic mammals, and so popular had his circus turn become, that it was decided to send him to the Falkland Islands to collect fresh specimens. He sailed from Swansea in June 1867 in the coal-ship *Epsilon*, reaching Port Stanley (the capital) ten weeks later. A number of expeditions were made to the various islands, chiefly in a schooner kindly put at his disposal by the Governor; but though Lecomte eventually succeeded in getting four sea-lions from the Kelp Islands, all soon died. However, a further collection was made, and in due course he embarked for England in the packet *Fawn* with four more sea-lions, an Antarctic wolf and nearly eighty other animals, mostly birds. Before reaching Montevideo the ship ran into very rough weather which caused the loss of all but eleven of his collection, among the survivors fortunately being the four sea-lions and the wolf.

But worse was to follow. Soon after leaving Uruguay one of the passengers went down with yellow fever, whereupon the autocratic captain ordered all Lecomte's larder of fish to be thrown overboard 'on account of its smell'. Dependent now upon such flying-fish as fell on the deck at night, and which he had to purchase at a high price from the sailors, Lecomte fought a losing battle to keep his little menagerie alive; and it was through no fault of his that when he arrived in England in August 1868, all that remained were one emaciated sea-lion, the Antarctic wolf, and half-a-dozen relatively uninteresting birds.

Buckland, like everyone else who knew Lecomte, was fascinated by the almost hypnotic influence the man exerted over animals. He relates how one day they went together to Deptford to see several sea-lions which had arrived there, and how Lecomte at once won their confidence by talking softly to them: '*Vous ne connaissez pas encore votre papa, mon petit. Restez tranquil, mon cher. Vous avez faim? Je vous donnerai un poisson, voilà.*' Then, two years

Python incubating at Regent's Park. *Illustrated London News*, 8 February 1862

later, the Frenchman was discovered to have cancer of the throat and given only a few months to live. As he lay in his lodgings in Frederick Street he became obsessed with the idea that his 'children' (as he called them) were missing him and, desperately ill though he was by then, he insisted upon being taken to the great tank in Regent's Park to see them for the last time. But half way there he collapsed and was unable to complete the journey. He never left his house again.

Performing 'seals', so popular today, are of course really what are usually called sea-lions,[1] and François Lecomte was the first to give a hint of the astonishing feats of which they have since been found to be capable.

Considerable excitement was caused at the Zoo when on 12 January 1862 a 22-foot-long West African python, a resident of long standing, laid about a hundred eggs and proceeded to incubate them. This was not in any sense a European 'first': an unsuccessful incubation had been recorded in the Tower, and in 1841 eight out of a batch of fifteen eggs had hatched at the Jardin des Plantes; but the size of the clutch made it an event

1. But sometimes 'eared seals', to differentiate them from the true, or 'earless', seals.

of some importance, and the Zoo and the Press gave it plenty of publicity. Messrs Negretti & Zambra, the famous instrument makers, constructed a special thermometer of unprecedented sensitivity (it required a mere three seconds to record a temperature) with which Mr Negretti and Mr Zambra in turn took regular readings from the mother and her eggs.

The eggs at the Jardin des Plantes had taken nearly two months to hatch; but Sclater was impatient to know whether or not his were fertile, and at the end of a fortnight he extracted one which when opened was found to contain a living embryo. Meanwhile the python, who had water within reach but rejected all food, never stirred from the bed of moss that had been provided for her. Her husband, however, indulged in an occasional rabbit; but he was shouldered away when he approached her as if to inquire how things were going. For the benefit of the Fellows and the Press, the blanket covering the mother was removed from time to time—a practice which *The Times* and *Punch*, with the wisdom of hindsight, were later to condemn.

On the fifty-third day the python sloughed her skin and her body temperature dropped by ten degrees Fahrenheit; but her century of eggs—dirty white, leathery, and about the size of tennis-balls—still gave no sign of life, and time was fast running out. On 4 April all hope of hatching was finally abandoned, and a fortnight later *Punch* published a long poem entitled 'Pity the sorrows of a poor Pythoness':

> 'OD rot the British public, thanks to whom my eggs have rotted,
> Not one of all my brood preserved, except the one they've potted!
> And that's a half-grown thing, that gives impression false as may be
> Of the true length, breadth, and thickness of a new-born Python baby.

Young Python in Bottle. *Illustrated London News*, 20 November 1862

Zoology's a great thing, but humanity's a greater;
Just let *me* get a chance, some day, of squeezing Dr. SCLATER!
The coil that I'd keep about him, some small return should be,
For the coil that he's been keeping these eight [*sic*] months about *me*. . . .

All a snake-mother asks is peace to warm and range and rank its
Precious ovarian treasure, safe and snug, beneath the blankets.
But if folks keep pulling, poking, peeping, prying, fiddle-faddling,
It will end, as it *has* ended, sure as eggs is eggs, in addling. . . .

Like boys, who when they've sowed a seed, still of its progress doubting,
Will pull it up from time to time, to see if it is sprouting,
So you in your anxiety to see my Pythons small,
Have poked and pulled and fingered me, till you've got none at all. . . .

From time to time, rash youngsters or stupid adults risk their lives by disregarding the warning notices and approaching too close to dangerous animals; on these occasions the victims or their relations, to excuse their folly or their negligence, almost always unjustly blame the authorities. There was once a craze (and it has recently been revived) for writing or carving one's name on the rump of a rhinoceros—an act of daredevilry that is in fact usually performed without the punishment it invites. But sometimes an animal does not seem to know the rules: does not understand that it is expected to turn the other cheek when teased or molested, and to ignore the presence of an unauthorised intruder in its cage. As a witty Frenchman, 'Théodore P. K.', wrote in *La Ménagerie* (1868):

> *Cet animal est très méchant,*
> *Quand on l'attaque il se défend.*

One July day in 1867 a youth up from the country, leaning unwisely far, let his hat fall into the bear-pit:

The circumstance does not appear to have been noticed by the visitors until the owner of the hat had the foolhardiness to descend into the pit, much to the consternation of those who observed his movements. Their alarm was increased when they saw him seized by one of the bears upon his arriving at the bottom of the pit. No sooner had this taken place when two other bears immediately came from their cave and also seized him, and began dragging him towards it. The confusion and consternation was now at its height. Many of the excited visitors threw sticks at the bears, in the vain hope that the animals might release their hold and betake themselves to their cave; but in this they were doomed to be disappointed.

In alluding to this subject, a morning contemporary says: A man will do astonishing things to recover his hat! A peculiar sentiment, seems, indeed, to attach to that objection-

'A Man seized by Bears in the Zoological Gardens'. *Illustrated Police News*, 6 July 1867

able head-dress, resembling the feeling with which an ancient Roman or Greek regarded his shield. . . . This rural enthusiast for hats would have been hugged to death, had not the keeper been at hand. That official hastened to the assistance of the foolish fellow, the bears slinking away in a moment when they heard his voice.[1]

On 11 August 1861 the *Observer* reported 'a frightful occurrence' in which a certain Harriet Ford, a married woman, lost the thumb and a finger of her right hand when bitten by a young wolf. The writer considered it 'unpardonable in the Society not to provide for the safety of those who visit the Gardens'; but Sclater quickly weighed in to point out that anyone who, in defiance of two large notices, deliberately put her fingers through the bars had only herself to blame.

More deserving of pity was a little boy of nine, who innocently took shelter from a

1. *Illustrated Police News*, 6 July 1867. Could this episode possibly have suggested the couplet quoted above?

shower too close to the bars of the leopard's cage and was badly mauled. A correspondence ensued in the *Evening Post*, in which 'THE BROTHER-IN-LAW OF THE LITTLE SUFFERER' blamed the Zoo, maintaining that there was no keeper within sight and alleging that he himself had had to rescue the child by repeatedly thrusting his umbrella down the animal's throat. On this occasion the Press sensibly supported the authorities and reprimanded the brother-in-law for his negligence.

Exotic visitors to the Zoo were almost as entertaining as was the resident fauna. In 1873 the Shah of Persia, Nasr ed-Din, came to Europe, and a year later John Murray published an English translation of the diary kept by His Majesty during his tour. The Shah was keenly interested in animals, successively visiting the 'Gardens of Wild Beasts' in Berlin, Cologne, Brussels, Paris and London. Of Regent's Park, he wrote, 'the Director of the Gardens, an old man hard of hearing, came forward, and as he knew a little French, we conversed with him'. In fact, the Shah had been expected at a different hour, and the President was not there to receive him; thus it was an elderly Fellow who had gallantly come to the rescue of poor Bartlett, innocent of French and Persian alike. The *Daily News* (23 June 1873) had a long account of the visit, from which this extract is taken:

> In the Monkey-house, the total absence of respect of persons which marks the character of the occupants was exemplified in a forcible manner. The Shah offered his stick to a monkey who, probably regarding it as a new growth of nut, seized it with avidity and wrenched it out of his Majesty's grasp. A vain attempt to crack the cane demonstrated the fact that it was not edible, and the monkey, with indignant snarls, ran off with it up the tree, and when at a safe distance sat and grinned at the King of Kings. A keeper was sent into the cage, and after some trouble succeeded in getting back the stick, which was returned to the Shah.
>
> From the monkey cage his Majesty passed in succession by the chimpanzee, the Chinese and Indian pheasant, the home of the seal and the sea-bears, where Le Comte went through his performance, the elephants, the rhinoceros, the hippopotamus, and the giraffes. There still remained much to be seen, but at this point his Majesty declared himself to be '*un peu fatigué*', a matter of small wonder under the circumstances. . . .

Less exotic perhaps, though hardly less improbable, was a party of more than a hundred elderly seamstresses:

> On Friday, by the kind permission of the Royal[1] Zoological Society, the members of the Baroness Burdett-Coutts' Sewing School, Brown's-lane, Spitalfields, were permitted to spend a day in their beautiful gardens in the Regent's Park. About 130 aged women, most of them having long passed their three score years and ten, were conveyed by the kindness of Lady Coutts by train to Chalk Farm; a short walk brought

1. The Zoological Society of London was frequently, though wrongly, described as 'Royal'.

them in sight of the gardens, and exclamations of delight at seeing green trees and beautiful flowers and breathing the fresh air were neither few nor far between.

The society's servants did their best to put the animals through their tricks, to the great delight of the old people, and the baby hippopotamus met with a large amount of amusement from them, as did the monkeys. But the amusement did not reach its highest pitch until two of the old ladies (both of them turned 80) accepted the invitation to mount the elephant for a ride. This was the signal for the rest to try their hand at mounting, and, with the exception of about half-a-dozen, every woman honoured the elephant with her patronage. Mrs Sapsford, the hon. lady superintendent of the sewing school, was indefatigable in helping them to gratify their wishes and encourage them in their fun. She had amply provided them with creature comforts for the day, and a plentiful tea awaited them on their return to the school. Singing and recitations succeeded, and the old folks, in passing a vote of thanks to Mrs Sapsford, declared they had never in their lives spent so happy a day. The ordinary visitors to the gardens seemed highly amused at the novel sight.[1]

The seventies were memorable for the building of the new lion house, in its day the finest in the world. Scherren[2] gives a detailed account of the 'flitting' (transferring) of the big cats from their squalid dens under the terrace walk to their new cages. The public was keenly interested, offering innumerable and largely futile suggestions as to how this delicate and potentially dangerous operation might be carried out: one idea was the construction of an iron tube connecting the old dens with the new. In the event the simplest means were (as our picture shows) successfully used by Bartlett and his men.

Not long after the opening of the house there occurred a battle royal between a tiger and tigress, which with possible mating in view had been placed in the same cage. Buckland, though not an eye-witness, relates what took place:

They were playing together quietly when, by accident (I suppose), the lady tiger suddenly struck one of her sharp claws completely through the septum of the gentleman tiger's nose. The male tiger immediately pulled back his head with a jerk, and the lady's claw in consequence cut its way out of the tender skin of the nose, causing naturally great pain and bleeding.

Not liking this sort of courting the male tiger immediately turned upon and pitched into his sweetheart, rolled her over, and gave her a good thrashing. There the matter would have ended, but as he was walking away the lady unwisely—and wishing to 'have the last word'—followed him and bit him in the thigh. War to the knife was then proclaimed. The male, the stronger of the two, rushed at her, rolled her over, pinned her

1. *East London Observer*, 6 September 1873.
2. *Op cit.*, pp. 155–8.

Moving the Big Cats to the new Lion House. *Illustrated London News*, 29 January 1876

by the throat, and the two, as I understand, fought most desperately. The sharp, sabre-shaped, razor-edged canines of the male tiger made a terrible wound in the female's neck, while there was plenty of blood on both sides. . . .

Hearing the fight going on with the tigers, the lions at the other end of the house thought that they too might as well have a bit of a fight on their own account. They bristled their manes and hair, lashed their tails, swore a good deal, but luckily did not pitch into each other, although a Frenchman, *to quiet them*, to use his own expression, writes, 'I ran up and down; I made great noises; I agitated my hat; I waved my handkerchief to disturb them; but they were agitated by so strong anger, that my efforts were of little effect.'[1]

In the end the tiger and tigress came close to the bars of their cage, where one of the keepers succeeded in making the former release its hold.

The first of April is a day dreaded by zoo authorities throughout the world. Dr Hediger relates that on April Fool's Day those inhabitants of Zürich who happen to be called Herr Fisch, Fräulein Wolf, and so on, are rung up and asked to call a certain number, which is that of the Zürich Zoo. After one year receiving more than a hundred such time-wasting calls, Hediger rashly anticipated the next April Fool's Day by a monitory letter to the local paper; but, as he should have foreseen, this resulted in there being more callers than ever. An article in the San Diego Zoo's periodical *Zoonooz* (May 1958), entitled 'Zoo Unintelligence', reported eight hundred such calls being received there, one of them from a Miss Ella Fant; and on 1 April 1950 the London Zoo refused even to answer the telephone.

The custom of April-fooling at zoos is an ancient one, as an extract from a newspaper of 1771 in the British Museum testifies:[2]

Yesterday being April day, two men went to the Tower to see the annual ceremony of washing the lions. On enquiring what time they would be washed they were told by a waterman in about ten minutes; he, at the same time, advised them to have a boat, as they might see better on the water. They had no sooner got into the boat but the waterman pushed them off, without any oars, and being immediately surrounded by a number of watermen in their boats, were well splashed by them for about a quarter of an hour, to the great diversion of the spectators.

The above cutting is attached to an invitation card which shows that after nearly a century the leg-pull had not staled:

TOWER OF LONDON

Please to admit the Bearer and Friend

to view the

Annual Ceremony of

WASHING THE LIONS

on Wednesday, April 1st, 1857

N.B. *It is requested that no Gratuity will be*

given to the Attendants.

Visitors admitted only at the White Gate

Percy B. Greville

1. *Land and Water*, 1 November 1879.
2. Quoted in Colin Clair's *Unnatural History*.

A somewhat similar farce occurred at Regent's Park in 1866, and one cannot but feel that the Society showed a certain lack of humour by taking the matter to court:

Old customs are not observed as once they were, but still it would seem April fooling is not quite forgotten. A ridiculous instance of the ease with which silly people are to be found was given at the Mansion House the other day—the Zoological Society prosecuting. Mr Mullens, who appeared for the Society, explained that several persons had been practising a fraud upon the public by selling tickets of admission to the Zoological Gardens. Sunday last, as everyone knew, or ought to know, was the first of April, 'All Fool's-day', and for that day those tickets were printed. They were printed upon green coloured cards, and the following was a copy:

'SUBSCRIBERS TICKETS. Admit bearer to the Zoological Gardens on Easter Sunday. The procession of the animals will take place at three o'clock, and this ticket will not be available after that hour.

(signed)   J. C. WILDBOARD, Secretary'

These tickets were sold at one penny each, and the lowness of the charge, and the probable fact of seeing all the animals—lions, tigers, bears and leopards—walking in procession at three o'clock, had the effect of drawing some 300 persons, who were foolish enough to purchase them, to the gates of the gardens. There they presented their tickets, said they had paid their penny for admission, and that they were determined to see the animals. The officials refused them admission, and told them (what was perfectly true) that they were a parcel of April fools, that admission to the gardens was never obtainable for a penny (the ordinary price being sixpence), and that no persons were admitted on a Sunday, except fellows or members of the Society and their particular friends.

This answer, however, did not satisfy the ticket-holders, who became exceedingly boisterous—so much so that it was feared a riot would ensue. Sir Richard Mayne, therefore, was communicated with, and a body of police had to be sent to convince the 300 simpletons that they really were the fools they had been represented as being. The whole affair is strongly provocative of a smile. . . .

The opening of the Zoo on Sundays to Fellows and their guests only, was over the years a continual source of irritation to the general public; but though there did exist sabbatarians who believed it to be sinful to look at animals on a Sunday,[1] Thomas Hood had missed half the point when, many years earlier, he had written in a long poem entitled 'An Open Question':

It is not plain, to my poor faith at least,
That what we christen 'Natural' on Monday,

---

1. In early days a bishop on the Council (the Bishop of Carlisle) had fought for keepers to be given the opportunity to attend Mattins.

> The wondrous history of Bird and Beast,
> Can be Unnatural because it's Sunday. . . .

For the principal reason for this regulation was that Fellows deserved certain privileges in return for their subscriptions. Moreover, it was illegal to take money at the gates on a Sunday.

Many of the Fellows treated the Zoo as a fashionable Sunday parade, and had about as little interest in zoology as have the Private Viewers of the Summer Exhibition of the Royal Academy in art. As a columnist wrote in 1869:

> The rage for the Gardens has run so far that they are looked on simply as one of the usual social markets where young ladies are exposed 'for sale', and where people greet each other with what Thackeray called the most affectionate animosity, and exchange criticisms on the dress of the period. So much has this been the case of late, that the story goes that a lady of fashion recently said to her companion, 'What a charming place the Zoo would be if it weren't for the animals!!'[1]

Another wrote sadly of 'the old Sunday at the Zoological before the name of the Fellows was legion and the style of their friends horrible.' As he saw it, the Zoo's function had been to provide an oasis on the day of rest:

> Then, those who had dinner engagements in town on the Sunday went to the Zoological Gardens in the afternoon as the nearest place where they could find coolness, shade, quiet, and tolerable imitation of greenery. Now, there is no coolness save in the vulgar women who sit on one chair and put their legs on another, lying so complacently about 'the lady who is coming back', and in the little boys in the big curly-brimmed hats, who yawp, and stare and smoke, while the large lawn is about as quiet as a parrot-house, and about as green as the Desert of Sahara.[2]

During the First World War, wounded soldiers and sailors were admitted free to the Gardens on Sundays and others in the forces and their friends on payment.[3] However, with the passing in 1932 of the Sunday Entertainments Act the taking of money at the gates became legal, and in the summer of 1940 the Gardens were opened to the public on Sunday afternoons on payment. This experiment, so rewarding financially, was continued, and in November 1957 the decision was finally taken to allow the public access on Sunday mornings also. Considerable discussion ensued in the press, and a number of Fellows resigned.[4]

In October 1874 the Zoo was shaken by an explosion: four barrels of gunpowder, which

1. *Scientific Opinion*, 30 June 1869.   2. *Morning Star*, 8 July 1867.
3. Perhaps this payment on a Sunday was temporarily legalised.
4. A full account will be found in the Report of the Council of the Z.S.L. for 1957.

Beasts at the Zoo.
Young Lady: 'Is this chair engaged?'
Perfect Gentleman (who does not stick at a lie): 'Yaas! I'm keeping it for a friend.'
John Leech, *Punch*, 16 June 1866

were being transported by barge along the Regent's Canal, blew up just under the bridge at the end of Avenue Road. A good deal of damage, most of it fortunately superficial, was done, creating 'commotion among the animals, whose howling added considerably to the excitement which the disaster caused in the neighbourhood'. A number of birds escaped, some never to return to their Ark; but no large or dangerous animal was injured or liberated, and jangled nerves were soon sedated. The Grand Junction Canal Company paid up in full, and the Society breathed again.

During the Second World War the possibility of lions and tigers at large after an air raid was to be a perpetual nightmare of the authorities, but happily this was something that the London Zoo was spared. Nuremberg, however, was not, though bands of hooligans, rather than bombs, were the immediate cause of the bestial happenings that occurred at its Zoo soon after the Armistice. I allow myself a digression—and why not?—to give some idea of what *might* have happened at Regent's Park or Whipsnade had we lost the War and been overrun. My authority is Franz Nadler, the author of an absorbing but scarifying book entitled, *Ich sah wie Nürnberg unterging*—'I saw Nuremberg die'.[1]

1. Fränkische Verlagsanstalt, Nuremberg, 1955.

In May 1945, after the bombing and capture of the city, an American armoured division was encamped in its Zoo, which lies in wooded country outside the city. It so happened that the commanding officer was an enthusiastic lover of animals; 'I'll turn my tanks on anyone who interferes with them,' he is reported to have said. Then he and his division were moved on. Hooligans who had been looting Nuremberg were at that moment encamped on the outskirts of the city, and 'no sooner was the Zoo left unprotected [wrote Nadler] than a yelling, shrieking horde of foreigners of all nations, appeared from the direction of Mögeldorf. They carried shotguns, hatchets, axes, iron railings sharpened on grindstones, and other lethal weapons, and with these they began a pitiless hunt. . . .'

First it was the turn of the bisons. They were pursued and cornered, speared to death, and their flesh cut up and roasted. Next came the thirty Sika deer, the fifteen zebus, the water buffaloes and the highland cattle—slaughtered and eaten to the accompaniment of gallons of looted alcohol. More animals, however, were killed than could be consumed, the unwanted carcasses being left to putrify. For a sadistic blood-lust had now seized the mob. Ostriches, antelopes and springboks were decapitated and their heads carried in bacchanalian procession through the suburban streets. All the camels were killed—all but Suleika, who was found at Fischbein, tied to a tree, and rescued by military police just as the murderers were whetting their knives. Two zebras let themselves out by a back door and made for the Lorenzerwald, where they caused not a little astonishment to walkers in the woods. The mob pursued the wretched animals, but in vain. They were finally recaptured by warders, and returned to the Zoo after order had been restored.

Perhaps the saddest fate was that of the brown bears. Having enticed the animals to the edge of the pit by means of scraps of bread, the murderers proceeded to lasso them with nooses of wire which cut into their flesh until the animals were strangled. Alone 'Der grosse Hans' resisted every blandishment, thus surviving to become the most admired quadruped in Bavaria.[1]

Could such things have happened in England? We shall never know.

---

1. See also a terrible account of the bombing, on 25 July 1943, of Hagenbeck's Zoo at Stellingen, in *Animals are my Life* by Lorenz Hagenbeck, pp. 216–22.

❧ 19 ❧

A very tame Wolf

THE most prolific of all zoological artists was probably Joseph Wolf (1820–99); he was for zoology what his exact contemporary, Walter Fitch, was for botany: the leading illustrator of the age in his chosen field.

Josef (or, as he later wrote it, Joseph) Wolf, the eldest son of a farmer, was born at Mörz in Rhenish Prussia. His passion for animals, especially birds, and his talent for drawing showed themselves at an early age, but his parents, like most parents, did not want their son and heir to become an artist; for one day the farm would be his. However, in the end the '*Vogelnarr*' (bird-fool)—as the villagers called him—was to have his way. After brief spells as a farm labourer, a lithographer's assistant and a 'wine-reviser',[1] he attracted the attention of a Frankfurt naturalist, Dr Rüppell, who employed him to illustrate a book he was writing on the birds of Abyssinia. This led to the youth's attending an art school in Darmstadt, and subsequently the Antwerp Academy.

'In 1848,' wrote Wolf, 'Sceptre and Crown tumbled down, and all over Europe the artists hung up their palettes and took to rifle-shooting. I made up my mind to see what London was like, so here we are.'[2] In England he soon won the friendship of the zoologists at Regent's Park and the British Museum, and of deaf old Lord Derby at Knowsley who talked 'like a gobbly turkey-cock' and was pushed around in a bath chair. Thereafter Wolf was never to lack employment, and the Zoo was of course the focal point of his activities; when he first went to draw there he was almost alone in this, but later the place was always swarming with artists. Between 1848 and 1880 he made nearly three hundred and fifty lithographs for the *Proceedings of the Zoological Society*, and many more for its *Transactions*. In addition there were a hundred watercolours for the two handsome folio volumes of *Zoological Sketches* (1861, 1867), made for the Society, and fifty-seven drawings for Gould's *Birds of Great Britain* (1873). Details of the vast number of other works illustrated by Wolf, many of them ornithological, are given at the end of Palmer's biography.

Henry Dresser, a distinguished ornithologist, claims that Landseer once said to him,

---

1. An official who visits wine-producing villages to search for concealed liquor.
2. Certain French Impressionist artists, it may be remembered, did the same at the time of the Franco-Prussian War.

Joseph Wolf in old age.
From a photograph

'Joseph Wolf is *without exception* the best all-round animal painter that ever lived. When a good many artists of the present day are forgotten, Wolf will be remembered.' Two of the Pre-Raphaelite Brotherhood—Thomas Woolner and D. G. Rossetti—also praised Wolf's minute observation, delicate precision and unswerving faithfulness to nature; but neither seems to have mentioned the word 'artist'. And alas! who now remembers Joseph Wolf?

It was certainly Landseer who saw to it that Wolf's 'Woodcocks seeking shelter', the first picture he submitted to the Royal Academy, was not only accepted but hung on the line in the summer exhibition of 1849—though if Landseer really said to Dresser what the latter alleged, then surely the Academician was exaggerating. But the savage attack on Wolf and on his biographer, A. H. Palmer,[1] which appeared in the *Saturday Review* of 14 December 1895, gives an equally distorted picture and must have deeply wounded the old painter. Landseer also once said that so full of *expression* were Wolf's ornithological paintings

1. *The Life of Joseph Wolf, Animal Painter*, Longmans, 1895. The artist must not be confused with that remarkable clergyman, Joseph Wolff, nor the former's biographer (A. H. Palmer—Samuel Palmer's son) with the latter's (H. P. Palmer). The two Wolves could hardly be more different.

that he thought he must have been a bird in a previous incarnation; to our reviewer, Wolf was, and had always been, the dreariest of sheep in sheep's clothing. Dipping his pen in vitriol, he wrote:

It is true that we find a prefatory hint that 'the story of a perfectly uneventful life . . . must often be dull reading', but torrents of eulogy overwhelm this stray eddy of mock modesty, and we find ourselves wading into the book wholly unprepared for the morasses of dullness, and the wildernesses of tedious facts about an individual as tedious as he is obscure. . . .

The endless lithographs of birds seem taken from amateur photographs in a museum rather than from drawings of live models. Each bird appears glued to an unnatural perch, and, when backgrounds are added, they suggest stage scenery. . . . These backgrounds are rendered peculiarly foolish by the author's utter lack of the sense of proportion: a Guatemala swift might be 200 yards long, and a rough-legged buzzard as big as a sphinx, did we credit the surroundings.[1] A young horned owl from Africa has below it a full moon for background, and recalls a hackneyed Christmas card. . . .

'The amusing thing,' the reviewer continues, 'is that the painter fancied that, if anything, his work was not wooden enough' to please the naturalists. Indeed, Wolf was flattered when they pronounced his pictures too 'artistic', whereas in fact many artists found them too 'scientific'. 'But both [the reviewer maintains] in a derogatory sense. We, for our part, who cherish a respect for both the artist and the naturalist, should be loth to give either name to Wolf.'

Having savaged the pictures, the reviewer again attacks the biography, which he finds 'as uninteresting as the illustrations to which it plays chorus'. Then he turns to the man himself. Whereas Palmer clearly admires his hero (whom he describes as 'sound as a bell, upright as a corporal, and with the eyes of a hawk') for dodging military service by a fiction of ill health, the reviewer equally clearly condemns him as a shirker. Finally comes the monstrously mendacious *coup de grâce*: 'Perhaps the only surprising fact revealed by the book is that a man can have lived to the age of seventy-five without encountering a single incident of interest, without contributing even in the smallest particular to our amusement, instruction, or edification.' The plain truth is that Wolf was a knowledgeable zoologist, a skilful observer, and a man of almost superhuman industry. As an artist—in the sense that Stubbs or Lear was an artist—he was almost nowhere. He was an extremely competent illustrator, but little more.

Palmer's book, though admittedly less exciting than a Le Carré thriller, is far from dull; but it should be read in a deck-chair in a country garden when the thrushes are singing. We are shown its hero in his studio, wearing his fez or his beloved tam-o'-shanter, puffing ceaselessly at his pipe and working on until he is 'giddy'. We see him painting the Queen's

1. This is completely untrue.

pet bullfinch. We see him much disliking the 'grand visits' he is obliged to make to some of the great houses of England and Scotland. 'I *hate* a Pheasant,' he told Palmer one day when the latter was collecting material for his book. 'So aristocratic, you know; so oriental. His call seems to say, "I am a Pheasant; and I am under the protection of Lord So-and-So; and I may come into your garden and scratch it all to pieces if I like, and you mustn't touch me." Put that down.' And we see him condemning the senseless slaughter of wild animals by Gordon-Cumming and his ilk, who 'have no desire to *know* about a thing. Their only desire is to kill it.'

On first arriving in London, Wolf had taken rooms in Fitzroy Square; but by stages he drew closer to the Zoo, settling finally in 1878 in a studio on Primrose Hill. It was here that Palmer came, in the early nineties, to worship and to catechise:

> In answer to the tinkle of the bell, a tall, broad-chested old gentleman appears, pipe in hand, at a door which is fringed with climbing convolvulus and ivy. Happily there is nothing 'artistic' about him, unless it be a knitted 'Tam o'Shanter' cap. His hale, upright figure is clothed in the well-cut vestments of a quietly disposed Londoner (to whom eccentricity would be as unnatural as slovenliness), and his short, grey beard and moustache are neatly trimmed. A pair of very large round spectacles rests on a nose which has the strong angular bend of the Eagle's beak about it. . . . Behind the spectacles are very kindly, true-looking, grey eyes, in which a merry twinkle is not unknown.

Here, among his drawings, his trophies, his pets and his flowers, Wolf died on 20 April 1899, in his eightieth year. He had never found time to get married.

20

Snake Troubles

She died because she never knew
These simple little rules and few;—
    The snake is living yet.

More Beasts for worse Children: the Python, Hilaire Belloc

THE serpent got off to a bad start, and it has never recovered the ground it lost in the Garden of Eden. 'No beast,' wrote Norman Douglas in *Alone*, 'provokes human hatred like that old coiling serpent. Long and cruel must have been his reign for the memory to have lingered—how many years? Let us say, in order to be on the safe side, a million.' An attempt once made by a little group of religious maniacs to banish original sin by plying the snakes in the terrarium of the Basel Zoo with pious tracts proved unsuccessful.

Bartlett found it 'consoling to know how few people are injured or killed by these creatures'; but the fact remains that they still account for the deaths every year of between thirty and forty thousand people, mostly in Burma and India. The individual Guinness record is, however, held by a Rhodesian black mamba with a bag of eleven humans to its credit. Perhaps by 'people' Bartlett—like so many Englishmen in those far-off days when we ruled the world—meant '*English* people'. Conservationists would naturally be reluctant to see the extinction of any species, however vicious. But to the inhabitants of Indian forests or the banks of African crocodile-infested streams there may well seem a case for removing from general circulation and closely confining such species as threaten their daily lives. It is very agreeable that we were able to send Père David's deer to China, where they had become extinct; but as someone has pointed out, English conservationists have shown no great eagerness to reintroduce the timber wolf into the home counties, where it flourished until our brutal ancestors hunted it to death.

Where snakes are concerned, we in England are fortunate in having only the adder to fear. On the average there is in this country hardly more than one death in a decade from its bite; there is far less chance of being killed by an adder than of being struck by lightning. As for Ireland—well, St Patrick, as everyone knows, drove its snakes out long ago.

In the summer of 1849 the old carnivora house—a seventy-foot long building in the Swiss chalet style—was converted into a reptile house, reptiles having previously been tucked away in boxes where they were barely visible. This was the first building of its kind in the world, and in it twenty-one different species, principally snakes, were displayed in large glass-fronted cases provided with branches of trees and given at all events 'comparative liberty'. It continued in use until 1883 when a new house, described by Chalmers Mitchell as 'in many respects the worst that was ever built', was erected with the blood money from the sale of Jumbo.

The public were soon flocking to see the seventeen-foot-long African boa constrictor, the deadly puff-adders, the rattle-snake with young born in captivity, and the tree-frogs. In general there was approval; but the animals had to be fed (though only once a week), and thus visitors became for the first time aware that their diet consisted of *live* ducks, rabbits, rats, mice, and other birds and small mammals. One correspondent protested about this in the columns of the *Athenaeum* (15 December 1849), and so did Dickens in *Household Words*; but these were still voices crying in the wilderness, and nearly twenty years were to pass before their challenge found support elsewhere.

Soon, however, it became apparent that all was not well with the staff of the new reptile

The First Reptile House (1849). *Illustrated London News*, 2 June 1849

house, and possibly the two above-mentioned protesters may have seen a certain poetical justice in the death, several years later, of Edward Girling, 'head keeper of the serpent room', from the bite of the Zoo's most recent acquisition, a hooded cobra.

Edward Horatio Girling, aged thirty-one, had been a guard on the Eastern Counties railway before joining the staff of the Zoo. He may have been qualified to deal (when sober) with trains, but events were to show that he should never have been put in charge of poisonous snakes. The circumstances of his death were reported in *The Times* (23 October 1852):

> Edward Stewart, one of the attendants of the humming-bird collection, said that he helped Gurling [sic] in the mornings, and had been with him on the evening preceding his death; he was also present when the fatal accident took place, and was going out of the room with a basket of sparrows, a little after 8 o'clock, when the deceased, who was in an excited state, walked inside of the railing which fenced off the compartments in which the serpents are confined, and lifting up the glass front took out a Morocco snake by the middle.

The Second Reptile House (1883). *Illustrated London News*, 8 September 1883

Another man entered the room at the time, and witness, turning round to Gurling, said, 'For God's sake put it back again!' He replied, 'I am inspired,' and laughed at witness. He then laid the snake round the shoulder of witness, who stooped down, and said, 'It will bite me in a minute'; after which he put it back. Witness then walked down the room, going on with his work, when the deceased, who was close beside him, inside the railing, exclaimed, 'Now for the cobra!' Witness called out, 'Good God! what are you about?' but he had the cobra out before he could prevent him, and put it under his waistcoat. It coiled round his waist and came out behind. When taking hold of it, about a foot from the head with one hand, and with the other lower down, he held it up in front of his face. It then flew at him, and witness saw the blood flowing from the bridge of his nose. Gurling said to him, 'Run for Hunt,' and he ran off accordingly.

How long he was away he could not tell, being in a maze, but deceased must have put the snake back in the interval, for he was in his compartment and the front glass closed down. Witness was perfectly sober at the time. He had seen deceased excited with drink once or twice before, but never so bad, and when he was intoxicated he generally went home. They had been together all night, and had not slept at all. They went to see a friend of Gurling's who was going to Australia, and there they had three pints of beer; after which they went to a public-house in Shoe-lane. Gurling was not tipsy when he got back to the gardens, but was in an excited state. They had a quartern of gin at the public-house in Shoe-lane, another afterwards, and again another at 8 o'clock. . . .

Girling was rushed in a cab to University College Hospital; but 'artificial respiration and galvanism' proved unavailing, and an hour later he died.

Various facts emerged at the inquest. Girling's widow assured the Coroner that her husband was a most sober man—except when drunk—and another witness testified that both Stewart and Girling had been drunk at the time. The Coroner said that some one should have sucked the wounds immediately, and, safe in the knowledge that his bravado could not be put to the test, added that 'he would not, had he been present, have hesitated to do so'. David Mitchell, the Secretary, explained that there was an alleged antidote to snake bites, called *Libama Cedron*, but that he personally had little faith in it; Girling had been provided with it but had not used it. The jury returned a verdict to the effect that 'the deceased had lost his life by the bite of a serpent known as cobra de capella [cobra di capello], when in a state of intoxication, and in consequence of his own rashness and indiscretion'.

A spate of letters, many of them from Anglo-Indians, informed readers of *The Times* how the situation should have been handled. 'A Constant Reader' spoke highly of the use of a cupping-glass, whereas 'Fanny Parkes' had found a 'teaspoonful of eau de luce[1] in a wine-glass of water' efficacious in the case of her Indian groom. The latter treatment met with the approval of 'E.St J.M.', who when a cornet in the 22nd Light Dragoons and

1. Eau de Luce (from *Luce*, the name of the inventor), a compound of mastic, alcohol, oil of lavender, oil of amber, and aqua ammoniae. It is stimulant and antispasmodic.

quartered at Bangalore had witnessed it successfully applied to a servant 'bitten in the great toe by a venomous snake'. One correspondent pointed out that in such cases sleep was always fatal, and that he had seen a life saved by two sepoys ceaselessly dragging the victim up and down a verandah for three-and-a-half hours. Almost all the writers also recommended enormous quantities of rum or gin—a remedy which in Girling's case had already been administered.[1] Old wives' remedies, such as burying the victim up to his neck in manure, received no mention; nor did one which in the nineteenth century still made sense: 'Death,' wrote F. B. Simson, was certain in the case of the cobra bite, 'except perhaps if a bystander should have an axe in his hand and should chop off the limb a good way above the bite'.[2]

Most verbose of those who rushed into print after Girling's death was a Mr D. Wilson, who begged leave 'to occupy a small space' (his letter ran to two thousand words) to recommend and quote extensively from *Wirkungen des Schlangengiftes*, the *magnum opus* of a certain Dr Constantine Hering of Philadelphia. Hering principally advocated holding a red-hot iron or lump of burning coal (or, failing that, a lighted cigar) close to the wounds 'until the patient begins to shudder or stretch. If this should occur soon, continue the application for an hour if he can bear it.' At the same time he should be persuaded to swallow a variety of unattractive substances such as gunpowder, arsenic, phosphoric acid and mercury, though brandy might also be tried.

And so on. But the surgeon at University College Hospital was not impressed. While admitting that he had never heard of Dr Hering or his book, he yet begged leave to doubt whether even the Doctor's last desperate remedy—the use of a second snake 'to neutralise the poison of the first, and so bite the man back again to life and health'—would have succeeded where he had failed. 'Though Mr Wilson may deeply lament the omission,' he added, 'I am inclined to hope that the public will believe the time to have been better employed.'

With the arrival of the great ant-eater, the troubles in the reptile house were soon forgotten. Year after year the snakes continued to be fed with live animals every Friday in the presence of an unprotesting, indeed enthusiastic, audience which usually included a fair number of small children. But the climate of opinion had gradually been changing, for when, on 17 May 1869, 'TELAM' wrote to *The Times* to condemn this barbarity he lit a great fire which continued to smoulder over the years, periodically to burst into flames, and finally to burn the Zoo down:

Sir,—The English sometimes boast of their humanity, and as a characteristic of their nation. But does bull fighting for instance, or even vivisection, present an idea more

1. Buckland, who several years later absorbed at second hand a small amount of venom while dissecting a rat that had been bitten by a cobra, gives a horrifying account of his experience; he failed to find any eau de Luce, but saved his life by ammonia and more than half a bottle of brandy.
2. *Letters on Sport in Eastern Bengal*, 1886.

repugnant, more inhuman than the spectacle offered at the Zoological-gardens of trembling rabbits devoured by a serpent?—a monster reptile maintained and thus feasted for the pleasure of the English—for their children, in many of whom the duty of humanity can only be inculcated in early life by enforcing tenderness towards the harmless part of the brute creation—God's way, if we would but bear in mind, to teach the infant his first and may be his best lesson. . . .

I firmly believe, could the question be put to the vote, a majority of the public would be contented with a stuffed boa, if once informed of the reason why only a dead reptile was presented to their gaze. Then let us in the name of all that is kindly—aye, and wise— consign this exhibition to the same grave as cock-fighting, bull and bear baiting. . . .

The Times, unlike the *Daily Telegraph* in those 'Muddle at the Zoo' days already described, was pleasantly impartial in the letters it chose for publication. To 'Y' the issue seemed simple enough: 'God made the boa. God made the rabbit, and God made one to prey on the other.' And how about man?

Does he never fatten upon rabbits? Does he never cut the throats of sheep and pigs, poleaxe oxen, bleed calves to death, wring the necks of fowls, tear the entrails of fish with barbed hooks, and boil lobsters alive, that he may subsist upon their miserable corpses? Away, then, with the wretched cant about the inhumanity of the 'spectacle offered at the Zoological Gardens of trembling rabbits devoured by a serpent' . . .

'H' warmly supported 'TELAM', stressing as the worst aspect of the case that this feeding was done in the presence of '"sweet little dears" of both sexes, who accompany their friends and parents'. 'V', balancing the arguments sensibly, agreed with 'Y' that God intended boas to eat rabbits, but reminded him that it was not

a Divine ordinance that a rabbit should be shut up in a cage with a snake without any chance of his life, deprived of the means of escape allotted to him by nature, and subject to the exquisite torture of terror prolonged by factitious circumstances and enhanced by despair. . . . Further, it is no part of the Divine ordinance that his sufferings should be witnessed by nursemaids and children. . . . To say that a process is the result of natural laws is one thing; to say that men ought to derive pleasure from the frequent contemplation of it is another. By Divine ordinance we have eyes; by Divine ordinance we have also the minds to regulate their use.

'W. Matchwick', a zoologist writing from the South Kensington Museum, maintained that no cruelty was involved: 'On the contrary, there is much to instruct and to wonder at.' It was easy, he said, to see that the little victims enjoyed almost every moment of it— the rabbits frisking about in the cage, the little birds 'flitting and fluttering all round'— until in a flash their lives came to a painless end. As for substituting dead animals for living (as one writer had suggested)—'You might as well offer a python a plumcake as a dead kid'.

Boa Constrictor and Rabbit. Beata Francis, *The Child's Zoological Garden*, 1880

Finally came a letter from 'Frank Haes' telling of happy, carefree mice 'nibbling the nose of a snake that did not seem inclined to devour them at once. . . . You will perhaps allow me to mention that the snakes are only fed on Fridays at 7 p.m., that the doors are closed, and that persons wishing to be present must make especial application to the reptile keeper. So much, therefore, for a public exhibition of cruelty.'

It was generally believed at that time that snakes would not touch dead food, and if Frank Haes was speaking the truth about those closed doors, the public seemed to have small cause for complaint. But was he? There can be little doubt that the keeper of the reptile house had an accessible palm, and that the feeding could be seen by all who greased it; moreover, it was later to be established that snakes could almost always be brought to accept freshly-killed animals.

Bartlett remained in general deaf to all entreaties to change his method of feeding his serpents; but at some unspecified moment he yielded to a request from tender-hearted women and children to substitute house mice for the white mice normally used. Why less cruelty was thus involved is not clear, and he may well have been motivated by economy rather than by compassion. He was soon, however, to discover his mistake: brown mice (unlike white), if not killed directly, gnawed their way out, thus providing a hole through which snakes could escape:

> The keeper of the reptile house came to me one day and told me that he had missed one of the cobras. I examined the empty cobra case, and found a mouse-hole in the corner leading into the water-viper's case. The water-viper appeared to have lately fed and to be well filled out, and I had some misgivings that the lost cobra, in creeping through the mouse-hole, had been caught and swallowed by the water-viper. The fear, coupled with the anxiety of thinking that so dangerous a serpent as a cobra was at liberty, caused me to determine to settle the question at once. I had the water-viper killed and, upon examination, found the nearly digested cobra. . . .

Though there is indeed a professional snake-eating snake—the king cobra (or hamadryad) —such acts of cannibalism in other snakes are usually the result of a misunderstanding. In 1894 a nine-foot boa-constrictor in Regent's Park swallowed an eight-foot boa-constrictor when the two began simultaneously to eat the same pigeon from opposite ends. The larger snake 'gradually enveloped, not only the bird, but the head of the other snake. Once begun, the swallowing process would go on almost mechanically.'[1] The swallower suffered no permanent ill effects, though it became lethargic and for many weeks showed no interest in food.

This sad story provoked the exchange of the two following letters:

To Mr Abraham Bartlett, 13 November 1894:

Dear Sir,—I should take it as a favour if you would be good enough to settle a wager,

1. *The Times*, 23 October 1894.

by letting me know by return if there be any serpent that can swallow a horse. Thanking you in anticipation and apologizing for the trouble,

Truly yours
S.M.

Mr Abraham Bartlett to S.M., 14 November 1894:
Sir,—There is no serpent living capable of swallowing a horse, or an ass.

Yours faithfully
A.D.B.

A python is on record as having swallowed a four-foot leopard, and another disposed of a 130-lb impala; but this is probably about the maximum any snake can manage.

In December 1869 James Edmonds, the proprietor of Wombwell's Menagerie, was summoned before the Liverpool magistrates for causing a live rabbit to be fed to a python; but Mr Horace Mansfield, the presiding magistrate, 'was compelled to decide—and he could not do otherwise—that a rabbit was not a domestic animal within the meaning of the Act of Parliament', and though 'strongly expressing his own abhorrence of the whole proceeding' he was obliged to dismiss the case.[1]

The editor of the *Daily Telegraph*, a paper that was soon, as we know, to become the Zoo's bitterest enemy, seized the opportunity to devote a leading article to the subject, painting a horrifying picture of the anguish suffered by the rabbit but directing his attack principally at the London Zoo and at those sadists who went to the reptile house 'to gloat over the death-throes of an inoffensive little creature'. He begged that an attempt be made to discover whether reptiles would accept dead animals. Edmonds replied that this was out of the question. If it was cruel (which he very much doubted) to give a live rabbit to a python, was it not even more cruel to allow a python slowly to starve to death? And there, for the time being, the matter rested.

In 1878 the *Whitehall Review* attempted to fan the embers once more into flame with an article entitled 'Sepoyism at the Zoo' in which the Zoological Society is begged to do its 'dirty sacrifice'—if do it, it must—in private. 'The *abattoir* has not yet become a raree show in this country, and vivisection is done on the sly. We protest against an exhibition which combines the devilry of an Inferno with the hideous details of the shambles and torture-trough.' But it was left to *The Animal World—A Monthly Advocate of Humanity*,[2] to make (in 1881) the most savage indictment to date of the Zoo, by publishing extracts from no less than forty letters attacking the Society in general and its Secretary, Sclater, in particular

1. The first Protection of Animals Act (1822), which led to the founding two years later of the R.S.P.C.A., dealt principally with cruelty to domestic animals. Further important and more comprehensive legislation was passed in 1911 and 1964, and over the years there have been many other Acts dealing with particular problems. The R.S.P.C.A. issues an informative leaflet, *Cruelty to Animals and the Law*.
2. The organ of the R.S.P.C.A.

for tolerating the public display of this cruelty. All tell the same story of the long-drawn-out agonising deaths of the victims and of the sadistic pleasure taken in them by the spectators (one writer noted thirty-nine children among the hundred and forty-five persons present); such a wealth of detailed evidence could not be shrugged off as merely the fanaticism of one or two cranks.

To these charges, Sclater replied:

1. That there was no cruelty in the practice conducted under his direction in the reptile-house every week during feeding-time.
2. That there was no attempt made by the management to attract persons to the gardens, by advertising the feeding-time in the reptile-house, and by making such occasions sensational as shows.
3. That the serpents living in the reptile-house could not be kept in health unless living prey be given to them.
4. That it was necessary for educational and scientific purposes to preserve ophidians in menageries.
5. That this spectacle of serpent-feeding in the reptile-house was not repulsive and demoralising, but was a reasonable and desirable source of healthy amusement [sic] to children and young persons.

But *The Animal World* had won, and at the next Meeting of the Council it was decreed that henceforth the reptiles would be fed after closing-time. As one writer put it, Medea was in future to slay her children 'off-stage'.

However, this was only the first round of the fight; in 1894 the *Echo* opened the second by giving publicity to a correspondence on the subject of whether, even in private, the practice of live feeding could be tolerated. Most of the arguments adduced were already familiar, though the field of discussion was now widened. Further, whereas the forty who wrote to *The Animal World* all adopted the same attitude, the *Echo* was impartial. How, asked one writer, could those who condone grouse-shooting, eat oysters, and celebrate Christ's birthday by a 'gigantic slaughter of geese and turkeys', wax so indignant at the cruelty of the boa? Perhaps the most valuable fact to emerge—if fact it be—was that during the siege of Paris in the Franco-Prussian War French snakes had learnt to accept dead meat.

Then, once again, snake-feeding vanished for a time from the headlines.

The final act of this drama was to take place in the opening years of the twentieth century, and in order to describe it we must anticipate an important event which had meanwhile occurred: the appointment of a new secretary.

As the old century drew towards its close it became increasingly evident that radical changes were needed at the Zoo; but so long as the Sclater-Bartlett duumvirate continued to rule, nothing could be done. In 1897 Bartlett died—still in harness in his eighty-fifth year, but only to be succeeded by his son Clarence, who had virtually been acting for him for some time past. Clarence is described by Sir Peter Chalmers Mitchell in his *Centenary History* as quite second-rate—'a sycophant with his superiors and a bully with his inferiors'; the situation, already bad, now became worse. A great deal of general unpleasantness ensued, and further personal attacks made on Sclater led to his resignation in 1902; that of Clarence Bartlett, already a very sick man, followed a few months later.

Sclater had also hoped to be succeeded by his son, who was at that time director of the Museum at Cape Town; this too would have been a mistake, for what was needed was a complete break with the past. Young Sclater was, in fact, temporarily so appointed by a Selection Committee; but his appointment had to be ratified at the Annual General Meeting, and he was then outvoted by the supporters of Chalmers Mitchell, who was to hold the position with great distinction for more than thirty years.[1] So a second Mitchell to the fight and to the rescue came, under whom it was possible for a new team to clear up the mess and give the Zoo a fresh and a better image.

One of the new secretary's first tasks was to deal with the still smouldering situation in the reptile house. Chalmers Mitchell tells his story so well that it seems best to give it, slightly abbreviated, in his own words:

When I became Secretary of the Society in 1903, I found that the reptiles were fed in private on Friday afternoons, and living animals, except frogs, were not always given. On the other hand, there is no doubt but that a gratuity to the keeper secured a rabbit being put into the cage of a python, and particular visitors were even treated to the spectacle of a goat being seized. Behind the scenes living prey was used freely. I stopped all public exhibitions of the kind, and gave orders that except in cases of necessity, the feeding in private should be done only on animals already killed.

But the practice of long years here and elsewhere, and the authority of those who themselves had kept living reptiles, was against my view, not only then but for long afterwards. On the one hand, I was told that I was killing the snakes because of a silly sentimentalism; on the other, from time to time, violent attacks were made on our supposed practices by various organisations and by individual Fellows of the Society. I took the line, supported by the Council, of being ready to explain our practice to any Fellows, or to responsible people for their private information, but I declined to place the Society in the position of appearing to have been bullied into treating our animals according to the views of persons who had no responsibility for them.

In the meantime, I used every opportunity of making personal observations in the United States and in various Zoological Gardens on the Continent so that I could amplify the knowledge I could gain here, from my own study of the actual practice, and not merely the professions of other institutions. There was then no Curator of

1. In spite of protests by some of the Fellows, Sclater was awarded a pension larger than the initial salary of his successor.

Reptiles, superintendence of the house being part of the duty of Mr Pocock, the Superintendent of the Gardens, the actual work being done by the keeper, J. Tyrell, who had been with us for many years and was extremely competent in the management of reptiles. Quite certainly he did not believe in giving killed food, [and] laughed at the idea that the animals used suffered more when they were killed by reptiles than when they were seized and killed by his own staff.

I was in some doubt as to the strictness of his interpretation of the order that the 'snakes were to be fed on dead animals wherever possible'. And so from the beginning of May to the end of October, 1907, I arranged that I myself or Mr Pocock, or both of us together, should be present every week during the feeding of the reptiles and make notes and observations. We published the results of our observations in a joint paper in the Proceedings of the Society (*Proc. Zool. Soc. Lond.*, 1907, pp. 785–94). I quote the summary of our record from that memoir:—

'It will be noticed that throughout the many months over which our observations extended, our snakes fed with great regularity, and at much shorter intervals than is generally reported, especially in the case of the pythons. It is also noteworthy that we found no species of snake, poisonous or non-poisonous, that would not take dead food, and that it was unnecessary to give live food to any individual snake. In these respects, however, other observers of at least equal experimental enthusiasm, have had a smaller measure of success in inducing snakes to take dead prey. Private persons who have kept snakes, and Directors of Zoological Gardens in Europe and America, have spoken to us of getting only one snake in four to take dead food. We set it down, therefore, not as a matter of scientific fact that all snakes can be persuaded to this non-natural form of diet, but as one of some interest that with the large collection in the Society's Gardens we have been, and hope to continue to be, more uniformly successful in this mode of feeding reptiles than have been the owners of any other public or private collections with the exact details of which we are acquainted.'. . . .

Meantime, the agitation against our supposed behaviour blew up into a gale. I was always ready to explain, and frequently did explain, our rules to any person who wished to know what they were, for his private information. But I continued to refuse to make an official reply to outside bodies which they could publish, and above all I declined to issue any statement which could be used in condemnation of other Zoological Gardens which might use other methods of feeding.

Also, it happened that our own reptiles during these years were not living well; they frequently refused to feed; I refused to relax my rules although the keepers begged me to do so, and were supported by Dr Plimmer, then our pathologist, an able microscopist who, however, had some extraordinary half metaphysical belief that some virtue passed from the living prey to the creature that devoured it. Questions were asked in the House of Commons as to why the Society was not prosecuted; letters and articles of an amusing violence were published, a famous one, afterwards reprinted under the title 'Secrets of the Reptile House', denounced me personally as well as the alleged practices of the Society. I suppose it was trying, but I survived.

In 1911, Mr E. G. Boulenger was appointed Curator of Reptiles, and I explained the general position and my rule to him. He told me frankly that he did not believe in it, but, of course, undertook to do his best to carry it out with absolute strictness. In a few months he was convinced that to get reptiles to take dead food was almost entirely a matter of skill and patience, on the one hand, and on the other of their being warm and in full activity at feeding times. He introduced various improvements into the house, and arranged that on feeding days the furnaces should be stoked a little more vigorously. With his concurrence, I was able, after a few months, to open the house on Fridays during the hours of feeding, by which those who cared for the spectacle, certainly interesting, if rather disgusting, could see the snakes taking their already killed food, and unbelievers be convinced from actual observation what our practice really was. . . .

My rule about no living prey being given except with special and direct authority is faithfully kept, and permission has to be given only in the rarest cases, these generally of very delicate or new-born snakes which are given new-born mice, creatures still blind and entirely unconscious of their surroundings.[1]

A third reptile house—the one still in use—was built in 1927. 'Today,' says Hancocks, 'it looks quaintly archaic with its neo-classical façade, reminiscent of some provincial railway station, with rather bored and elegant crocodiles lounging in the pristine waiting rooms.' But it is still a very serviceable building and will probably have to wait some time before being replaced.

1. *Centenary History*, pp. 224–8.

21

Eighties and Nineties

AFTER the sensation caused by the sale of Jumbo to America in 1882, public interest in the Zoo, though aroused from time to time by the arrival of some unusual acquisition, was in general to wane for more than two decades. In 1887 the attendance was the lowest for twenty years; the annual income declined; and if in the later nineties the number of Fellows appeared to rise, this was only because (it was later discovered) quite a lot of those still listed had in fact been dead for many years. As has already been told, Sclater and Bartlett were impatient of criticism, too set in their ways to move with the times and too arrogant to give ear to criticism. It was not until the advent in 1903 of Chalmers Mitchell that the rot was arrested and the Zoo began to march triumphantly forward into the twentieth century. But before the end of the nineteenth there were to be further innovations at Regent's Park.

In 1870 the Society had received a legacy of £2,000 (reduced by legacy duty to £1,800) from one of its Fellows, Mr Alfred Davis. The interest on this was at first used to support the publication of the *Zoological Record*—a notable comprehensive bibliography of zoological literature including abstracts and a full index. But in 1874 the Council decided, in spite of opposition from some of the Fellows, to divert it to the promotion of courses of 'popular' lectures throughout the summer months. They were to be given twice weekly, and without additional charge to those who had already paid for admission to the Gardens. The lecturers, says Scherren, were eminent zoologists, the subjects varied and well chosen; but the experiment, though persisted in for many years, failed—because the experts, as so often happens, could not find the 'wave-length' of their audiences. Of the inaugural lecture, given by Sclater, the *Echo* said:

> The beasts did not personally attend, as some of the junior portion of the audience obviously expected, and their feelings would have been hurt had they done so to find themselves constantly described as 'specimens' of their respective classes and species, without any attempt at those personal sketches of character and biography to which many of them might, not unreasonably, have aspired. Even the lamented Joe was referred to as 'an Anthropoid Ape' of the 'Species Chimpanzee', and the affecting narrative

of his last moments, given by a contemporary, was trivially touched upon as 'sensational'.[1]

On one occasion, however, the animals *did* attend, for Sclater made an innovation by talking about the big cats in their own home, the new lion house, instead of in the formal and depressing surroundings of the lecture hall:

> The quadrupeds themselves seemed to take a great interest in the proceedings and, as though instinctively aware that something concerning them was going on, not only kept in front of their cages during the delivery of the lecture, but from time to time sought to testify their appreciation by applauding roars. Indeed, it was noticed that by some peculiar divination on the part of the beasts, or else by telegraphic signals communicated by the keepers, each class of the great felidae passed under review began to utter remarks in its native tongue directly its name was mentioned.[2]

But the lion house was the only venue in the Gardens suitable for such treatment, and in the lecture hall the addresses were less attractive to the layman. Take, for example, Sclater on Waterfowl, thus reported in *Nature*:

> Of the whole number of 174 generally recognised species of Anatidae, 77 may, I think, be best set down as Arctic, although some of them, such as *Tadorna rutila*, *Fuligula rufina*, and *Marmaronetta angustirostris*, cannot be strictly so termed, as they inhabit only the temperate portion of the Palæarctic region. Very many of the Palæarctic species also, as will be noted below, go far south in winter, and intrude into the Æthiopian, Indian, and Neotropical regions. . . .[3]

What could an ardent but ignorant young zoophile have made of that?

Throughout the lean later eighties, as the Zoo steadily declined in popularity, lectures became fewer, duller, yet more poorly attended. Then in 1887, in the hope of augmenting its dwindling annual income, the Society decided to make a separate charge for admission to them. This was all that was needed to seal their fate, and five years later—to the undisguised satisfaction of the small band of earnest Fellows who had always resented the legacy being squandered on what it considered the mere entertainment of the public—the money reverted to supporting the publication of the *Zoological Record*.

In March 1889 Regent's Park acquired a mermaid—or rather, a merboy—from Demerara: a year-old male infant not much more than a yard in length. The authorities called it a manatee; the public, who flocked to see it, knew better. . . . It was not, in fact, the first manatee to reach this country; but it got some splendid publicity.

The Order *Sirenia*—the sea-cows or sirens—comprises the dugongs, allegedly the mermaids of classical mythology, and the manatees, the mermaids which renaissance voyagers

1. 15 April 1874.   2. *Daily Express*, 25 May 1877.
3. *Nature*, 20 July 1880, quoted by Scherren.

found in the tropical coastal waters and river estuaries of the African and American shores of the Atlantic. A third genus, the immense Steller's Sea-cow, found by Bering in 1742 in large quantities near the Strait that commemorates him, was believed to have been exterminated in 1768. In 1962, however, the crew of a Russian whaler reported the sighting of half a dozen twenty-foot marine animals, which from the description given would appear to have been the allegedly extinct monsters.

Columbus was the first to report factually upon the manatee, three of which he saw off Haiti in January 1493, but only to dismiss it as 'not half so beautiful as old Horace's'.[1] To be honest, the beauty of sea-cows is in the eye of the beholder, and their 'singing' (horrid snufflings) unlikely to lure any sensible sailor to his destruction. In fact, Thomas Beddoes seems to be differentiating between manatee and mermaid when he wrote:

> The dolphin wheels, the sea-cows snort,
> And unseen Mermaids' pearly song
> Comes bubbling up, the weeds among. . . .[2]

Once the manatee had been discovered, no seaman worth his salt dared to return from the New World without reporting a sighting of one, even in waters far too chill to sustain it, and soon no cabinet of curios was considered complete without its shrivelled fish-and-monkey fake.[3] Take, for example, John Smith of Pocahontas fame, who in 1610 saw 'with these my own eyes' off the coast of Newfoundland 'a marine monster' swimming swiftly towards him: 'Lovely was her shape; eyes, nose, ears, cheeks, mouth, neck, forehead, and the whole face was that of the fairest maiden; her hair, of azure hue, fell over her shoulders. . . .' And then take a look at the picture in the *Graphic* of Regent's Park's manatee alongside the mermaid of fiction.

How on earth, then, did this extraordinary myth arise? There are, it must be conceded, certain human qualities in sea-cows, and even Columbus managed to find something human in the manatee's homely face. First, 'married' couples are touchingly faithful and devoted to one another (this was formerly considered to be a human characteristic). Then the female sea-cow has breasts placed as in the human body, and when she took her pink infant in her 'arms' to suckle it, even the most stonyhearted sailor thought of home and shed a tear. Finally, the sea-cow too can weep: or rather, when excited, a tear-like secretion streams from her eyes. Thus was the myth born; wishful thinking did the rest.

The first attempt to transport a live manatee to Europe—a young female caught off Puerto Rico—had been made in 1866; but ten days out to sea she died. A little later Clarence Bartlett was despatched to Surinam to collect another infant, for some unknown reason

1. The myth dates back to at least the third century B.C.
2. *Death's Jest-Book.*
3. In the nineteenth century the ingenious Japanese did a roaring trade in these. (See Carrington, *op. cit.*, chapter 1.)

'"Real and Ideal"—A Suggestion which occurred to our Artist on seeing
the new Manatee at the Zoological Gardens.' *Graphic*, 18 May 1889

named Patchly. On board it seemed to thrive, accepting fresh goat's milk from a bottle
and an occasional banana; but it too died, as the ship entered the English Channel. Then
in 1875 one actually reached Regent's Park alive from Demerara. Its arrival was, however,
badly timed, for the public had already chosen as its 'lion' of the season a pair of giant
tortoises from the Seychelles; and within five weeks it was dead.

In 1878 another manatee reached Glasgow and continued its journey to London by
train, buckets of hot water being in readiness at every halt along the line. It was taken to
the Westminster Aquarium, where it went on hunger strike; but after forcible feeding with
a mixture of milk and castor oil (someone had suggested it might be constipated) it suddenly
began to eat prodigious quantities—about 100 lbs a day—of very expensive French lettuce,
scornfully rejecting cheaper English cabbage. It showed little gratitude, choosing to sleep
by day and eat all night; but those fortunate enough to catch a glimpse of it awake reported
'a cunning leer' in its eye, in which 'elephantine roguery seemed mingled with porcine
obstinacy'. Then one December morning of that same year it was discovered, high and
dry and very cold, in an empty tank. Had its keeper left the waste plug improperly fixed?

Or had the manatee attempted suicide? We shall never know. But thereafter it began to languish, and with the coming of the first crocus it died.

The public is an unpredictable animal. It had been given more than one opportunity to see a manatee, but it had not responded. In 1889, however, it suddenly became manatee-conscious and rushed to Regent's Park to welcome the newcomer, which survived until the end of July.[1]

Some of those who came to the Zoo thought that the mermaid[2] must be a reptile—because, for convenience, it had been given a tank in the reptile house. Others were sure that, since it lived in the water, it was a fish; and so, perhaps, were the members of the New York Ichthyophagous Club, who included manatee cutlets in the menu of one of their club dinners.[3] In fact the manatee is an archaic elephant that took to the water; it is, along with the hyrax and the rhinoceros, the elephant's closest living relative. Like the elephant it is a vegetarian, consuming large quantities of water-weed and using its 'hands'—another human touch—to direct the food to its mouth. And here it employs an ingenious instrument: a prehensile, cloven, fleshy upper lip which can grasp the food independently of the lower; Alfred Garrod, when lecturing on the manatee, used to demonstrate this by means of two bolsters operated by a cord.

The papers of the day were full of the new arrival. The reporter of the *Globe* wrote:

> He has no ears apparently, no voice, no temper, and but very little intellect. But he is tractable, gentle, and not incapable of affection. His daily routine at present is to have his house and himself thoroughly washed every morning and his tank refilled. He is sponged and rubbed all over, submitting passively, and permitting himself to be turned this way and that and laid on his back as if he were in unconscious slumber or enjoyed the ceremony rather than otherwise. . . .

Being obliged to come constantly to the surface to breathe, the manatee catnaps at the bottom of the tank, its hands neatly folded across its chest like a Muslim acknowledging a greeting. But none of the articles drew attention to one of the oddest things about the manatee: unlike almost every other mammal in the world it has *eight* neck vertebrae. Why the extra one?

At Georgetown manatees have for many years helped to keep the pools in the Botanic Garden free from weed; however, an attempt made in 1960 to persuade them to clear the country's choked waterways of water hyacinth met with little success. The manatee may be stupid, but it refuses to be pushed around; and that, no doubt, is one reason why it

---

1. Since 1889 the London Zoo has exhibited eight further manatees. Two which were there when the Second World War broke out, had to be shot. One acquired in 1955 lived on for six years; this was the last, and so far as is known there is none in any British Zoo at the present time.
2. It was, as we have already said, a male.
3. In Guyana the flesh of the manatee was considered so nasty that it was given to slaves.

Sally the bald-headed Chimpanzee.
Photograph by J. F. Nott in *Wild Animals Described*, 1886

has rarely survived for long in captivity. And for how long will it survive in the wild? For today it is being persecuted, and in a letter to the *Guardian* (3 October 1974) captioned 'Man's inhumanity to Manatees' Nigel Sitwell, Director of Information of the World Wildlife Fund, appealed to 'the British soldiers stationed at Belize (and, of course, other people as well)' to stop hunting it—before it is too late.

One of the Zoo's most celebrated inhabitants in the nineteenth century, and certainly its most famous chimpanzee, was the bald-headed Sally, who lived at Regent's Park from 1883 to 1891. She had a nice sense of fun:

> At this moment in the Zoo, an acquisition in anthropoid circles holds well-attended *levées*, and is daily enlarging a wide list of acquaintances. Sally, a highly cultivated chimpanzee of tender years, amiable temper, and affectionate disposition, has become an adept in tricks, and a madcap romp in amusements with the friendly, and particularly with her keeper. At the rate of education she is now keeping pace with, her accomplishments may be worth a separate biography a few years hence.
>
> Some time ago, Sally displayed a diplomatic tact for feminine but unworthy objects for which few would have given her credit. An elderly lady, with a sprightly bonnet,

happened to be standing by making a benevolent calculation of Sally's characteristics. Sally had a fond desire to see how the bonnet was put together, and in a very innocent fashion dropped a handkerchief just outside her cage, and looked forlorn as it fell out of sight. The lady knelt to pick up the lost article, and Sally reached out a brown hand, with an exultant croak of satisfaction, and instantly had the sprightly bonnet in her hand for examination.[1]

Sally 'recognises those who have made her acquaintance, and pays marked attention to men of colour, by uttering a loud cry of *bon, bun, bun.*'

But the real cult of the chimpanzee at Regent's Park began with the inauguration in 1926 of the 'chimps' tea-parties' and the birth in 1935 of its first baby chimp, the famous 'Jubilee'. Since then, the chimpanzee has never looked back.[2]

It is the unanimous opinion of those who have worked in zoos that the behaviour of the animals is in general gentlemanly, while that of the visitors is on occasions bestial. This is an unpleasant subject, but it cannot be passed over in total silence.

Zoos, according to Hediger,[3] attract more than their fair share of undesirables. He divides these into three classes: the petty criminals, the murderers and suicides, and the psychopaths. He cites only a single example of murder—one which occurred at Regent's Park but which might just as well have happened in Soho. Suicides do occur from time to time, the victim usually selecting for his purpose one of the larger carnivores. Among the psychopaths he places sexual perverts, voyeurs (who come to watch sex play), sadists (who torment or kill animals), and publicity-seekers of various kinds; but English readers will probably learn with surprise that in Continental zoos attempts by visitors to have sexual intercourse with animals are not unknown, though often 'defeated by the railings'. In what follows we see a psychopath at work:

MARYLEBONE.—DEATH OF THE BELL-BIRD AT THE ZOO. Walter Hamilton, 27, described as a gentleman, of 13, Ladbrooke-gardens, Notting-hill, was charged with stealing a Bell-bird, worth £10, the property of Mr. Philip Lucas Slater [sic], the secretary of the Zoological Society. Henry Preston, keeper in the parrot-house at the gardens, said he heard a great noise amongst the birds about two o'clock, and on going into the house he saw the prisoner hurrying away from the cage where the Bell-bird was. On looking about he missed the bird and then went after the accused, whom he overtook in the Gardens. He stopped him and asked him about the bird, and

1. *Echo*, 14 April 1887.
2. Neither here nor anywhere else. Only today (4 May 1975) I read in the *Sunday Telegraph* of the 'American' chimp J. Fred Muggs, aged 23, who performs several times a day in an amusement park in Florida, plays an octave of bells, finger-paints, imitates Richard Nixon and Pop-eye the Sailor, has his own chauffeur-driven limousine, and last year earned £86,950. His wardrobe includes two thousand pairs of tennis shoes.
3. *Op. cit.*, pp. 265 ff.

The Bell-bird at Regent's Park.
Illustrated London News,
22 September 1866

he replied that he knew nothing about it.

Witness saw a feather on his coat, and when another keeper spoke to Hamilton the latter put his hand into his pocket and pulled out five feathers like that of the Bell-bird. Jeffcoat, the keeper of the elephant-house, had just previously seen the accused enter the gentleman's lavatory, and immediately afterwards leave. Jeffcoat searched the place, and found the bird in a pocket-handkerchief with the name 'Goodfellow' on it in a closet. . . . The bird was dead and very wet, apparently having been drowned. . . .[1]

This had been the only specimen in England of a rare Brazilian bird. The prisoner was fined £5 and ordered to pay £10, the value of the bird. He was lucky to get off so lightly.

Unfortunately, sadism at the Zoo is not merely a thing of the past. Oliver Graham-Jones, writing in 1970, mentions that after a recent record-breaking bank holiday week-end nine animals—including a llama, a bison and a buffalo—were found dead. 'One sadist had fed his victim a banana that concealed a sharpened knife. Others had found fun in injuring the wing membranes of "flying foxes" by applying to them lighted cigarettes.' 'Spitting at the chimps'—another popular pastime of the day—degraded the spitter but did little harm to the 'spittee'.

There was often an exotic element to be seen at Regent's Park. Scherren mentions the arrival

1. *The Times*, 28 July 1888.

in 1884 of a male Burmese elephant (alleged by its depositors, Messrs Barnum, Bailey and Hutchinson, to be a sacred white elephant) accompanied by a band of alleged Burmese priests. But, as *The Times* said, 'The title priest might be used in their case with some such modifications as attach to the white of the elephant', and they were soon exposed as fraudulent and banished from the Gardens.

Still more colourful was a party of sixty-one Somalis, who came in June 1895 with their wives and children from the Crystal Palace to see animals familiar and unfamiliar:

> The excursion was evidently regarded as a great holiday, and the men, whose teeth were already of a wonderful whiteness, rubbed them to the last moment with the bits of root which they use as toothbrushes, so that their ivories shone again. To the few Europeans who accompanied the West Africans it was most amusing to watch the intense astonishment with which they received the sights of the streets. In the Brixton-road, for example, the cable tramcar puzzled them greatly, and they attributed its propulsion to satanic agency. The florally-decorated houses at the West-end also astonished them.
>
> But it was at the Zoological Gardens that the most curious incidents took place. The Somalis were less surprised to see the lions than the lions to see the Somalis. With every sign of fright the beasts ran roaring from den to den, and Mr Bartlett attributed this panic to the fact that the lions in some cases recalled their Somaliland experiences when they were accustomed to regard these black-faced, white-robed, spear-brandishing human beings as their natural foes. Possibly it was an inherited instinctive feeling in the case of animals that have passed their lives at the Zoo.
>
> The Somalis took very little interest apparently in animals with which they were unfamiliar, but manifested the liveliest pleasure upon visiting the camels, antelopes, snakes, hyenas, zebras, leopards, and elephants. The latter began to trumpet, and they were fed with biscuits. An old friend was found in the 'gurree', which was the name the Somalis had for the giraffe, and they crowded round the tank of the 'jerre', or hippo-potamus, a beast of which they knew something by repute but had not previously seen. But the 'hippo', which is a Cockney by birth, took alarm at them, and plunged into the water, and was not to be tempted with a handful of hay to face these unusual visitors. The only animals which appeared to take the Somalis as ordinary Bank Holiday folk were the monkeys and the chimpanzee, which amused the party immensely. The kanga-roos, which they called 'jumping rats' were also popular; but the visitors soon vacated the cockatoo house, the parrots making, as they said, too much noise.[1]

There was, however, one large and remarkable African animal which the Somalis did not see at Regent's Park—and for the simple (though it may seem improbable) reason that it *had not yet been discovered*! This was the okapi: the subject of the chapter that follows.

1. *Daily Telegraph*, 10 June 1895.

22

Okapi

A CENTURY ago it was generally and very reasonably believed that the giraffe was the only surviving member of the ancient family of Giraffidae.

Travellers' tales of the existence of an unknown and fairly large mammal in the innermost recesses of the great Central African forests had indeed been current since the eighteenth century; and had not Pliny said, '*Ex Africa semper aliquid novi*'? But eighteen hundred years had passed since then, and could Africa still have any major novelty to offer? Few any longer took these legends more seriously than most people today take the alleged sightings of the Loch Ness monster, and nobody had ever suggested that such an animal, did it exist, might be a kind of giraffe. There was, however, one man at least who did not scoff: that great pioneer of Central African exploration, Sir Harry Johnston (1858–1927); and it was a chance observation in Philip Gosse's *The Romance of Natural History* (1860), which he had read as a boy, that had first aroused his curiosity and made him determined one day to see for himself whether Gosse's conjectural 'unicorn' was pure fiction, or something at all events based on fact.

It was another great African explorer, Stanley, who in 1899 gave Johnston, the newly-appointed special commissioner in Uganda, a valuable hint. 'If you ever get a chance,' he said, 'mind you take a dip into that wonderful Ituri forest [in what was then the Belgian Congo]. I'm sure it contains some strange beasts not yet made known to science. You may find there the donkey that the pygmies told me they caught in pitfalls. . . .' They called it, he said, 'atti'. The following year Johnston found himself in the Belgian Congo on a mission on behalf of the Belgian Government. Through an interpreter he cross-examined some of the natives, who confirmed the existence of a rare animal, something like a cross between a zebra and a mule, which they trapped in pits. Their name for it was 'o'api' or 'o'ati' (or, as European zoologists soon decided to call it, 'okapi').

Johnston's services to the Belgian Government—he had rescued some pygmies who had been abducted by an enterprising showman hopeful of taking them to Paris for display at the 1900 Exhibition—had made him *persona grata* with the local authorities, and at Mbeni he was warmly received by a Belgian officer, Lieutenant Meura, and his Swedish colleague Lieutenant Eriksson. These men both knew of the existence of the animal and had indeed eaten its flesh, but they had never seen it alive. They believed it to be more like an antelope than a horse, and were sure that it had more than one toe on each hoof. An expedition was immediately organised, and a guide and porters engaged.

Now Johnston had got it into his head that he was looking for an *odd*-toed[1] ungulate, 'possibly a surviving three-toed horse which had taken to the densest forest in Africa as its last refuge'; when, therefore, on the second day the guides excitedly drew his attention to cloven-hoof marks and declared that they were those of the okapi, he disbelieved them. He was not going to waste time pursuing some already familiar forest eland or bongo. Three days later, however, when the sickness of several of his porters necessitated a halt at a village, he noticed and quickly acquired two strips of hide,[2] handsomely marked with brownish-black, orange and creamy-white, which he was told was that of an okapi; the animal appeared to be an entirely new type of zebra. Back at Mbeni, his porters' assurance that he was indeed the possessor of pieces of the hide of an okapi was confirmed.

Johnston had to return to Uganda; but he left with Eriksson's promise of the skin and skull of the next specimen taken. When in due course a skin and two skulls reached him in Uganda, he saw with amazement their 'giraffine characters'. Having taken careful measurements and attempted a reconstruction in water-colours of the living animal, he despatched the sketch to the Royal Society and the material to Professor (afterwards Sir) E. Ray Lankester, 'half in fun' labelling them '*Helladotherium*', an extinct giraffid. He also wrote a letter to *The Times* entitled 'A New Mammal'.

The drawing, which reached England first, was exhibited at a soirée of the Royal Society, where it was denounced by Lankester as a joke in very poor taste; but with the arrival of the skin and skulls he had to change his tune. The new animal, which had tentatively been named *Equus johnstoni* on the strength of the strips of skin which appeared to associate it with the zebra (*Equus zebra*), now became *Okapia johnstoni*. This important discovery caused a worldwide sensation in scientific circles, and for his contribution to zoology Johnston was honoured in 1902 by the Zoological Society of London with its gold medal; it was only the second time that this had been awarded, the first recipient having been the Prince of Wales (Edward VII).[3] In 1907 Jules Fraipont produced a fine folio monograph on the new mammal.

The first okapi to leave Africa reached the Antwerp Zoo in 1919 but died within a few weeks. Okapis, which in 1933 were accorded total protection in the Congo and allowed to be caught only by the official 'Groupe de Capture d'Okapis', are still prestige animals in European zoos, and James Fisher estimated £3,000 as a fair price for one in 1966. Because of their tendency to harbour innumerable parasitic worms they are difficult to keep in captivity, and today are subjected to quarantine in Zaire before being despatched abroad.

In the summer of 1935 King Leopold III of the Belgians presented one (named Congo)

1. *Odd*-toed ungulates include the horse, zebra, rhinoceros, etc. *Even*-toed ungulates include cattle, sheep, antelopes, giraffe, deer, etc.
2. One of these strips is now exhibited in the Natural History Museum, South Kensington.
3. See p. 189.

Okapis. Watercolour drawing by Sir Harry Johnston, based only on two
skulls and a skin yet remarkably accurate.

to the Prince of Wales (King Edward VIII), who passed it on to the London Zoo; it survived only four months and never aroused the interest of the public. A post mortem revealed that it harboured fifteen different species of intestinal parasites. In 1937 the Superintendent of the London Zoo went to Antwerp at the invitation of King Leopold to select another okapi from a number being held there. By examining the droppings under a microscope he was able to pick out an animal, Zanba, which was relatively free of parasites and which lived on at Regent's Park for thirteen years. The Paris (Vincennes) Zoo succeeded in breeding the okapi in 1961, and two years later a birth occurred at the Bristol Zoo; but both animals soon died.

Michelangelo is alleged to have said that 'something strange in the proportions' was an important ingredient of beauty, and it is the whimsical improbability of the proportions of the giraffe that contributes so much to its charm; indeed, many early authors believed it to be a cross between a camel and a big cat (hence 'camelopard'). As the French had said of their animal, '*On la trouve belle sans pouvoir dire pourquoi*'. Spinage considers the okapi 'an extraordinarily handsome animal'; but I find it aesthetically a failure. It is ungainly, and that stale joke about the camel being designed by a committee might equally well be directed at the giraffe's unsatisfactory cousin. Its four striped stockings suggest an amateur knitter, moreover one who had run out of lighter-coloured wool with the job only half finished. The animal somehow lacks appeal, and one can sympathise with the small boy who, when taken by a conscientious parent to admire the newly arrived Congo, observed witheringly, 'What of it? You can see a lion *killed* at the cinema!'

Postscript

Plus je vois les hommes,
Plus je respecte les chiens

Madame Roland

I HAVE more than once, in the course of this book, broken out from the nineteenth century into the twentieth; the time has now come to call a halt.

A rather abrupt halt—which demands an explanation. I had originally intended to include—had indeed already written—two perorating chapters, the one discussing the pros and cons of zoos in general, the other giving a brief survey of the progress of the Z.S.L. since 1900. But the authorities of the Society considered that so important a subject as the rights and wrongs of the keeping of animals in captivity could not be treated adequately in the space I could afford to allot to it, while with regard to my account of the recent history of the Society various points were raised, among them that to devote only a single chapter to one half of the life of the Society would give too unbalanced an impression—even in a book that makes no claim to being balanced. I have therefore consented—though with regret—to the omission of both these chapters. However, possibly the book is in any case long enough already.

Moreover, the turn of the century is in some ways a good place to stop. For with the new century came the ascendancy of the camera, with popular zoological illustrations beginning to wear a fresh look. Today's brilliant photographs of polar bear cubs, pandas and infant chimps would appear out of place alongside the relative austerity of Victorian wood-engravings or the paintings of Joseph Wolf.

So my curtain falls—but leaving (one must hope) an audience wishing for more. And doubtless it will be offered more; for the sesquicentennial of the Z.S.L. must surely also see the publication of a serious work by a trained zoologist describing in detail the many triumphs of the Society in the present century, culminating in the scientific field in such exciting projects as the building and establishment of two new research departments (the Wellcome Institute of Comparative Physiology and the Nuffield Institute of Comparative Medicine), a zoological Education Centre, and the first zoological teachers' centre ('Teachers'

Centre for Life Studies') in the country—and perhaps the first anywhere in the world. There are also a few other centres with courses for teachers, pupils and friends. This resurgence of science and education is, of course, of fundamental importance at a time when many people believe these aspects of zoos to be the main justification for their continued existence.

W.J.W.B.

'Llama and Man'.
H. Hediger, *Man and Animal in the Zoo*, 1969

Officers of the Z.S.L.

Presidents

1826	Sir Stamford Raffles
1827	The Marquess of Lansdowne
1831	The Lord Stanley (Earl of Derby)
1851	H.R.H. the Prince Consort
1862	The Rt. Hon. Sir George Clerk, Bt.
1868	The Viscount Walden (Marquess of Tweeddale)
1879	Professor (Sir William H.) Flower
1899	His Grace the Duke of Bedford
1936	The Earl of Onslow
1942	Henry Gascoyne Maurice
1948	His Grace the Duke of Devonshire
1950	Field Marshal the Viscount Alanbrooke
1954	Sir Landsborough Thomson
1960	H.R.H. the Prince Philip, Duke of Edinburgh

Secretaries

1826	Nicholas Aylward Vigors
1833	Edward T. Bennett
1836	William Yarrell
1838	The Rev. John Barlow
1840	William Ogilby
1847	David William Mitchell
1859	Philip Lutley Sclater
1903	William Lutley Sclater
1903	(Sir) Peter Chalmers Mitchell
1935	Professor (Sir Julian Sorell) Huxley
1942	Sheffield Airey Neave
1952	The Viscount Chaplin
1955	Professor Sir Solly (later Lord) Zuckerman

Treasurers

1826	Joseph Sabine
1830	James Morrison
1831	Charles Drummond
1858	Robert Drummond
1881	Charles Drummond
1932	Major Albert Pam
1945	The Rt. Hon. Sir Francis O. Lindley
1950	Sir Terence Morrison-Scott

Bibliography

This brief bibliography contains only a handful of the books I have read or consulted. In addition to those listed, I have made use of the *Proceedings*, *Transactions* and other publications of the Z.S.L., and in particular of its invaluable collection of Press-cuttings. The extracts from Queen Victoria's Diaries are quoted by gracious permission of H.M. the Queen.

AVERY, G. *The Elephant War*, Collins, 1960
BALLANTYNE, R. M. *The Gorilla Hunters*, Nelson, 1862
BARTLETT, A. *Wild Animals in Captivity*, Chapman & Hall, 1898
——*Life among Wild Beasts in the Zoo*, Chapman & Hall, 1900
BATES, H. W. *A Naturalist on the River Amazons*, John Murray, 1863
BENNETT, E. T. *The Tower Menagerie*, Robert Jennings, 1829
——*The Gardens and Menagerie of the Zoological Society Delineated*, C. Whittingham for Z.S., 1830, 1831
BOUDET, J. *Man and Beast*, Bodley Head, 1964
BOULGER, D. C. *The Life of Sir Stamford Raffles*, Horace Marshall, 1897
BRIGHTWELL, L. R. *The Zoo you knew*, Blackwell, 1936
——*The Zoo Story*, Museum Press, 1952
BRODERIP, W. J. *Zoological Recreations*, Henry Colburn, 1847
BUCKLAND, F. *Curiosities of Natural History*, Richard Bentley, 1857–72.
——*see* BURGESS, G. H. O.
BURGESS, G. H. O. *The Curious World of Frank Buckland*, John Baker, 1967
BURTON, M. *Infancy in Animals*, Roy, New York, 1956
CARRINGTON, R. *Mermaids and Mastodons*, Rinehart, 1957
CLAIR, C. *Unnatural History*, Abelard-Scherman, 1968
CLARK, R. W. *The Huxleys*, Heinemann, 1968
COLLIS, M. *Raffles*, Faber & Faber, 1966
CRANDALL, L. S. *The Management of Wild Mammals in Captivity*, University of Chicago Press, 1964
DARWIN, C. *Life and Letters*, John Murray, 1887
DU CHAILLU, P. *Explorations and Adventures in Equatorial Africa . . .*, John Murray, 1861
EDINBURGH, H.R.H. the Prince Philip, Duke of, and FISHER, James. *Wildlife Crisis*, Hamish Hamilton, 1970
FISHER, James. *Zoos of the World*, Aldus Books, 1966
FRANCIS, Beata. *The Child's Zoological Garden*, Strahan, 1880
GOSSE, P. *The Romance of Natural History*, J. Nisbet, 1860
GOULD, J. *Monograph of the Trochilidae, or Family of Humming-Birds*, published by the author, 1849–87
GRAHAM-JONES, O. *Zoo Doctor*, Fontana/Collins, 1973
GROVES, C. P. *Gorillas*, Arthur Barker, 1970
GRYLLS, R. G. *Portrait of Rossetti*, Macdonald, 1964
GRZIMEK, B. *Four-legged Australians*, Collins, 1967

——*Twenty animals, one Man*, Deutsch, 1963

Guinness Book of Animal Facts and Feats, ed. by Gerald L. Wood, Guinness Superlatives Ltd, 1972

HAGENBECK, C. *Beasts and Men*, Longmans, 1909

HAGENBECK, L. *Animals are my Life*, Bodley Head, 1956

HAHN, E. *Zoos*, Secker, 1968

HALLIBURTON, R. *Seven League Boots*, Bles, 1936

HANCOCKS, D. *Animals and Architecture*, Hugh Evelyn, 1971

Harmsworth Natural History, Educational Book Co., n.d.

HEDIGER, H. *Wild Animals in Captivity*, Dover, 1950

——*Man and Animal in the Zoo*, Routledge, 1969

HUXLEY, Sir J. *Memories*, Allen & Unwin, 1970; Penguin, 1972

ILES, G. *At Home in the Zoo*, W. H. Allen, 1960

JENNISON, G. *Noah's Cargo*, Black, 1928

JESSE, E. *Gleanings in Natural History*, John Murray, 1832–5

JOHNSON, T. *Personal Recollections of the Zoo*, published by the author, 1905–7

KIRCHSHOFER, R. *The World of Zoos*, Batsford, 1968

KNIGHT, C. (ed.). *London*, published by the editor, 1841–4

LAUFER, B. 'The Giraffe in History and Art' (*Field Mus. Anthrop. Leaflet* 22), Chicago, 1927

LEAR, E. *Illustrations of the Family of the Psittacidae, or Parrots*, published by the author, 1832

LILLY, J. *Man and Dolphin*, Gollancz, 1962

——*The Mind of the Dolphin*, Doubleday, New York, 1967

LOISEL, G. *Histoire des Ménageries . . .*, O. Doin, Paris, 1912

London Zoo Guides, various editions

MATHIESON, E. *The True Story of Jumbo the Elephant*, Hamish Hamilton, 1963

MITCHELL, Sir P. C. *Centenary History of the Z.S.L.*, Z.S.L., 1929

——*My Fill of Days*, Faber, 1937

'MORUS' (LEWINSOHN, R.). *Animals, Men and Myths*, Gollancz, 1954

NADLER, F. *Ich sah wie Nürnberg unterging*, Fränkische Verlagsanstalt, Nuremberg, 1955

NOTT, J. FORTUNE. *Wild Animals photographed and described*, Sampson Low, 1886

OWEN, The Rev. R. *The Life of Richard Owen*, John Murray, 1894

PALMER, A. H. *The Life of Joseph Wolf*, Longmans, 1895

POCOCK, C. I. *Highways and Byways of the Zoological Gardens*, Black, 1913

Purnell's Encyclopedia of Animal Life, B.P.C. Publishing Ltd., 1968–70

RAFFLES, Sir Stamford, *see* BOULGER, D. C. and COLLIS, M.

READE, Winwood. *Savage Africa*, Smith, Elder, 1863

RUSSELL, W. H. *The Prince of Wales's Tour: a Diary in India*, Sampson Low, 1877

SCHALLER, G. *The Mountain Gorilla*, University of Chicago Press, 1963

——*The Year of the Gorilla*, University of Chicago Press, 1964

SCHARF, G. *Six Views of the Z.S.'s Gardens . . .*, published by the artist, 1835

SCHEITHAUER, W. *Hummingbirds: Flying Jewels*, Arthur Barker, 1967

SCHERREN, H. *The Zoological Society of London*, Cassell, 1905

SCHOMBERG, G. *British Zoos*, Allan Wingate, 1957

SCLATER, P. L *Record of the Progress of the Z.S.L.*, Zoological Society, 1901

——and THOMAS, O. *The Book of Antelopes*, R. H. Porter, 1894–1900

SCULLARD, H. H. *The Elephant in the Greek and Roman World*, Thames & Hudson, 1975

SIDEBOTHAM, H. *Behind the Scenes at the Zoo*, Cassell, 1925

SILLAR, F. C. and MEYLER, R. M. *Elephants, Ancient and Modern*, Studio Vista, 1968

SITWELL, S. *Fine Bird Books*, Collins, 1953
SPINAGE, C. A. *The Book of the Giraffe*, Collins, 1968
STENUIT, R. *Dolphin, Cousin to Man*, Dent, 1969
STREET, P. *The London Zoo*, Odhams, 1956
——*Whipsnade*, University of London Press, 1953
SWAINSON, W. *Taxidermy, with the Biography of Zoologists*, Longman, 1840
TOPSELL, E. *The History of Four-footed Beastes*, London, 1607
WATERTON, C. *Wanderings in South America*, J. Mawnan, 1825
WENDT, H. *Out of Noah's Ark*, Weidenfeld & Nicolson, 1956
——*The Sex Life of the Animals*, Arthur Barker, 1965
Whipsnade Zoo Guide, various editions
WOLF, J. *see* PALMER, A. H.
Zoological Keepsake, Marsh & Miller, 1830
ZUCKERMAN, Professor Solly, *The Social Life of Monkeys and Apes*, Kegan Paul, 1932

Notes on the Black-and-White Illustrations

14 Mauritshuis, The Hague
16 Mansell Collection, London
17 Mansell Collection, London
18 Radio Times Hulton Picture Library, London
20 F. Buckland, *Curiosities of Natural History*, third series, Richard Bentley, 1888
22 National Portrait Gallery, London
27 Z.S.L. Photo: J. R. Freeman
28 Z.S.L. Photo: J. R. Freeman
33 Photo: J. R. Freeman
36 Mansell Collection, London
39 Z.S.L. Photo: J. R. Freeman
42 National Portrait Gallery, London
44 Museum Press. Photo: Jeremy Marks
47 Photo: J. R. Freeman
48 Photo: Jeremy Marks
53 Photo: J. R. Freeman

55 Photo: J. R. Freeman
59 *Top and bottom* Photos: J. R. Freeman
66 Photo: J. R. Freeman
69 By courtesy of the Trustees of the British Museum
75 Crown copyright. Victoria and Albert Museum, London. Photo: J. R. Freeman
77 Musée des Beaux Arts de Beaune. Photo: Georges Stevignon
78 Collection M. Gabriel Dardaud, Beirut. Photograph lent by Sheila Cunningham Scriven
81 *Top Harmsworth Natural History*, Educational Book Co., n.d. Photo: Jeremy Marks
    Bottom Z.S.L. Photo: J. R. Freeman
83 Photo: J. R. Freeman

87 Photo: J. R. Freeman
89 Photo: Jeremy Marks
90 Z.S.L. Photos: Michael Lister
91 Photo: J. R. Freeman
93 Photo: J. R. Freeman
94 Photo: J. R. Freeman
97 Sir P. C. Mitchell, *Centenary History of the Z.S.L.*, Z.S.L., 1929. Photo: J. R. Freeman
99 Royal College of Surgeons of England
101 *Punch*, 10 August 1850. Photo: J. R. Freeman
109 Photo: J. R. Freeman
111 Photo: Jeremy Marks
113 Z.S.L. Photo: J. R. Freeman
114 Photo: J. R. Freeman
115 Photo: J. R. Freeman
116 Photo: J. R. Freeman
118 Photo: J. R. Freeman
120 Photo: Jeremy Marks
123 Photo: J. R. Freeman
126 Photo: J. R. Freeman
128 Photo: J. R. Freeman
131 Photo: J. R. Freeman
134 Photo: J. R. Freeman
138 Photo: J. R. Freeman
141 Z.S.L. Photo: J. R. Freeman
142 *Harmsworth Natural History*, Educational Book Co., n.d. Photo: Jeremy Marks
148 Photo: J. R. Freeman
153 George Rainbird Ltd. Photo: J. R. Freeman
162 Published in Paris by P. Patte. By courtesy of Suzette Morton Davidson
164 Photo: J. R. Freeman
165 Photo: J. R. Freeman

166 Photo: J. R. Freeman
167 Photo: J. R. Freeman
171 Photo: J. R. Freeman
174 Sir P. C. Mitchell, *Centenary History of the Z.S.L.*, Z.S.L., 1929. Photo: J. R. Freeman
179 Photo: J. R. Freeman
181 Photo: J. R. Freeman
183 Photo: J. R. Freeman
184 Photo: J. R. Freeman
185 Photo: J. R. Freeman
186 Photo: J. R. Freeman
191 Photo: J. R. Freeman
192 Photo: Jeremy Marks
193 Photo: J. R. Freeman
194 Photo: *Illustrated London News*
197 Photo: J. R. Freeman
199 Photo: Jeremy Marks
200 Photo: *Illustrated London News*
202 Photo: Jeremy Marks
203 Photo: J. R. Freeman
204 Photo: J. R. Freeman
206 Photo: J. R. Freeman
209 Photo: J. R. Freeman
213 Photo: J. R. Freeman
216 A. H. Palmer, *Life of Joseph Wolf*, Longmans, 1895. Photo: J. R. Freeman
220 Photo: J. R. Freeman
221 Photo: J. R. Freeman
225 Photo: Jeremy Marks
235 Photo: J. R. Freeman
237 Photo: Jeremy Marks
239 Photo: J. R. Freeman
243 By courtesy of Mr J. Henderson. Photo: W. W. Winter Ltd.
246 Routledge and Kegan Paul Ltd. Photo: J. R. Freeman

Index

Page numbers in italics refer to illustrations or their captions. The letter n after a page number refers to a footnote.